TRANSCENDING CHILDHOOD TRAUMA
THROUGH SOMATIC THERAPY

Relieving Trauma Symptoms Across the Life Span

Jean Bragg Schumaker, Ph.D., S.E.P.

Transcending Childhood Trauma through Somatic Therapy:
Relieving Trauma Symptoms Across the Life Span
by Jean Schumaker

1. PSY075000 PSYCHOLOGY: Trauma psychology
2. PSY006000 PSYCHOLOGY:
Child & Adolescent
3. HEA009000 HEALTH & FITNESS: Healing

ISBN (b&w paperback): 979-8-88636-079-0
ISBN (ebook): 979-8-88636-060-8

Library of Congress Control Number: 2025915650

Cover design by Lewis Agrell
Internal figures by Chris Lorenzen
Cover photo by Shellie Bender

Printed in the United States of America

Authority Publishing
13389 Folsom Blvd #300-256
Folsom, CA 95630
800-877-1097
www.AuthorityPublishing.com

WHAT ARE PROFESSIONALS SAYING ABOUT *TRANSCENDING CHILDHOOD TRAUMA*?

"Despite its deep subject matter, *Transcending Childhood Trauma* is accessible, lucid, and easy to read. It is a valuable resource even for those with little prior knowledge of the field. This book effectively helps readers identify how early trauma manifests in behavior. As someone who has been involved with community service activities for children for years, I believe this book will be very helpful to professionals working in this area."

Paula Martin, J.D.
Retired District Court Judge
Co-Founder of the Children's Advocacy Center of
Douglas County, Kansas

"Dr. Schumaker, an early student of Peter Levine, is a gifted and generous trauma therapist, educator, and researcher. Her book invites us to witness the application of Somatic Experiencing (SE) through her gentle, patient, and interpersonal/psychodynamic lens. The cases presented in her book illustrate how trauma energy moves through the body and is released and integrated as an essential tool for SE therapists whose clients experience symptoms that traditional medicine and psychology fail to understand. She gives us a roadmap for hope."

Molly Glauner, D.P.N., A.P.R.N., P.M.H.N.P.-B.C., S.E.P.
Psychiatric Nurse Practitioner

"As a former teacher at the high-school and junior-high levels, I recommend *Transcending Childhood Trauma*. This book offers valuable insights on dealing with students with trauma issues. Teachers armed with methods that calm troubled students will create classrooms where all students can learn."

Michel Loomis
Retired Secondary Teacher

"When we hear or think about Post Traumatic Stress Disorder (PTSD), military veterans usually come to mind. Most of us don't realize, however, that statistics for children and teens are also alarming and that childhood trauma results from many common events in today's world. Given the alarming prevalence of childhood trauma, Dr. Schumaker's *Transcending Childhood Trauma* should be on every educator's bookshelf. Calling on her extensive experience as a therapist, as well as her stellar career as a researcher, Dr. Schumaker presents case studies of several of her clients. Like flies on the wall, we listen in on the intimate interactions between Dr. Schumaker and these traumatized youngsters. These conversations help us understand the pervasive damage traumatized children endure. Thankfully, she also describes how somatic therapy can play a role in helping these children transcend their trauma and find peace."

Daniel P. Hallahan, Ph.D.
Professor Emeritus
School of Education and Human Development
University of Virginia

"This book is a stellar example of descriptive research translated into relevant practice. Dr. Jean Schumaker's decades of experience as an honored national educational researcher are evidenced through her deep and thorough analysis of the case studies discussed in this book. Dr. Schumaker outlines detailed rationales and processes tying important concepts to effective somatic therapeutic interventions. Importantly, Dr. Schumaker offers extensive accounts of her personal and professional utilization of these techniques. This book offers clarity about the causes and treatments of trauma. It is an eye opener! It frees the reader of false and inaccurate hypotheses and offers paths to effective treatment. It is a one-of-a kind book that should be read and utilized across schools, mental-health clinics, and social-service organizations. Parents and persons suffering from trauma will also be enlightened and empowered once they utilize this valuable resource."

Rosemary Tralli, Ph.D.
Educational Consultant and Author
Former Assistant Superintendent of Schools
Former Special Education Director
Special Educator

"As a practicing psychologist, I am continually interested in innovative and emerging approaches to therapy. Dr. Schumaker's book not only challenges conventional trauma treatment models but also illustrates, through compelling case examples, an alternative therapeutic framework. She clearly explains the principles and practice of Somatic Experiencing Therapy, introduces the concept of 'stored trauma energy,' and demonstrates through multiple cases how this approach has benefited her clients. Her work has the potential to reshape how trauma is understood and treated.

I have known Dr. Schumaker for over forty years, and she is a nationally recognized expert in learning and behavior. The same thoroughness and meticulous attention to detail that define her previous professional work are evident throughout this book."

J. Stephen Hazel, Ph.D.
Licensed Psychologist

Dedication

This book is dedicated to my children, grandchildren, and all children everywhere. May you discover many ways to transcend trauma in your lives and find peace.

TABLE OF CONTENTS

Preface xiii

PART I: A PRIMER ON TRAUMA

Chapter 1: Trauma Defined. 3
What is trauma? 3
What is a traumatic event? 3
Types of traumatic events. 4
Shock trauma. 4
Developmental trauma. 4
Continuous trauma 5
Complex trauma 5
A continuum of traumatic events 6

Chapter 2: The Body's Reaction to a Traumatic Event 9
How does the body react to a traumatic event? 9
Fight or flight 11
Freeze 12
How does the body deal with extra trauma energy? 13
What happens when trauma energy is stored? 14
How can different people react differently? 15

Chapter 3: Symptoms 19
What are the body's signals about stored trauma energy? . . . 19
What is important to know about stored trauma energy? . . 21
What symptoms can be linked with trauma energy? 22
What combinations of symptoms can occur? 25

What kinds of diagnoses are associated with symptoms? . . . 25
How is the term "mental illness" related to symptoms,
     diagnoses, and labels?. 27

Chapter 4: An Option for Healing—
Somatic Experiencing (SE) Therapy. 29
     What can people with symptoms do? 29
     What does Somatic Experiencing (SE) Therapy look like? . . 30
     What does SE Therapy feel like?. 31
     What can SE Therapy accomplish?. 32
     How does an SE Therapy session proceed? 32
     What happens with a fearful client? 36
     What are the goals of a course of SE treatment? 37
          Ensuring release from the "freeze" state. 37
          Discharging energy associated with specific
               traumatic events. 40
          Dealing with new traumatic events. 41
     Summary. 42

PART II: STORIES ABOUT TRAUMA AND HEALING

Reading the stories 43
A dynamic phenomenon 45
Is this a new way to look at trauma?. 46

Chapter 5: Injuries 47
     The Boy Who Stepped in a Deep Hole. 47
     The Boy Who Couldn't Stop Vomiting. 50
     The Boy Who Did a Flip and Landed Wrong 54

Chapter 6: Falls. 59
     The Girl Who Tumbled Down a Slide 60
     The Boy Who Nearly Swallowed a Ruler 66
     The Girl Who Didn't Let Go 73
     The Girl Who Stopped Short. 76

Chapter 7: Vehicle Accidents. 81
   The Boy Who Lost His Ear 81
   The Girl Who Lost her "Mary Janes" 85
   The Toddler Whose Mother's Arms Served as Her Seat Belt . . 88
   The Girl Who Was Hit by a Train 93

Chapter 8: Loss. 99
   The Girl Who Wanted to Say More 100
   The Girl Whose Eyes Itched. 103

Chapter 9: Parental Abuse. 109
   The Boy Who Could Not Speak. 109
   The Girl Who Spent an Evening by Herself in NYC. 112
   The Girl Who Hid Her Mother's Riding Crop 115
   The Girl Who Hated to Bathe 117
   The Girl Who Was Determined to Get Better 120

Chapter 10: Inescapable Attack 125
   The Boy Who Was Attacked on the Playground 125
   The Girl Who Got Arrested AND Kidnapped the
     Same Night 128

Chapter 11: Medical Procedures 135
   The Boy Whose Brain Exploded. 135
   The Girl Who Was Constantly Typing 140
   The Boy Who Tried to Jump Out of a Moving Car. 144
   The Boy Who Took Some Scary Showers (as a Man). 150
   The Girl Who Got Left Out in the Cold 152
   The Girl Who Was Trapped in Concrete 158

PART III: CONCLUSIONS

Chapter 12: Lessons Learned. 165

Chapter 13: Some Caveats. 177
    Caveat #1: The storage and discharge of trauma energy
      is a dynamic phenomenon 177
    Caveat #2: The body's reactivity to traumatic events
      appears to decrease over time, with fewer symptoms
      arising over years 184
    Caveat #3: People can reenact previous traumatic events . . 191

PART IV: RECOMMENDATIONS

Chapter 14: Recommendations for You!. 203

Chapter 15: Recommendations for Parents 221

Chapter 16: Recommendations for Teachers. 235

Chapter 17: Recommendations for Our Society 251

APPENDICES

Appendix A: Biological Connections 263

Appendix B: Lessons Learned Summary. 273

Appendix C: References. 279

Acknowledgments. 283

The Author. 285

PREFACE

This book contains many stories told to me by people about their lives. All of these people have something in common. They experienced traumatic events during childhood, and those events severely affected their lives. Many of these events, like falls, accidents, and medical procedures, are very common in everyday life. Others are less common but result in serious consequences, nonetheless. Most importantly, all the stories show how these people transcended the consequences that befell them.

How did I come to learn these people's stories? Well, in the early 1990s, as a university researcher in the area of child learning, I became very interested in the consequences of these types of traumatic events on children. I was perplexed by a subgroup of learners who weren't benefiting from the instructional programs my colleagues and I had developed. Even though their teachers were doing their best to use the programs faithfully, the students, if they came to school at all, simply could not stay in their seats or concentrate long enough to be in contact with the materials and the instruction. They had difficulty putting any effort into their work, and they did not complete assignments. Some were disruptive and prevented other students from doing their work.

About this time, I met with one of my colleagues and close friend for lunch and asked her how her own children were doing. We had been exchanging news about our children for at least ten years, and I had watched her daughter, Cammie,[1] grow from a toddler to a high

---

[1] Fictitious names have been used in this book to protect the identity of the people who have been so gracious to allow their stories to be told herein.

school student. She had always been a wonderful child and very successful in school. In tears, my colleague reported that she was very worried about Cammie. All of a sudden, Cammie had refused to come home and was not attending school. She was wandering around town in bare feet and sleeping on her friends' parents' couches each night. Different parents were feeding her, watching over her, and giving reports to my friend, but my friend was worried, and her heart was breaking as she was desperately trying to figure out ways to help her daughter and bring her home.

This situation really bothered me. First, I dearly loved my friend and wanted to help her. Second, her daughter had been a very success-ful student who was no longer living at home nor going to school. In my mind, this was a dire circumstance that needed to be addressed. The next day, I went to the university library and read all the journal articles that I could find that might provide answers for a situation like this. I started to understand that Cammie might have experienced a traumatic event, which was at the root of her rather sudden and drastically changed behavior. At that time, though, I could not find any solid research about possible treatments or therapies that might be helpful for Cammie.

I continued my search for an answer, and I spoke with everyone around me who might have knowledge about the general issue of children who simply cannot concentrate long or hard enough to learn, or as in Cammie's case, were not even attending school. One day, I was getting a massage, and I posed the issue to my massage therapist. She told me that she had recently attended a week-long retreat where she had learned about a new therapeutic method for treating trauma, called Somatic Experiencing™ (SE) Therapy. She willingly shared with me the materials given to her at the retreat. What she handed to me was a draft of Dr. Peter Levine's now famous best-selling book, *Waking the Tiger*. I took the manuscript home and devoured it. Then I signed up for the next available retreat with Dr. Levine, and I asked my massage therapist (who had been trained to provide SE sessions) to provide three SE sessions to me. I wanted to experience the therapy firsthand. After I had experienced the therapy and the alleviation of symptoms that had been bothering me for years, I suggested to Cammie's mother that she make appointments with my massage therapist to work with her daughter, which she did. She reported to me that after a few SE sessions, Cammie was living at home and back in school. Soon, she was attending her classes daily and earning good grades. Now, twenty years later, Cammie is very successfully working in a helping profession after earning her bachelor's and master's degrees.

After witnessing Cammie's transformation and experiencing a reduction in symptoms myself, I definitely wanted to learn more about this type of therapy. Over the next five years, I attended the full series of retreats offered by Dr. Levine and became certified as a Somatic Experiencing Practitioner (SEP). I also assisted Dr. Levine in training other practitioners. I began providing sessions and watching traumatized people as they navigated the difficulties associated with the aftermath of traumatic events. I started observing everyone and everything around me with a "trauma" filter. I watched my fellow trainees transforming across five years as we practiced on each other and had the good fortune of Dr. Levine giving us treatments. I became convinced that Somatic Experiencing Therapy was very effective in helping people.

Throughout these years, I continued my "day job" as a researcher at my university, and thus I had rigorous research on my mind every day. I continued to develop new educational programs and test them in rigorous research studies. Now, though, I began to feel driven to do research that would show the successful outcomes that SE can provide. I especially wanted to show that individuals who initially cannot concentrate and learn can become successful learners and performers if they receive SE Therapy.

That was easier said than done! Unfortunately, I was not able to raise sufficient funding that would enable me to do the kinds of research that I was used to doing—namely, research involving large numbers of individuals who are randomly assigned to one of two groups where one group receives treatment and the other group receives no treatment. Finding large numbers of children who had experienced the same traumatic event proved difficult, indeed. I encountered many complexities, including ethical issues, which might be involved in doing a large research study with traumatized people and especially traumatized children. I resorted to doing the next best thing: I started seriously studying the effects of SE on individuals, and I have looked for patterns across those individual cases. My initial research question was this: Does participation in Somatic Experiencing sessions improve individuals' concentration and ability to do academic work? Gratefully, across the last thirty-plus years, I learned so much more!

In order to do this type of case-study research, I have provided SE sessions to people who volunteered to work with me. Sometimes, I offered to help them after hearing about their struggles. Other times, they have shown up at my door or called me after hearing about the help I have given to others. I have worked with adults, and I've worked with children after hearing from their parents that help was needed.

I have told them (and/or their parents) the following. First, I said that I was willing to work with them for no charge, as long as they were willing to come to a weekly one-hour session regularly. I figured this was the best way to see the effects of SE over time, with no limitations on the number of sessions a person might have. Second, I told them that they must come at a given time each week and be willing to sustain that schedule for at least several months. Third, I explained that they are to be respectful of my time and give me advance notice if they cannot attend a session. I added that they are to be sober and drug-free as we work together. I emphasized that if these conditions could not be met, our relationship would not continue.

Finally, I explained that I might someday write about my experiences related to working with them and others. I told them that if I happened to write about their case, I would do my best to contact them and show them what I had written for their review and their edits. I pledged that I would hold their identity in confidence. I asked for their advance permission to write about their case. They all agreed to my conditions, and many declared that if they could help other people, they would be happy to do so. Recently, I spent two months trying to track and reach each person. For those I reached, I sent the story I had written, and, if they wanted to change something, they sent me edits, which I incorporated in their stories. I encouraged them to change any details in the stories that might identify them. They chose the fictitious names they wanted me to use for them. If they told me not to use their story, I eliminated it from the book.

Thus, this book contains information about only those individuals who have worked with me voluntarily and gave me permission to tell their stories. I have been able to contact most of them, show them what I have written about them, and obtain their additions and corrections. I deleted anything that they did not want me to share. They each chose the fictitious name I've used in their stories. Although they are essentially my coauthors, they are not responsible for the conclusions I have drawn from my experiences with them and others. I have known some of them for twenty-nine years, because they continue to request a session now and then and continue to update me about their lives. I have watched some of them grow up, earn degrees, get married, create careers, and have children. Some of their children and grandchildren are now in college. I salute their courage and persistence in seeking healthy lives. They have enriched my life in incredible ways. I am truly grateful to them for all that they have taught me and for their desire to help others through participating in this work.

My goal in writing this book is to explain in a very simple way what I have witnessed and the patterns I have seen across individuals who have experienced traumatic events, have participated in SE Therapy, and have healed themselves. My goal is to help readers understand what they might be experiencing as the result of similar events and how help might be available to them. My hope is that each reader will work to transcend trauma in some way after reading this book.

This book begins with some basic definitions related to traumatic events and what happens in the human body during and after those events. Next, some principles associated with trauma are explained, and people's stories are told to illustrate those principles. Next, the lessons that I have learned across all the participants are shared. After those lessons are shared, some recommendations for you (the reader), parents, teachers, and our society are included. Finally, I have included a section at the end of this book that explains some of the biology associated with trauma. It is simply a layman's reference that provides a basic understanding of what happens in people's bodies during and after traumatic events. I've also included a list of other books and materials for people who want to delve into the topic of trauma in more detail. My hope is that the information and stories shared here will help you understand trauma in a new way. If, after reading this book, you conclude that you or your children are experiencing the effects of traumatic events, I hope that I will have given you a direction that you can take in terms of seeking therapy. At the minimum, my fervent wish is that you will find some relief and hope in reading this book and in understanding its messages. If you are a professional working with traumatized children and adults and looking for new ideas about how to help them, I hope that the information in this book gives you a new direction for your career and will lead to higher satisfaction in your life.

PART I
A PRIMER ON TRAUMA

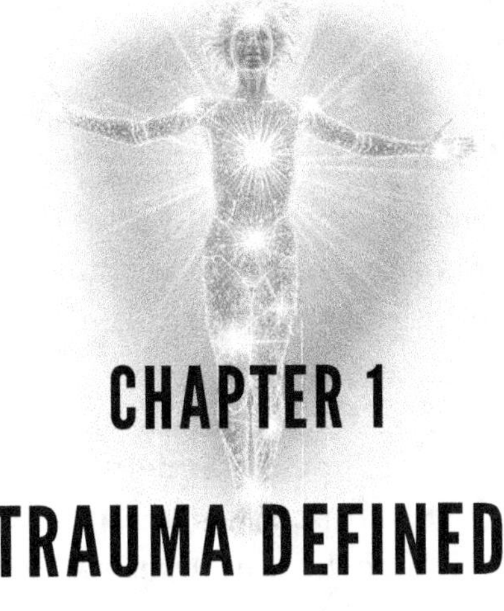

CHAPTER 1
TRAUMA DEFINED

What is trauma?

Every day, we see and hear reports in the news about traumatic events, and we hear about people suffering from "trauma," which will be defined here as a condition that can occur after a traumatic event. Typically, we think of war veterans or victims of mass shootings when we think of people suffering from trauma; however, truth be known, traumatic events are affecting you, me, and our children every day.

What is a traumatic event?

For the purposes of this book, a **traumatic event** will be defined as:

> **Any event that involves actual or threatened death**
> **or that is a threat to the integrity of a person or others**
> *(American Psychiatric Association, 2022).*

What does this mean? It means that any time people feel that their lives are threatened or that the life of someone close to them is threatened, that event is a traumatic event. It also means that any time their body or their self is invaded or any time they witness another person being invaded, that event is a traumatic event.

Types of traumatic events

Traumatic events have often been grouped as either shock trauma or developmental trauma. Another type of traumatic event appears to be occurring often in our world. Let's call it "continuous trauma."

<u>TYPES OF TRAUMA</u>
Shock Trauma
Developmental Trauma
Continuous Trauma

Shock trauma

Shock trauma is any type of physical trauma or insult to the body. Examples are accidents, falls, physical abuse, sexual abuse, kidnapping, surgeries, other invasive medical procedures, asphyxia, near-drownings, poisoning, gun injuries, combat, explosions, or violent war-like events. Accidents can include car accidents (even fender benders), sports accidents, motorcycle accidents, and bike accidents. Falls can include falling off a ladder, a roof, a trapeze, or a slide on the playground. Surgeries can include wisdom-teeth removal, circumcision, Cesarean sections, tonsillectomies, hernia repairs, tumor removal, open-heart surgery, plastic surgery, knee replacements, and gastro-intestinal bypasses. In all these events, the body senses that it has experienced a potentially mortal wound. General anesthesia adds another layer of trauma to the physical trauma of these medical events because the body senses that poison has entered the body. Many of these events are very common in our lives, and we accept them as part of the course of normal events.

Developmental trauma

Developmental trauma involves a threat to the integrity of the person and typically happens during the development of a child. It can happen before or after birth. Before birth, the fetus can be impacted by events surrounding the fetus such as the mother's use of cigarettes, alcohol, medications, or other drugs. Physical abuse, falls, and accidents experienced by the mother while pregnant can also affect a fetus. After birth, developmental trauma can involve lack of stimulation, abandonment, lack of food and water, loss of a parent, emotional and/or psychological abuse, immobilization, and witnessing violence.

Continuous trauma

Continuous trauma occurs when the events in a person's life are continuously threatening, such as when people observe or care for a loved one who is dying over a series of months or years, or when they are trapped in a situation that is continually threatening to their own lives and/or the lives of their children and other loved ones (e.g., an ongoing war, ongoing domestic violence, a neighborhood with frequent drive-by shootings). These people are living inside of a continuous traumatic event for a long time. These kinds of continuous threats can have serious consequences and may require therapy.

Complex trauma

The term "Complex Trauma" has been used in a variety of ways, but typically it is used when a person has experienced a variety of types of traumatic events, especially developmental trauma. It is often used when a person has experienced sexual abuse as a child at the hands of a relative; however, since most of the people I know and with whom I have worked have experienced a long list of a variety of traumatic events, I found that using this term does not really provide a helpful distinction. In fact, I can't think of anyone who has experienced only one traumatic event or no traumatic events (well, maybe a newborn baby who has had a perfect environment as a fetus, a natural birth with no medications, and no circumcision!). Thus, the term "complex trauma" will not be used in this book.

A continuum of traumatic events

Obviously, some events are more traumatizing than others, even of the same type. For example, let's think about bike accidents for a moment. A child who falls off her bike without injury does not typically have lasting repercussions as a result of the event. A child who falls off her bicycle, cuts her knee, gets yelled at by her mother, and has to go to the hospital for a pain shot and stitches might have some repercussions. A child riding on the handlebars of her mother's bicycle (or in a seat on the back of the bike), whose ear is ripped off because her mother loses control of the bike on gravel and the child's head hits the hard ground, will certainly have repercussions, and they may be serious.

Similarly, within a category of traumatic events, some events are more traumatizing than others. For example, wisdom-teeth removal is likely to be a less traumatizing experience than open-heart surgery, especially if the dental patient opts to stay awake and have local anesthesia. A twisted ankle on a baseball field is likely to be less traumatizing than getting hit in the mouth with a line-drive baseball. A fender-bender accident is likely to be less traumatizing than a roll-over car accident.

Likewise, some whole categories of traumatic events can be more traumatizing than others. Accidents are usually less traumatizing than kidnappings and rapes, for example. Injuries resulting within an active war zone are more traumatizing than most other traumatic events.

Another level of complexity is added when the complicating factors surrounding a traumatic event are considered. For example, how the victim is supported during and after the event and who is present during the event, how these people behave, and whether the victim is able to express any agency in the situation can be complicating factors that present more or less danger to the victim, and which, in turn, can be more or less traumatizing.

These comparisons across traumatic events are based on my personal experience with the number of sessions required to work with people who have experienced different types of traumatic events. Of course, everyone is different, and variability occurs; however, these comparisons are important to understand as readers make decisions about the kinds of experiences that they wish to undertake and in which they allow their children to participate. For example, people may decide not to have elective surgery that will have no effect on their longevity. Alternatively, others might decide to have elective surgery with local anesthesia and general anesthesia but take precautions to get adequate therapy before and after the surgery to alleviate any trauma issues. Understanding trauma can help people make important decisions about their future lives.

TRAUMATIC EVENTS

Now that you know a traumatic event is an incident where a person feels invaded, their life is threatened, or a loved-one's life is threatened, please list the traumatic events of your life (or the life of someone you know well) here.

Traumatic Event	Age/Year
1.	
2.	
3.	
4.	
5.	
6.	
7.	
8.	
9.	
10.	
11.	

CHAPTER 2
THE BODY'S REACTION TO A TRAUMATIC EVENT

How does the body react to a traumatic event?

An important concept to understand is how the human body responds during a traumatic event. When the body perceives a traumatic threat, it reacts. Its goal is to survive, period. Figure 1 shows many of the ways a body reacts immediately and simultaneously to a traumatic event.

1. The head and eyes turn toward the perceived danger.
2. The eyelids open wider to see the danger more clearly.
3. The pupils dilate.
4. The ears become more sensitive in order to hear everything possible.
5. The lungs breathe deeper and faster to bring more oxygen into the body.
6. The heart beats faster and stronger to pump more blood into the muscles.
7. The muscles in the hands, arms, feet, and legs get engorged with blood, so the person can fight or flee successfully.
8. Hormones and other chemicals are pumped throughout the body to give the body energy and super-human strength, and to dull pain.
9. Digestion is shut down to conserve energy, along with other organ functions not needed to fight and flee.

Figure 1: The body's reaction to a traumatic event.

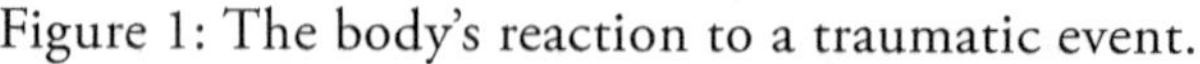

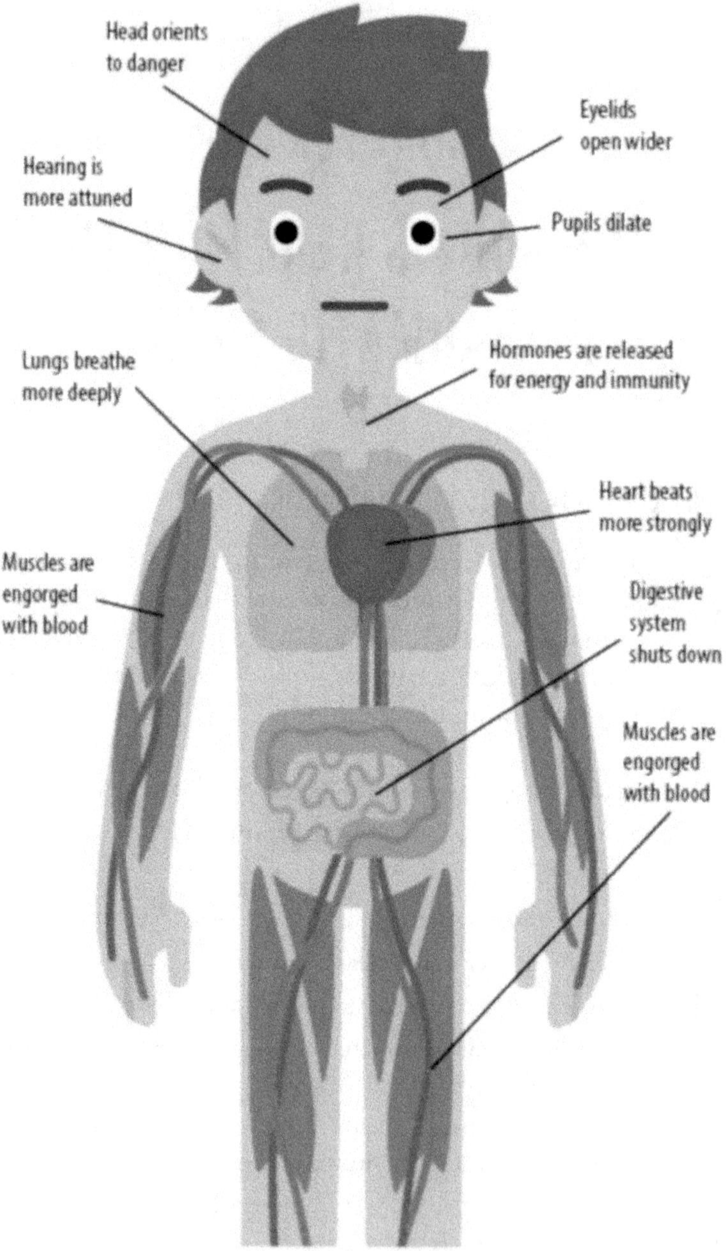

Fight or flight

In short, many parts of the body are involved when a traumatic event occurs. The body gets ready to survive the danger by fighting or fleeing. Every part of the body becomes prepared to defend or run. These survival mechanisms are built into the human body, which reacts instantaneously to danger. A person's thinking brain does not need to instruct the body to react. The body just reacts, *even if it is under general anesthesia*. It goes into a hyper-alert, hyper-vigilant, hyper-prepared state.

The graph in Figure 2 shows what happens when a person is walking along in a normal state of activity (represented by the graph at Point #1) and then senses a potentially dangerous situation (represented by Point #2 on the graph).

Figure 2: Graph showing the body's reaction to a traumatic event and then its return to baseline (Levine, 1994).

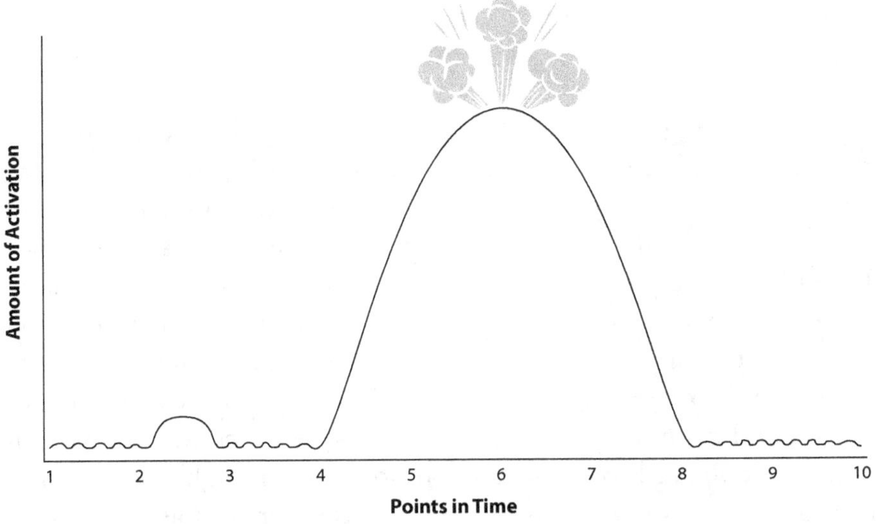

For example, a woman might be walking along a sidewalk (Point #1) and then see another pedestrian walking toward her on the opposite side of the street. Depending on how the other pedestrian acts, the woman's body might begin to activate (represented by the graph at Point #2). Her heart rate might increase, her eyes might get bigger and focus on the situation, and her hands might grip her purse more tightly; however, if the other pedestrian keeps walking and does not even look across the street, the woman's body is likely to return to its normal resting state at Point #3 in the graph. If the woman senses that the danger has passed relatively quickly, all of the survival functions typically can return to normal.

In contrast, if the other pedestrian crosses the street and walks quickly and directly toward the woman, her body will go into full activation mode (represented in Figure 2 at Point #4) so that she can fight or flee if needed. If she can pull out some pepper spray, get ready to aim it at her attacker, yell at the attacker to leave her alone, set off the pepper spray, fight off the attacker, and run away in order to use up the energy stored in her body (represented by the explosions in Figure 2), then all of the survival functions can return to normal (represented at Point #8).

Freeze

In contrast, Figure 3 (p. 13) shows at Point #4 what happens if the woman does not have the right conditions under which all the energy that has been generated can be used to defend herself or run away (e.g., the pepper spray doesn't work, the attacker is too strong). Instead, the energy that has been generated stays where it is located in her body at the time of the event. This same phenomenon occurs when the person is under general anesthesia and cannot fight back or flee. It also happens when a child is being attacked by a larger person and cannot fight back or flee, or when a child witnesses an adult attacking a loved one and cannot stop the fight. Sometimes, a traumatic event happens so fast that the person has no time to use up the energy that has been generated. For example, this might happen when an unexpected car accident occurs, and the person is seat-belted into the car and not able to move out of the damaged car for a while.

In all these instances, the person freezes. When a person freezes, all the energy that the body has generated for fighting or fleeing becomes stored or locked in the body. This "Locked In" state is represented by the flat horizontal line starting at Point #4 in Figure 3. This stored energy will hereafter be referred to as **trauma energy.**

Figure 3: Graph showing the body's reaction when fighting or fleeing are not possible. (Levine, 1994).

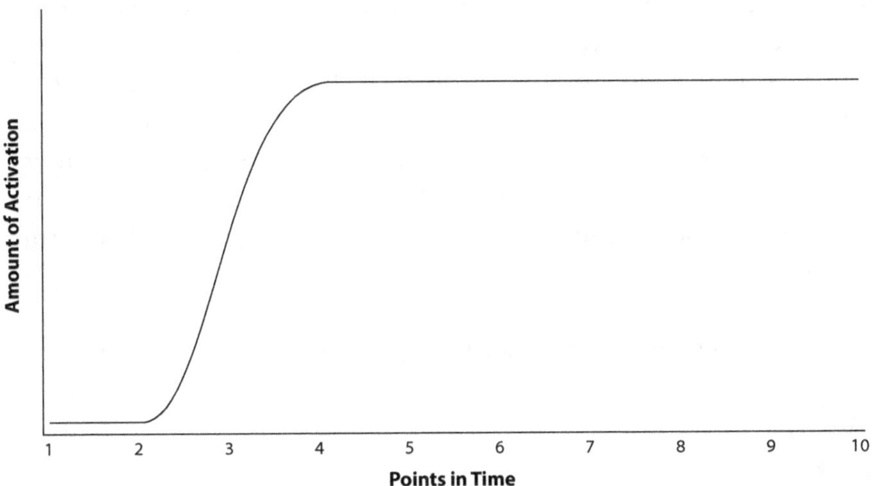

How does the body deal with extra trauma energy?

When the body freezes during a traumatic event or does not use up all the trauma energy that has been generated, it must deal in some way with the trauma energy that has built up. If the body cannot use the built-up trauma energy by fighting or fleeing, it stores the energy in all parts of the body; that is, the energy is stored in body parts like the eyelids, ears, muscles, skin, feet, hands, fingers, toes, neck, tongue, throat, heart, and face.

The body also reacts in other ways. Because chemicals and hormones have been released, they remain in the body, and the parts of the body which released these chemicals continue to release them. The body reacts as if a switch has been turned on but did not get turned off. Moreover, all the parts of the body that shut down during the traumatic event, such as the stomach and intestines, can be affected in a variety of ways.

What happens when trauma energy is stored?

For the most part, the human body is very resilient. After a single and simple traumatic event in which a person freezes (and cannot use up the trauma energy), the body stores up the energy relatively easily and adjusts to the new physical state. Indeed, the human body has a built-in capacity to store up trauma energy and continue to live.

You might think of the body's capacity to store up trauma energy as if it were a reservoir. As each bit of stored trauma energy is added to a person's body, another layer of trauma energy is added within that reservoir. (See Figure 4.)

Figure 4: Reservoir storing trauma energy for two traumatic events.

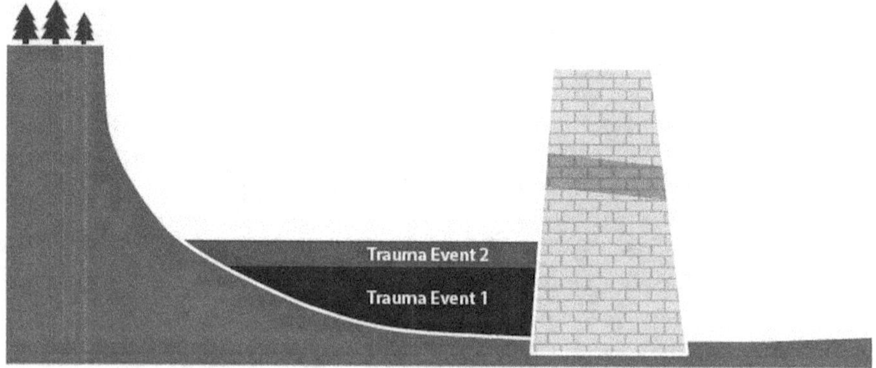

What is important to know is the idea that there is no single place in the human body where this reservoir is located. The reservoir is simply an analogy for understanding how the human body works. As more and more traumatic events occur, the body's capacity to store trauma energy fills up, just like a reservoir fills up. (See Figures 5 and 6.) This analogy is based on my observations and experience, and I created it to help people understand how traumatic events affect their bodies. You will not find this analogy in any biological descriptions of the consequences of trauma.

Figure 5: Reservoir storing trauma energy for four traumatic events.

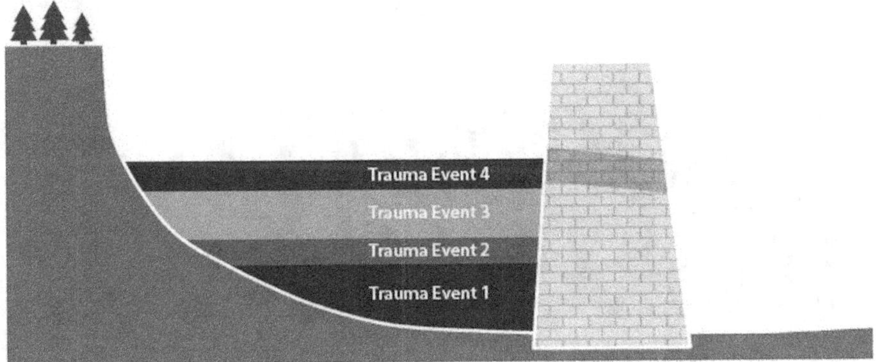

Figure 6: Reservoir storing trauma energy for six traumatic events.

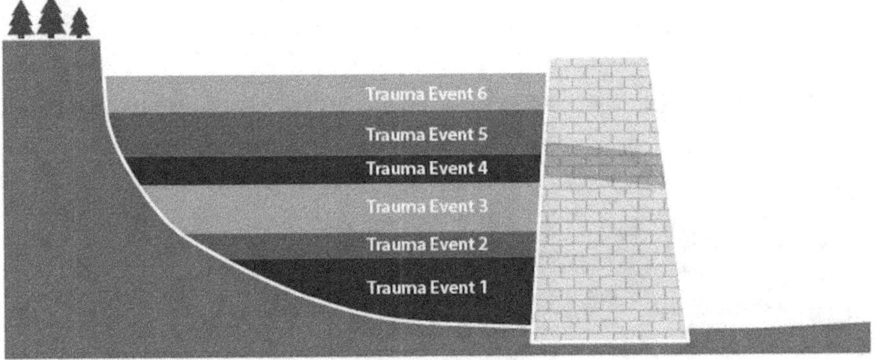

How can different people react differently?

Another important point is that different people have different capacities to store trauma energy based on their genetic heredity. For example, the reservoir shown in Figure 7 is a shallow reservoir with a small amount of capacity. After only a few traumatic events, this person's reservoir, or capacity to store trauma energy, can be filled. In fact, for some people, one traumatic event might fill their capacity to deal with the extra energy.

Figure 7: Reservoir with a shallow capacity for storage of trauma energy.

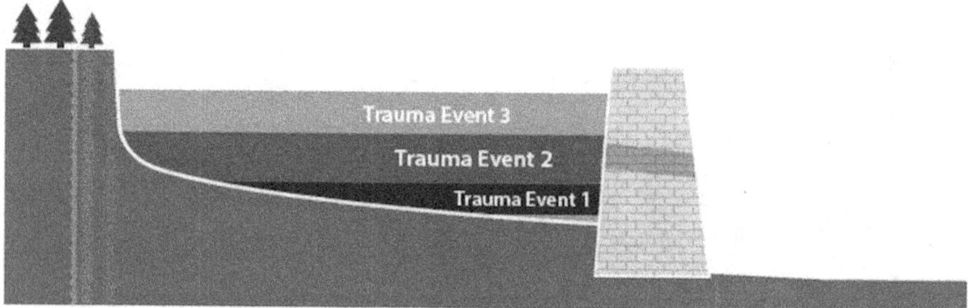

On the other hand, the reservoir shown in Figure 8 is a deeper reservoir with much more capacity to store trauma energy. A person whose capacity is like the capacity in Figure 8 can store trauma energy related to many more traumatic events, and possibly more serious traumatic events, than the person represented in Figure 7.

Figure 8: Reservoir with a deep capacity for storage of trauma energy.

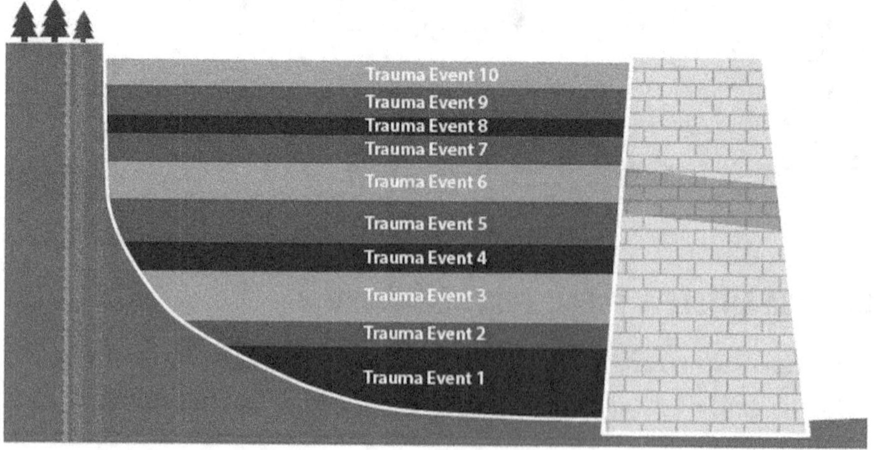

Nevertheless, because trauma energy is stored everywhere in the body, and there is no one place where the amount of trauma energy can be measured, or even a way to measure it, there is no way to determine how much energy is being stored by a person's body and how much capacity has been filled. Thus, people cannot easily determine whether their personal capacities to store trauma energy are shallow or deep, and there is no clear way to determine how full a person's capacity might be. Also, everyone's life experiences are different. Some people simply encounter larger numbers of traumatic events than others because of where they live and the activities in which they engage. The only way to know anything about one's capacity to store trauma energy is to observe oneself and notice the signals that the body is sending before and after the occurrence of traumatic events.

THE BODY'S REACTION TO A TRAUMATIC EVENT

Now that you have read how the body reacts to a traumatic event, please take a few moments to list what is new information for you and what questions you want the rest of this book to answer.

NEW INFORMATION

QUESTIONS

After listing some questions and reading the rest of the book, please send one remaining question to jschumaker@transcending-trauma. org to receive an answer and a bonus.

CHAPTER 3
SYMPTOMS

What are the body's signals about stored trauma energy?

When the body's capacity to store trauma energy is about to fill up, it starts to send signals. This situation can be illustrated by a picture of a reservoir that has water splashing over the dam. (See Figure 9.) The minimal splashes going over the dam in Figure 9 represent the signals which the body sends; they are called **symptoms.**

Figure 9: Reservoir that is at capacity and starting to send signals.

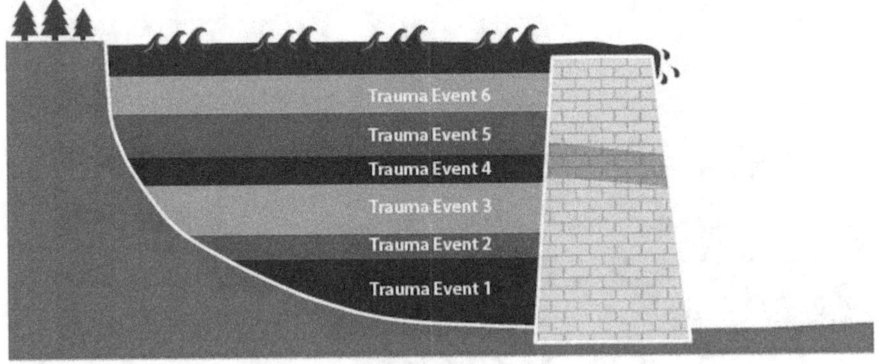

Examples of relatively minor symptoms are headaches, backaches, indigestion, irritability, and heartburn. These minor symptoms are an early warning system. People may choose to treat symptoms like these with over-the-counter medications that can be easily purchased at a grocery store or drug store. They might also seek out treatments provided by a body worker, such as a chiropractor, massage therapist, rolfer, acupuncturist, physical therapist, or cranio-sacral therapist. They might go to yoga classes, meditate, run five miles, or listen to calming music. These are all ways that people cope with the minor symptoms they experience.

When the body's ability to store trauma energy is severely above capacity (see Figure 10), the body starts to send more serious signals. A person in this state might experience serious difficulty sleeping, a constant feeling of unease or fear, depression, anxiety, compulsive behavior, or manic behavior. These symptoms are illustrated in Figure 10 with the larger waves going over the dam. To deal with these symptoms, depending on their severity, a person might go to a personal doctor or a psychiatrist and begin taking a prescribed medication. Alternatively, a person in this state might begin to self-medicate by drinking alcohol excessively or taking recreational drugs. Nonetheless, although the person's life might be somewhat hampered by the symptoms being experienced, the person continues to function in today's world.

Figure 10: Reservoir that is above capacity and sending serious signals.

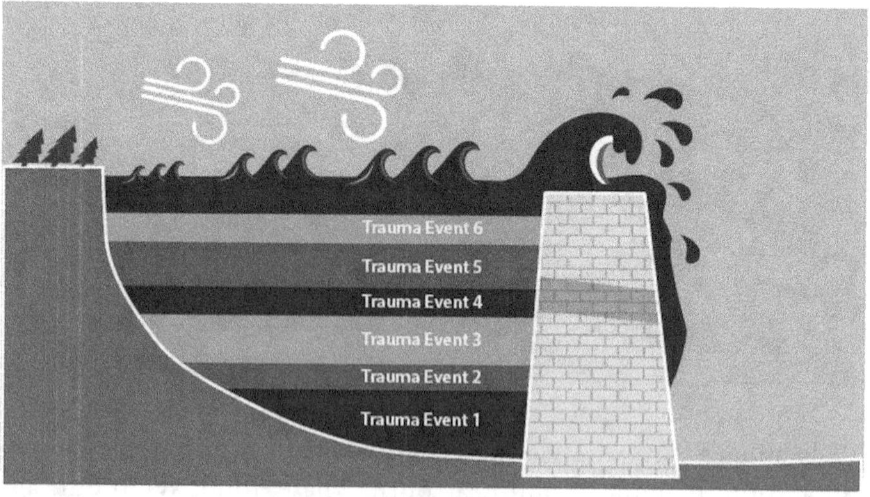

When a person's body is totally overwhelmed by the trauma energy that it is required to hold in storage, the situation can be illustrated by the reservoir pictured in Figure 11. Here, the land below the reservoir and the dam has become flooded. At this point, the person is no longer able to function in today's world. That is, the person is not able to engage in productive work, may not go to school, and may not leave the home. In this case, the symptoms are so severe that the person cannot tolerate being in the world at large.

Figure 11: Illustration showing flooding of the land below the dam, representing a person's inability to function at this point.

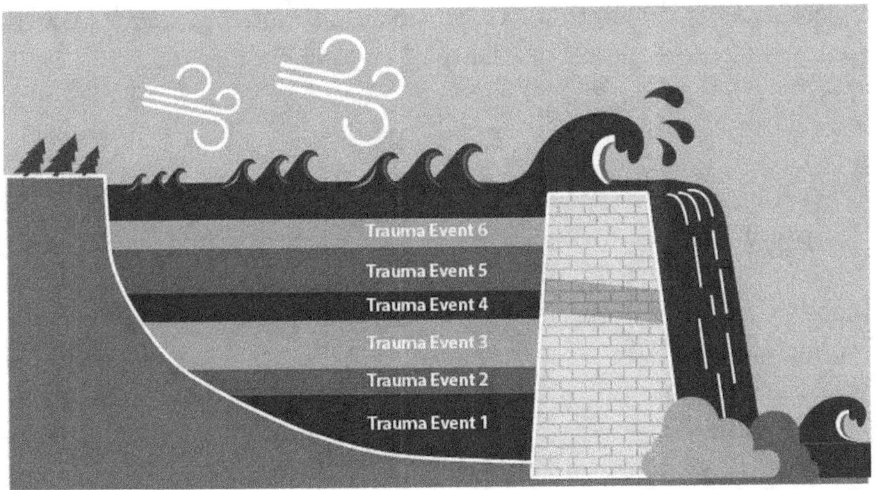

What is important to know about stored trauma energy?

Stored trauma energy has no expiration date. That is, once the body stores trauma energy, it remains in the body unless a specific method is used to release it. Trauma energy stored at birth is just as powerful as trauma energy stored in a fifty-year-old person, and it remains in the body as long as the person is alive if specific methods are not used to discharge it. In other words, when the body stores trauma energy, the energy is locked in the body unless the person takes specific actions to discharge it. The person cannot discharge the energy by pounding a punching bag or running several miles. Trauma energy is a special kind of energy that can only be discharged in specific ways.

What symptoms can be linked with trauma energy?

Figure 12 (pp. 22-25) lists a variety of symptoms which can be the consequences of traumatic events and which potentially can be alleviated. Some of these symptoms can be related to vitamin deficiencies, allergic reactions, toxic poisoning, or diseases, so these possibilities should always be ruled out by medical personnel. Nevertheless, my experience has shown that the symptoms in Figure 12 can be alleviated through the discharge of stored trauma energy.

Figure 12
Symptoms Related to Trauma*

Symptoms related to sleeping
Taking a long time to go to sleep
Inability to go to sleep
Inability to stay asleep for long
Waking up numerous times
    per night
Sleeping only a few hours
    per night
Sleeping during the day
Too tired to get out of bed

Bad dreams
Nightmares
Screaming nightmares

Symptoms related to digestion
Acid reflux
Heartburn
Stomach aches
Excessive burping
Avoiding breakfast

---

* These are the symptoms that have been reported to me as disappearing after participating in Somatic Experiencing (SE) Therapy. Some of them disappeared when I participated in SE Therapy. There are additional symptoms known to be associated with a traumatic history. For another extensive list, see Diane Poole Heller's Trauma Symptoms Checklist at https://traumasolutions.com/wp-content/uploads/trauma-symptons-checklist.pdf.

Overeating
Hardly eating
Eating only one food
Avoiding eating meat
Eating only comfort foods
Eating only one meal per day
Eating a lot and vomiting
Diarrhea
Constipation

Other symptoms related to the *timing* of bodily functions
Irregular heart rhythm
Racing heart beats
Irregular periods
No periods
Severe cramping during periods
Severe bleeding during periods
Irregular breathing
Holding one's breath
Taking frequent deep breaths
Irritable bowel syndrome
Frequent urination

Symptoms related to sensations
Tingling in any body part
Itching in any body part
Numbness in any body part or totally numb all over
Reacting to loud noises/loud voices/anger
Reacting to clothing tags or certain fabrics
Not wanting to be touched

Pressure on a body part (e.g., chest)
Touching others too much or annoyingly

Symptoms related to feelings
Feeling overwhelmed
Feeling "dead inside"
Feeling empty inside
Feeling of wanting to die
Feeling of not deserving to live
Feeling of not being a part of anything
Feeling of being left out of everything
Feeling dizzy
Feeling that one part of the body is larger (or smaller) than others
Feeling that one part of the body is less dense (or more dense) than others

Symptoms related to pain
Chronic pain in any body part (e.g., neck, back)
Headaches
Migraines

Symptoms related to mood
Irritability
Overreacting
Excessive worrying
Anxiety
Constant fearfulness
Frequent crying

Lack of facial affect
Hyper-alertness
Hyper-vigilance
Hyper-preparation
Repetitious/obsessive thoughts
Black days
Depression
Mood swings
Suicidal ideation
Suicide attempts

Symptoms related to behavior
Feet or legs always moving
Body rocking
Body swaying
Repetitive body movements
Hyperactivity
Low activity
Eyelid twitches
Rubbing eyes
Inability to speak
Hoarse voice
Speech disfluency
Spacing out/dissociation
Cutting one's skin
Picking at one's skin
Pulling on one's hair
Biting/tearing fingernails
Self-injuring (e.g., tattoos,
    piercings)
Black everything (clothes, hair,
    nails, make-up)
Disheveled appearance
Poor selfcare (e.g., bathing,
    grooming)

Loss of basic skills (e.g.,
    speech, potty training)
Absent protective reactions
Shaking throughout the body
Lack of physical exercise/poor
    coordination
Difficulty standing without
    support
Defiant behaviors
Perseverative behaviors
Compulsive behavior
Manic behavior
Panic attacks
Temper tantrums
Verbal and physical
    expressions of rage
Daily use of alcohol
Daily use of recreational drugs

**Symptoms related to mental
    functioning**
Inability to concentrate
Inability to learn
Disorganized behavior
Inability to keep track of tasks
Inability to plan
Inability to complete tasks
Inability to remember
    information
No childhood memories
Terrible memory
Blacking out when standing
    up from sitting
Flashbacks

Symptoms related to social interactions
Being bullied
Being socially shunned
Bullying others
Having few, if any, friends
Avoiding social activities

Avoiding crowded places
Self-isolating

Symptoms related to sexual behavior
Lack of sexual desire
Hypersexual arousal and activity
Fear of skin-to-skin contact

What combinations of symptoms can occur?

All combinations of symptoms can occur. My experience has taught me that very few people seek help for only one symptom. In fact, many people with whom I've worked have been experiencing fifteen or more symptoms.

What kinds of diagnoses are associated with symptoms?

The medical profession has associated certain diagnoses with certain symptoms. For example, a person who does not eat may be diagnosed with anorexia, and a person who lines up all her make-up tools in a row every day (and exhibits other compulsive behaviors) may be diagnosed with an obsessive-compulsive disorder. A few common diagnoses are listed in Figure 13. My experience has taught me that people diagnosed with the disorders listed in Figure 13 can, through the discharge of trauma energy, eliminate the symptoms listed in Figure 12. Indeed, some of them have been diagnosed with more than one disorder by more than one doctor, and they all have experienced a reduction of symptoms.

Figure 13
Diagnoses Related to Symptoms

Post-traumatic stress disorder (PTSD)
Depression
Psychotic depression
Bi-polar disorder
Anxiety disorder
Conduct disorder
Obsessive-compulsive disorder
Oppositional defiance disorder
Phobic disorder
Anorexia
Bulimia

Additionally, children are often given labels related to the symptoms that they are experiencing. Figure 14 lists some of these labels.

Figure 14
Labels Given to Children

Underachiever
Having learning disabilities
Emotionally disturbed
Behaviorally disordered
Attention deficit disorder (ADD)
Mentally disturbed
Oppositional defiant disorder
Hyperactivity disorder
Attention deficit hyperactivity disorder (ADHD)
Perceptually handicapped

How is the term "mental illness" related to symptoms, diagnoses, and labels?

The term "Mental Illness" is typically used when a person receives a diagnosis or label like those listed in Figures 13 and 14. The definition for the word "mental" is "of the mind," and "mental illness" is commonly defined as a "disorder of the mind." As previously explained, though, trauma energy is stored everywhere in the body of a person who has experienced a traumatic event or a series of traumatic events and who did not use up all the trauma energy generated. When a person's body becomes overwhelmed by the sheer volume of the trauma energy being stored, the body starts sending signals that "something is not right." This is not a case of a person's brain or mind being diseased or disordered. It is a case of a person's whole body becoming overwhelmed due to stored trauma energy. At the extreme, the person cannot function in any meaningful way, and the person has no mental ability to control or change this state. In other words, the person's state is not under the voluntary control (i.e., not under the conscious mental control) of the person. Thus, telling people who are experiencing symptoms to "pull themselves up by the bootstraps" or "fly right" does no good whatsoever. The person simply cannot control the presence of symptoms.

SYMPTOMS

Now that you have read about the symptoms that can follow a traumatic event or a series of events, please take a moment to list the symptoms you or someone close to you is experiencing.

	Symptom	For how long?
1.		
2.		
3.		
4.		
5.		
6.		
7.		
8.		
9.		
10.		

CHAPTER 4

AN OPTION FOR HEALING—
SOMATIC EXPERIENCING (SE) THERAPY

What can people with symptoms do?

A person who is experiencing trauma-related symptoms, like the ones listed in Figure 12 (pp. 22-25), can choose to enroll in some type of therapy. Figure 15 illustrates how trauma therapy can be used to reduce the level of trauma energy in storage. In this illustration, the outlet for the reservoir has been opened, and the stored reservoir water is draining out in a controlled way.

Figure 15: Illustration showing the gate in the dam is open, allowing trauma energy to flow out, much like the discharge of energy during a trauma session.

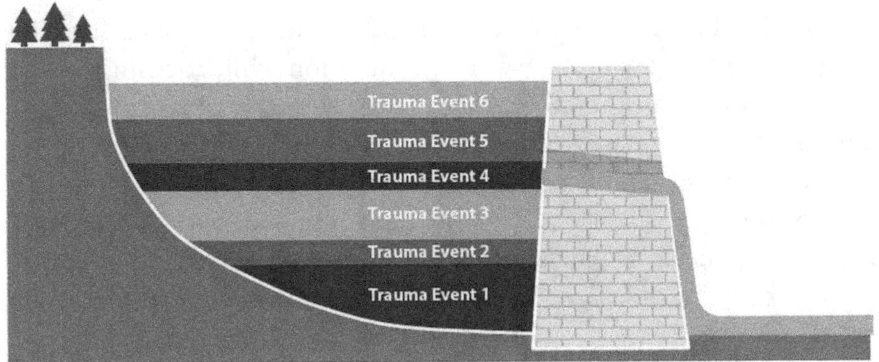

Somatic Experiencing (SE) Therapy is presented in this book as an example of a therapy that can be used to release the trauma energy. To use this type of therapy, the SE therapist teaches the traumatized person how to open the gate to the reservoir so that the energy can drain out or be discharged in a controlled way. To ensure that control, the SE therapist sets up regular sessions (e.g., hour-long sessions) that happen on a regular schedule (i.e., weekly). This type of schedule allows the body to readjust between sessions. It also gives the person a clear point in time when the gate will be opened and shut so that the person's body adapts to discharging the energy at that given time and does not discharge stored energy during other activities. Additionally, the therapist uses certain procedures to ensure that the stored energy is discharged slowly and gradually, and that periods of discharge are interspersed with periods of rest and peaceful recovery.

What does Somatic Experiencing (SE) Therapy look like?

When a person meets with an SE therapist to do SE work, the two individuals are typically present in the same room together, about four to six feet apart. The client may be standing, sitting, reclining, or lying down. The therapist engages the client by asking questions about the client's sensations, and the client answers those questions. For example, the therapist might ask the client to describe what sensations the client notices in the body. The client might state that he has a pain in his neck. The therapist would then ask a series of questions to determine the location of that pain, the intensity of the pain, the size of the area affected by the pain, the shape of the pain, and any colors associated with it. The client would answer each question while focusing on the pain. For example, the client might state that the pain is flat like a pancake and about the size of a fifty-cent piece. After further inquiry by the therapist, the client might state that the pancake is fiery red, and its intensity is at a level five on a ten-point scale, with ten being the most excruciating pain imaginable. By engaging in the act of focusing on the pain, the client "unlocks" the trauma energy stored in the neck; that is, simply focusing on the pain in this way allows the pain level to dissipate. Over a few minutes, the client reports that the neck pain is the size of a quarter, then the size of a nickel, then the size of a dime, then the size of a dot, then a shadow of a dot, and then finally that it is gone. Also, the client simultaneously reports that the color changes from red to pink to yellow to green, and the intensity of the pain gradually reduces from level five to zero. Through this simple exchange of questions and answers while focusing on the body, the therapist and client can keep track of and monitor the energy discharge from the neck and then from different parts of the body throughout a session. The therapist is a "guide on the side," and the client, through intense focusing, does the needed work.

What does SE Therapy feel like?

People often remark that SE Therapy feels weird and unlike anything they have ever experienced because their bodies are moving without them consciously asking their bodies to do so, and they are feeling sensations that they have never felt in the past. They may report that they feel an electrical force moving through their bodies in waves, tingles in their arms and legs, or hot or cold spots on their skin. They may report a hot, painful sensation, or a cool, pleasant sensation. Nevertheless, because SE therapists are skilled in ensuring that trauma energy is discharged in a controlled way, the client is gently coached, and the discharge is managed in such a way that the client stays comfortable throughout a session.

Indeed, clients report that the discharge feels like the body is doing something without their conscious effort to make the body do so. That is, they can see and feel parts of the body moving, feel sensations and emotions, experience memories, generate meaning related to their movements, or see images without asking the body to do anything. All of this happens in a very matter-of-fact way. The client and the therapist engage in a very matter-of-fact exchange about what is happening without assigning causes to anything that is happening.

What can SE Therapy accomplish?

The major goal of SE Therapy is to discharge the stored trauma energy. Over time, the goal is to reduce traumatized clients' symptoms such that they can live comfortable lives by learning, working, and interacting with others in positive and meaningful ways. Indeed, as the result of SE Therapy, traumatized clients can experience reduced symptoms in all the areas shown in Figure 12 (pp. 22-25), including sleeping, digestion, mental functioning, physical coordination and performance, social interaction, pain, bothersome behaviors, and undesirable sensations. This is typically accomplished when each client engages in regularly scheduled sessions over an extended period of time. Once symptoms have been reduced, it is also accomplished when clients monitor the trauma content of their lives, recognize the onset of new (or old) symptoms, and then engage in booster sessions as needed.

How does an SE Therapy session proceed?

The contents of SE sessions will obviously vary across therapists, but most of my sessions have a standard structure that helps clients know what to expect each time we meet. To begin, though, in the first session, I explain the reservoir analogy (see Chapter 2) and answer any questions. When we get to the part of the analogy where the reservoir fills up, most clients will spontaneously tell me something about the traumatic events they have experienced. Those discussions are limited to only a few minutes because I do not want people to become more traumatized or to experience symptoms as a result of describing their traumatic events. When we get to the part of the analogy about water splashing over the dam, most clients will sponta-neously tell me about the symptoms they are experiencing. I usually ask about the client's resources, such as places, people, activities, and things that bring peace to the client. Then I explain my expectations (e.g., about coming weekly, contacting me with schedule changes, etc.), and I ask clients to think about what I have said and to make another appointment if they are willing to meet those expectations.

From then on, sessions are divided into several parts. In the first part, we spend some time getting settled in and updating each other. I ask the client to report the latest developments in the client's life and any symptoms or improvements being experienced. If the client has questions, I answer them. In the second part of the session, I guide the client through a brief grounding exercise where I ask the client to focus attention on various parts of the body. For example, I say something like, "Take a minute to focus your attention on all the places your back is touching the back of the chair;" then "Now focus your attention on all the places your thighs are touching the seat of the chair;" and so forth. The point of this activity is to ensure the client is focusing on the body and the sensations in the body. I tell clients that this part of the session helps them to open the gate to their "reservoir."

> **Parts of an SE Therapy Session**
> - Update
> - Developments
> - Continuing symptoms
> - Improvements
> - Grounding exercise
> - Body scan for a sensation
> - Tracking changes in the sensation
> - Peaceful scene meditation
> - Questions and future plans

Once we have worked through this exercise by focusing on several major parts of the body, the next part of the session begins. Here, I ask the client to scan the body and report to me any sensation that draws attention to it. For example, the client might say, "I feel a tightness in my chest." From that point on, we continue to talk, back and forth, with me asking for more description, and the client describing what is being sensed. An example exchange might go as follows:

Me: "Just take a moment to scan your body from the top of your head downward, and let me know what you notice."
The Client: "I have a headache."
Me: "Can you describe where that is?"
The Client: "It's in my forehead."

Me: "And where in your forehead is it?"
The Client: "It's above my right eyebrow."
Me: "About how big is it? It's the size of a …"
The Client: "It's the size of a walnut."
    Client takes a deep breath (called a "Deep Breath" from now on).
Me: "And what color is it?"
The Client: "It's black."
Me: "On a scale of zero to ten, with ten being the most excruciating pain you can imagine, how painful is this headache?

The Client: "It's a '4'."
    Deep Breath
Me: "What size is it now?"
The Client: "It's like a grape now."
Me: "What color is it now?"
The Client: "It's light gray."
    Deep Breath
Me: "What level of pain is it now?"
The Client: "It's a '2'."

The Pain Rating System

0 = No pain
1 = Almost no pain
2 – 4 = Some pain
5 = A medium amount of pain
6 – 7 = Painful
8 – 9 = Very painful
10 = The most excruciating pain ever

Me: "And the size?"
The Client: "It's like a pea."
    Deep Breath
The Client: "It's gone. There's no pain."

Another way that I can begin the energy-discharge part of the session is by asking the client to state a couple of sentences related to a particular traumatic event in the client's life. The session might start like this:

Me: "Just take a moment to think of the day when you had your tonsils removed. Please share with me a little memory of that day. Perhaps you remember the weather or the place?"
The Client: "They had a little red wagon that they used to take me to the operating room."
Me: "Okay, so please scan your body, and let me know what you notice when you think of that little red wagon."

The Client: "My heart is beating fast."
Me: "Okay, just take a moment to focus on your heart."
The Client: "My heart is beating slower."
    Deep Breath
The Client: "Now my throat feels sore."
Me: "And where exactly is that soreness?"
The Client: "It covers my whole throat and the roof of my mouth."
....

As illustrated in the previous example, this exchange would continue until the color and intensity of the throat pain is described, gradually disappears, and the pain level reduces to zero. Then I would ask the client to scan the body and notice another sensation. Sensations might move around the body to various body parts, but we would continue to "track" those sensations through focusing on them and describing them. This laser focus on the body is like putting a key in a "lock" and turning it. The key serves to "unlock" the trauma energy that is stored in the body. The deep breaths that can occur throughout a session represent the body's natural tendency to rest and relax.

As a result of this process of discharging and resting as needed, the trauma energy continues to release. The release can be in the form of body movements, trembling, hot spots, cold spots, tingling, itches, twitches, pain, colors, memories, tension, tightness, statements of meaning, and images. If the person has difficulty describing a sensation, I might ask questions to provide example descriptive words. For example, I might ask whether the sensation is deep in the body or on the surface, how intense the pain is on a ten-point scale (with ten being the most excruciating pain imaginable), what color the sensation is, and how wide (or long) of an area the sensation covers. This part of the session takes up the majority of one hour, such as forty to forty-five minutes. With most clients, this major part of the session ends when the body stops discharging energy and the body becomes calm with no further sensations to be described.

During the next part of the session, I lead the client in a guided meditation about a peaceful scene that the client has chosen. For example, the client might choose to meditate on a hike in the woods, a beach scene, or even the painting of a sunset. I tell clients that this part of the session serves to "shut the gate to their reservoir," and I explain that the exercise is necessary to ensure that they do not experience energy discharge during the next week. Once this short meditation exercise is complete, for the final part of the session, I answer any questions or concerns the client has about the session that we just completed, and we make plans for the next session.

What happens with a fearful client?

The session sequence described above is adjusted when I learn that a person is very fearful. People can indicate this by telling me that they don't trust anyone. They might stand near the door. They might refuse to sit down or refuse to close their eyes in my presence. If they sit down when given a choice of chairs, they might sit on the edge of a chair seat in a chair that has a full view of the room, with a wall located behind the chair. The person might state, "I don't feel anything," when I ask to notice a sensation in the body.

In such a case, I engage the person in a series of what I call "Walk-Up Activities." To introduce the first activity, I ask if the person is willing to do a little exercise or experiment with me. If the person agrees, I have the person stand, usually near the door to the room. I stand about fifteen feet away, facing the person. I explain that I will

---

Steps of the Walk-up Activity

- The therapist and client stand fifteen feet apart.
- The therapist walks slowly toward the client.
- The client puts hands and arms up toward the therapist and says, "Stop!"
- The therapist stops walking.
- The client reports any change/sensation in the body.
- The therapist helps the client "track" the sensation as it changes and until it dissipates.
- The exercise is repeated.

start walking toward the person very slowly. I ask the person to "tune into" all parts of the body, and, as soon as the person notices any change in the body regardless of how small, to put up both hands with the palms facing me and say, "Stop!" I demonstrate how to put up both arms and how to say, "Stop!" I promise that I will stop walking toward the person.

I take note, the first time we do this activity, of how many feet are between us when the person tells me to "Stop." This distance is the distance in which the person feels safe. It is the radius of a circle that can be drawn around the person within which the person does not become triggered or activated related to that person's safety. I also note how strongly the person puts up the arms, the position of the arms and hands, and the strength with which the person says, "Stop."

Thereafter, each time we do the activity, we pause, and I direct the person to focus on the sensations that were felt and to allow the energy to discharge. For example, the person might say that she feels tingles in her arms and hands. We wait until the body is calm and no longer discharging energy by tingling before we do the activity again. Over time, across several sessions, the person will stop me at closer and closer distances until the distance is about three feet. We can do other similar exercises to help the person establish a feeling of safety within a three-foot bubble. Over a few sessions, the number of reported symptoms becomes fewer and fewer. The person may soon be willing to sit down to participate in a full-blown SE session to discharge energy continuously. In other cases, the person may need to stand for many sessions before being willing to sit down.

What are the goals of a course of SE treatment?

Ensuring release from the "freeze" state

Most clients come to trauma therapy in a relatively "frozen" state. That is, they have experienced trauma, and their bodies froze during at least one traumatic event. In other words, they were not able to use up the trauma energy generated in their bodies by fighting or fleeing. When these clients begin SE Therapy, their bodies do not move. They sit perfectly still in the chair or stand perfectly still. They do not move their heads, hands, or feet during initial sessions. One of the goals of the therapist in these cases is to ensure that the client emerges from the frozen state. As each body part starts to discharge energy and move, one thing the therapist can do is encourage that movement. Gradually, over several sessions, each part of the body starts to move, and as this happens, other body parts join in until, over time, all the parts are moving in a coordinated way. That is, they become synchronized. Typically, the movements mirror the kinds of movements that the person might have made during the traumatic event. A good example of this is a case where the person might have run away from the event. During an initial SE session, the person's toes might start to move. Later, the person's feet might start to move. Then in a later session, the legs might start "running," at first in unison, and later in alternation. Eventually, over a few more sessions, the arms, shoulders, torso, and head can join in with the feet until the whole body is engaged in synchronized running movements while seated or lying down.

As different parts of the body begin to move during sessions, the client will experience a new sense of freedom of movement and often will report starting to engage in dancing, sports, yoga, working out, or other physical activities, whereas none of those activities were occurring when therapy began. For example, one person may report playing tennis again after several years of not doing so despite winning tennis tournaments in the past. Someone else might report finding running shoes in the closet and running a couple of miles.

Besides engaging in running movements during a session, different parts of people's bodies might engage in the movements that might have taken place during a traumatic event. For example, a person who experienced a near drowning might begin to engage in tiny swimming movements in initial sessions and then engage in whole crawl strokes or dolphin kicks in later sessions. A person who experienced a collision on a ski slope might engage in arm movements related to protective reactions that might have cushioned the fall.

Additionally, another sequence of movements that helps discharge trauma energy and that is especially related to past vehicle accidents has been dubbed the "Cobra Sequence" (Levine, 1996). Like other movements, this sequence typically develops over numerous sessions. Initially, the person's head begins to move, even a smidgen during a session. Eventually, the head starts to turn left or right, or perhaps it tilts left or right very slowly. Next, the head starts to circle left or right. Also, the head can tilt forward and all the way back. Eventually, after a few sessions, the "Cobra Sequence" movement starts to appear as the head goes forward all the way down to the knees. Once down at the knees, the head may stay down for a while. Then it comes back up, the back arches, and the head goes back as far as it can. The arms reach up and back, and the whole body stretches. This movement sequence, including the head going forward to the knees, the head coming back up and going backward, the back arching, and the full-body stretch can be done numerous times in

> **Movements in the Cobra Sequence**
> - Head tilts forward
> - Head tilts forward and back
> - Head goes forward to knees
> - Head goes forward to knees, and hands go down to floor
> - Position is held
> - Head and arms come up
> - Back arches
> - Head goes back all the way
> - The whole body stretches
> - Head comes back up

one session and across numerous sessions. It represents the body coming out of its frozen state as the result of what is typically called "whiplash."

Thus, one of the main goals associated with a sequence of trauma therapy sessions is to ensure that the body comes out of its frozen state. This involves the body gradually experiencing a full range of motion in all body parts across sessions. For example, at the end of a course of treatment, the neck moves through a full range of motion in circles in both directions. Likewise, the arms, legs, wrists, and ankles do so as well. The fingers and toes move freely, often like they are playing a piano. The muscles in the face also move in all directions. All of these movements must be done involuntarily during SE sessions. That is, the client cannot do these movements voluntarily to achieve the trauma energy release; the movements must evolve involuntarily through focusing on the body during an SE session.

Discharging energy associated with specific traumatic events

A second main goal of a treatment program across time is to discharge the trauma energy associated with the major traumatic events the person has experienced. Choosing the right traumatic event to start can be difficult if the person has experienced many traumatic events. Fortunately, the body often spontaneously chooses where to start and then proceeds to discharge energy associated with other important traumatic events over time. Also, over time, symptoms will start to dissipate until the client reports no longer experiencing symptoms.

To begin a treatment program, a given traumatic event can become the focus of one or more sessions, based on the client's choice. For example, if a person had a bad fall during a ski trip, that fall can become the focus of one or more sessions until the trauma energy associated with that fall has discharged. For another example, if a person had a knee surgery, that surgery can be the focus of one or more sessions until the trauma energy associated with that surgery has dissipated. Likewise, if a person had a car accident, that accident can be the focus of one or more sessions until the energy associated with that accident has disappeared.

Typically, the client need only report a few details about the traumatic incident in order to trigger the discharge of trauma energy. For example, the therapist might ask the client who fell on a ski slope to start describing the day (e.g., the weather) and the particular ski slope on which the fall occurred. After a couple of sentences from the person, the therapist might ask the person to describe any current sensations in the body. From this point on, the client can begin describing the sensations in the body and tracking them as they move to different body parts. For another example, the therapist might ask a person who had a car accident to describe the location of the car accident (e.g., the road, the intersection, the direction the car was headed) and, after a couple of sentences, to describe the current sensations in the body. Once the person focuses on the body, especially in combination with a few details associated with the traumatic event, the key has been placed in the lock, and the trauma energy will begin to discharge (i.e., the client will notice a sensation [e.g., tingling, pain, heat], which can be reported and then tracked).

In other words, typically there is no need to review the whole traumatic event; just a few details are needed in order to initiate the discharge of energy related to that event. Once that happens, the therapist and client can track the energy discharge as it occurs throughout the body. Across more sessions and at the beginning of each session, the client can describe a few more details associated with that given event to discharge more energy in a similar way. Eventually, over time, as the trauma load associated with the event is reduced, the person typically becomes able to describe more and more details about the event until the description of the event is complete, and the energy discharge is also complete. Nevertheless, complete description of the event might not be necessary. After a few sessions focused on one event, no new sensations or movements of the body might occur, and the trauma energy associated with that event does not exist. Over time, as the trauma energy associated with several events are experienced in this way, more and more parts of the client's body start to move and become synchronized, and the client's symptoms are reduced.

Dealing with new traumatic events

Often, a client may experience a new traumatic event while being treated for a previously experienced event. For example, the client may experience a new car accident, or a loved one may have a heart attack while the client is participating in therapy related to a fall. In such a case, treatment for the previous event (the fall) might need to be interrupted until the client is treated for the current event.

Obviously, this will delay the conclusion of the treatment sequence for the previously experienced event; however, trauma energy related to both events may need to be released if the person is to become symptom free.

Summary

Thus, the major goals across a series of treatment sessions are as follows: (a) to educate the person about trauma, trauma energy, and the need for life-long care of the body by describing the reservoir analogy and reminding the client about its relationship to what the client is experiencing; (b) to ensure all parts of the body come out of their frozen state; (c) to integrate the movements of the parts of the body; (d) to discharge energy associated with particular traumatic events; (e) to reduce the symptoms the client has been experiencing; and (f) to help the person integrate the changes the person experiences and the meaning the person comes to understand into a new way of living. This is not to say that other positive changes do not happen across a course of treatment. For example, people who, during our first meeting, look disheveled, blurry eyed, and have a flat facial affect, can start to look bright-eyed, well-groomed, and smiling after a few sessions. They report engaging in social activities and physical activities. They report successful ventures at work and school. All of these changes can be expected as a result of a course of Somatic Experiencing Therapy, but Somatic Experiencing Therapy is not presented here as a panacea. As can be seen in the remainder of this book, Somatic Experiencing is an example of a type of therapy that can be used to reduce symptoms and improve people's lives.

PART II
STORIES ABOUT TRAUMA AND HEALING

Reading the stories

The next sections of this book contain stories about some of the people who have participated in Somatic Experiencing sessions with me. Each chapter covers a type of traumatic event that was experienced during *childhood*. I have focused on childhood trauma in this book because a wide variety of traumatic incidents can occur in childhood, and we can all learn a great deal from these stories about how to protect and help our children so that they can live productive lives.

Each type of traumatic event that is covered in the stories has factors associated with it that complicate the way that a person might react to therapy. Thus, in each section, the type of traumatic event is defined, and the complicating factors associated with it are also described. Then a few stories associated with that type of event are told. For each story, the person is described briefly while keeping personal identity confidential. The symptoms that each person specified and the traumatic events described to me are briefly summarized. Then excerpts from my notes are listed in a way that shows the unfolding of the therapy sessions that focused on a given traumatic event.

Because of the constraints of time and energy, the notes I took during sessions covered what the person said to me and what the person was doing. I did not take notes about the words I said to the person except in a few important instances when I asked the person to do something. This is a book about the traumatic events people have experienced as children and their journeys in seeking a life free of symptoms. It does not describe how to conduct Somatic Experiencing Therapy. Information about therapeutic techniques can be obtained in other books and through training workshops. (See Appendix C for references.) I found taking notes difficult enough when tracking what the other person was saying and doing without taking notes on the therapeutic process. Throughout every session, my statements were made to help the person maintain focus on sensations in the body. Very occasionally, I wrote a note about what I asked the person to do. Those occasions appear in my notes, and I have listed them in such a way that they can be separated from what the person was doing and saying.

The symbols used in the stories are as follows.

- Quotation marks are used for the exact words the person said (e.g., "I feel pain in my right shoulder").

- Quotation marks are <u>not</u> used when I observed a movement (e.g., Left head turn). Descriptions of movements have been indented from the left-hand margin.

- Brackets are used when I specifically asked the person to say or do something (e.g., [Please say, "I'm alive!"]).

- Ellipses (…) are used to indicate "more of the same" or "repeated similar sensations" to save space. For example, if the person was doing a series of left head circles and then continued making more left head circles for the next two minutes, an ellipse is used to indicate repetition of the previous notation and the passage of time. Ellipses are also used at the beginning and end of a group of notes to indicate that more happened before or after the excerpted notes.

Most sessions lasted about sixty minutes in total length but sometimes as long as two hours. On average, my handwritten notes cover four pages per session but sometimes covered eight pages. Thus, representing everything that occurred in each session is not possible here. I have selected the most important sections of my notes to provide the most meaning within brief snippets. Also, please understand that time is not represented in my notes. Several seconds, if not minutes, may have transpired between statements made by the person. During that time, trauma energy was being discharged through the same sensation, body movement, or trembling as previously listed.

A dynamic phenomenon

Recognizing that the storage of trauma energy is a dynamic phenomenon is very important. That is, the human body is designed to do certain things and react in certain ways. When traumatic events occur and symptoms present themselves, trauma therapy can be used to discharge the stored trauma energy and alleviate symptoms. When additional traumatic events occur, new trauma energy will be stored. As more and more traumatic events occur, even though a person has had a series of trauma sessions, the chances will increase that the person's capacity to store the extra trauma energy will be overwhelmed again. More and more serious symptoms may be experienced if the person does not seek additional sessions. Additionally, as this occurs, stressful daily events such as dealing with an abusive boss, having financial difficulties, and experiencing serious illness in the family can exacerbate the situation, making symptoms more pronounced.

In summary then, although the human body is incredibly resilient and can heal in many ways, SE Therapy does not "cure" a person from ever experiencing trauma-related symptoms again. The ability of the human body to store trauma energy and send signals when it is overwhelmed is a wonderful thing. The ability of the human body to discharge trauma energy when taught to do so is also a wonderful thing. The human body is designed to do these tasks well. Our task as humans in our traumatizing world is to monitor our bodies and seek the help we need to keep functioning at our best, relatively free of symptoms.

Is this a new way to look at trauma?

Absolutely. We have been taught to think of "mental illness" as something to whisper about and keep secret instead of feeling proud that our bodies are working well, protecting us, signaling us, and helping us. According to the old way of looking at symptoms, people who experience symptoms have been told that they have a "brain imbalance" that can be "rebalanced" only through the use of prescribed drugs. Then, when the medication does not work very well, they may be told to add another drug. When the medication causes side effects, they are told to add another drug to counteract those side effects. Sometimes, they have been told that they must be on prescribed drugs for the rest of their lives. They have been told that people with symptoms inherited those symptoms from their parents. In fact, our whole culture holds that people with symptoms are somehow "defective" and to be shunned.

In contrast to this "brain-disease model," the new way of looking at trauma allows people to have pride in themselves and their bodies and hope for the future because they know how to take care of themselves and can seek the help they need to heal and transcend trauma. The new way of looking at trauma gives them agency and the ability to act in productive ways. It gives them a future with productive lives.

CHAPTER 5
INJURIES

A wide variety of injuries can occur as people go about their daily lives. They participate in sports activities, go hiking, go up and down stairs, and walk on the ice in front of their homes. These activities may or may not result in injuries and the storage of trauma energy; however, when they do, trauma treatment can be very helpful in terms of reducing the swelling and pain. It can also be helpful in stopping the cycle of re-traumatization of the same body part over and over again. Moreover, trauma treatment can be helpful in improving the likelihood that people will take better care when engaging in a variety of activities because they understand the risks they are taking when doing so.

The Boy Who Stepped in a Deep Hole

Lawrence* was an eighteen-year-old boy and a senior in high school when I met him. He had a long history of traumatic experiences, including years of physical and emotional abuse by his father, sexual abuse by a friend of the family at around age five, a broken left leg and surgery when he was eleven years old, a broken right ankle when

---

*   This is a fictitious name. All the names of individuals in this book are fictitious.

he stepped in a hole while jogging at age fourteen, and a separated shoulder as a result of playing football at age seventeen. He had set fire to the family home, threatened suicide, and had cut and burned his arms with wires and candles. He had been hospitalized five times for periods of time ranging from three days to three months as a result of his behavior. He complained that his energy level was at "3" on a ten-point scale, that it took one hour to go to sleep at night, and that he woke up about three times per night. He had scary dreams. In the morning, he felt terrible, like he hadn't slept at all.

Lawrence exhibited similar patterns as other youths who had been abused. He was continually having accidents and getting injured. Despite being handsome, tall, and well-built, he was the target of bullies who punched and injured him.

Because he was very uneasy in my presence, I asked him whether he preferred to sit or stand. He chose to stand. Thus, in the first five sessions, we did a series of Walk-Up Activities (see Chapter 4 for an explanation), where I walked toward Lawrence until he felt a change in his body and stopped me from approaching him. The distance between us decreased across sessions from ten feet to three feet in the first five sessions. He tracked sensations in his body and patiently allowed those sensations to dissipate after each approach. We also did some exercises where we pushed against each other's hands. He tracked sensations in his body after each right- or left-handed push.

In the sixth session, Lawrence reported that he had sprained his right ankle. (This was the same ankle he had broken at age fourteen.) For the first time, probably because his ankle hurt, he sat on an exercise ball in my presence. Despite the pain in his ankle, each time I walked toward him in this session and the next four sessions, he reported a band of pain across his back that was about an inch wide. He said that the band reminded him of his father beating him on his back with a belt. With regard to a positive improvement, he reported after these four sessions that he was feeling different in athletic activities, more coordinated and graceful.

Lawrence arrived at the eleventh session with a cast on his right ankle and foot, reporting that he had broken it while playing basketball. Since he was in pain, we began by focusing the session on his right ankle and leg. About halfway through the session, he started to move his head left and right and then began moving his head in circles for the first time.

By the thirteenth session, Lawrence reported that he was running on his ankle again and that he had run a mile in six minutes and sixteen seconds, a new personal best. He said his running was feeling very smooth and coordinated. In following sessions, Lawrence sat on the couch with his foot on a stool. He felt tingling in his right foot but then the tingling moved to other parts of his body, often focusing on his shoulder and back. He was able to track the tingling continuously across all parts of his body. He exhibited full motion in his neck, doing head circles in both directions.

By the seventeenth session, Lawrence excitedly reported that he had run a mile in five minutes and fifty-five seconds. He also reported having lots of energy (rated at an "8" or "9" on a ten-point scale) and receiving a $1,000 scholarship for college for his academic work and extra-curricular activities. A couple of sessions later, he reported that he had graduated from high school and that he was no longer the target of attacks from others. He worked all summer, and then he moved into a dorm and started college. He had completed twenty-five sessions.

Sadly, when I tried to trace Lawrence's whereabouts, I learned that he had passed away at age thirty-four after being treated for pancreatic cancer. He had been working, had married, and had one child.

Lawrence's case is significant because it is an example of how a youth who has been abused will continue to experience abuse, through injuries or attacks from others. (For more on this pattern of reenactment, see Chapter 13.) His story and others in this book are testimony that trauma therapy can serve to interrupt this pattern of abuse. It also shows that over the course of trauma treatment, a person can become more and more adept at a physical activity or sport as a result of his body becoming more coordinated and synchronized.

The Boy Who Couldn't Stop Vomiting

Thomas was a college freshman when we first met. He experienced several injuries to his head, starting when he was two years old. He had pulled on the cord to a radio, which fell on his head and created a cut over his left eye. When he was seven and eight years old, he had a couple of bike accidents; one caused a big bruise over his right eye. When he was eight years old, he slipped in the shower, cut his chin, and had to have stitches. When he was fifteen years old, a large mirror fell on his head, and a shard of glass cut his right shoulder. In junior- and senior-high-school wrestling, his nose was broken by opponents three times. He had all four of his wisdom teeth taken out at the same time when he was seventeen years old after receiving a general anesthesia. Also in his seventeenth year, when he was at a party in a very crowded space, someone smashed an elbow into the base of his neck, and he was diagnosed with a concussion. In the same year, he had a car accident when another driver ran a stop sign and plowed into Thomas's car.

With regard to symptoms, Thomas reported that he was sleeping ten to twelve hours per night. Sometimes, he'd sleep for days. He often could not go to sleep for one or two hours. He would wake up as many as ten times per night. In the morning, he had a terrible time waking up; sometimes, he couldn't really become alert until the afternoon. Once, he slept for a whole week without getting up. He felt tired all the time. His pupils were very large all the time (eight millimeters. according to his doctor); they didn't adjust to light. He appeared dazed and disheveled. He reported that he could barely get through a few essential tasks each day. He had no idea what school-work needed to be done during a given week, and his grades were poor. He had not completed two of his college freshmen courses. He walked slowly, taking very small steps, as if he were afraid of falling. As we talked, he yawned and cracked joints in his neck, back, toes, and ankles often. He rated his energy at the "3" level on a ten-point scale and his concentration at the "4" level.

During the first few sessions, Thomas's eyelids blinked tiny blinks and his eyeballs rolled constantly. He also reported twitches of pain in his head, jaw, and the back of his neck, and he began moving his head to the right and back to center as well as upward and downward very slowly. After the first two sessions, he reported that his pupils remained small (three to four millimeters) and had become responsive to light for increasing numbers of days after each session. After the fourth session, he noticed that he was feeling just as alert when he woke up in the mornings as he normally felt in the afternoons. He reported that he was making fantastic catches when he played Ultimate Frisbee with his friends. He was waking up about one or two times per night, and he rated his energy at the "6" level on the ten-point scale.

By the sixth session, Thomas's head began to circle to the right and to the left, and he exhibited a full range of motion in his neck. He said he was sleeping straight through the night, his energy was at the "7" level, and his happiness was at a "6" or "7" level on a ten-point scale. He yawned only once during the ninety minutes that we were together. In the seventh session, he said that he required only thirty minutes to get into gear for the day as opposed to half a day previously. Nevertheless, he reported having a migraine accompanied with nausea for one day in the previous week. He did not attend his next appointment. During the eighth session, Thomas looked really dazed and wore a black T-shirt. The illustration on his shirt depicted a man with a smashed brain that was sitting on top of his head. The man's face and body were covered in blood.

Then Thomas missed his next session. His mother called that following Sunday to report that he was admitted to the hospital on Saturday with constant vomiting. During the next week, doctors conducted a number of tests but could not determine why he was vomiting. He returned home the next Saturday, but he could not stop vomiting and retching. Naturally, he was unable to eat. I visited him at his home, and I guided him as he mentally envisioned a peaceful place that he had previously described to me. (He did not think he could concentrate enough to do a Somatic Experiencing session.) The vomiting stopped for several days and then started up again. The next Thursday, I visited his home, and we did a Somatic Experiencing session. His head moved through the following sequence many times very slowly:

...

Head turn right and down
Head moving up and back to center
Yawn
Head moving forward and down
Head up while centered
Deep breath

...

Throughout this repeated sequence, his closed eyelids were blinking, and his eyeballs were rolling. The yawn reflects the respiratory system coming back on line. The deep breath signifies the end of a sequence of trauma energy release and a short period of rest. At the end of the last cycle in the sequence, he put his head back, gave a big sigh of relief, and his whole body relaxed into the chair. His face had a very peaceful expression on it.

Within the next few sessions, which took place at my office, he reported continuing improvements, cut his hair, and started dressing nicely and greeting me with a big sparkling smile. He reported that when he was taking a college test, he could remember what the professor had said in class and what he had studied. He was moving with a fluent gait, more energy, and some spring in his step. He said that everything was easier for him. He finished all his college courses with grades of C or above. He was experiencing no depression, and he rated his happiness at the "8" level on a ten-point scale.

Unfortunately, in the next couple of weeks, his parents decided to get a divorce, and his great-grandmother died. He missed three weeks of appointments with me. He became dazed. He didn't take an exam because he didn't know where it was being administered.

He stopped getting up in the morning. He described himself as going across the room to shut off his alarm and then going back to sleep on the floor near the alarm clock. When I saw him next, he lamented that his family home in which he had lived his whole life was being sold.

Nevertheless, he continued to occasionally come to sessions at my office. Below are some of the notes I took during his twentieth session. I asked him to briefly describe the party where he got a concussion.

"My friends and I went to this party. It was wall-to-wall people."
    Taking deep breaths
"There's pressure inside the top of my head."
"It's tennis-ball sized and one-inch deep."
"The pressure moved forward now."
"There's an itch on my left big toe."
"It's painful."
    Both feet moved under body more
"The itch is less intense."
    Head tilt right
    Head is shaking
    Big impact/shudder to head
"The pressure in my head is less."
"The itch on my toe is gone."
"The back of my neck is sore on the right side especially."
    Head is shaking with small shakes
    Several head jerks/shudders
    Head going down very slowly
"The pressure inside my head continues to be less."
    Head is going down more
    Head is all the way forward
    Lots of impacts to head and shoulders
"The pressure in my head is less."

    . . .

This sequence of his head moving downward and engaging in big shudders continued until he reported that the pressure in his head was gone at the end of the session. He attended a few more sessions like this one. Along the way, he announced that he decided to drop out of school and start a job delivering pizzas. He moved into a townhouse with his father. At the end of the spring semester of his sophomore year, he stopped coming to appointments. When I tracked him down twenty years later, I learned that he had graduated from college, had a professional career, and had a family.

Thomas's case illustrates how difficult working with head injuries can be. Working with concussions is especially time-consuming, and progress can be slow. The chance of nausea and vomiting is worrisome and requires extreme care and a slow pace. Moreover, even after twenty-five sessions, some of them lasting two hours, the majority of Thomas's body remained frozen; his arms and legs had not begun to move. Thomas's story also shows how sensitive a traumatized client can be to stresses in his life. Even though he had made considerable progress and most of his troublesome symptoms had disappeared, some of those symptoms quickly reappeared when major traumatic events (his parents' divorce, his great-grandmother's death, and moving out of his childhood home) occurred. After these events, he was not able to concentrate at the level required for college work.

The Boy Who Did a Flip and Landed Wrong

Jerry was a freshman in college and had just turned nineteen years old when I met him. He had had a Cesarian-section birth and had been suffering from asthma throughout childhood. He had been diagnosed as having ADHD for which he had taken medication. He got better scores on tests when he was on the medication, but he didn't like to take it because it made him anxious. He had broken his right arm when he was in elementary school by getting the arm caught in the spring of a trampoline. He broke his right leg in seventh grade while playing basketball. He had been earning As and Bs in high school until the end of his sophomore year. He fractured his right hand during his junior year of high school. He had had several car accidents. His grades deteriorated during his junior year.

Jerry's mother was divorced twice. His father left the home when Jerry was one year old, but he stayed in touch with Jerry and Jerry's older brother. Jerry's father learned that he had a brain tumor on Jerry's sixteenth birthday, and Jerry became closer with his dad while his dad's condition deteriorated. Jerry's dad died when Jerry was a senior in high school.

With regard to symptoms, although Jerry graduated from high school and was accepted into college, he was not doing well in relation to academic studies. He said he had trouble concentrating. He had withdrawn from his courses during his first semester of college. He had no appetite, and it had been years since he had eaten three meals a day. He didn't eat regularly, often eating only one meal a day for several days in a row. He sometimes avoided eating meat because his stomach hurt when he did. He was having trouble following through on promises and activities, and he frequently missed appointments. Although he had been an athlete throughout high school and had played one sport at a very competitive level, he had stopped participating in sports except for Frisbee golf. He rated his energy at the "3" level on a ten-point scale but said he was not depressed.

During his second session, Jerry focused on the incident where he had broken his arm and his hand in two separate incidents. I began the session by asking him to think of the day when he fell off the trampoline and describe something about it. Below are some notes I took during that session.

"It was a sunny day in the backyard of my neighbor. We were having fun
    jumping on the trampoline."
"My arms are more tense."
    Yawn
    Hands on thighs
    Hands on knees
"My arms are less tense."
    Yawn
"Now I have a headache in the back of my head at the '2' level of pain."
    Yawn
Rubbing nose

Yawn
"The headache is now grape size."
Yawn
"The headache is now gone."
"My right arm got caught in the spring of the trampoline."
Demonstrates how his arm was bent outward
"I feel tingling in my right hand."
Moving head randomly
Moving right hand around
"There's tingling in the middle of my right palm only."
Yawn
Scratching the top of his head
Rubbing both eyes
"My palm feels numb."
Deep breath
"The broken bone in my right hand aches at the '3' level."
"My right foot hurts on the outside edge."
"My stomach hurts like it's hungry."
"My hand bone aches at the '1' or '2' level."
...

Moving right fingers around
Sat up straight and crossed left leg over right knee
Yawn
"My stomach is a tad nauseous."
"There's no more tingling or aching in my hand, but it feels really weak."
...

The session continued until Jerry said that his right hand felt stronger than before the session and the nausea had disappeared. He also said that he could make a fist without feeling pain. During the next session, he focused on the trampoline accident again. Below are a few of the statements he made, along with my observations, after I asked him to think of the day he fell off the trampoline.

"I remember falling head first and hitting the trampoline on the left side of my body."
Cough

Both hands on thighs
"I have an itch in my right eye."
"My right arm was caught in a coil, my left side swung down to the ground,
    my right arm was still caught, and my right side was facing the sky."
"I took my right arm out of the coil, got in the van, and went to the hospital."
"It wasn't broken all the way through. I could move it."
    Hands clasped between legs
    Head tilt right
"That area of my arm feels lighter."
"There's a subtle pressure on my right forearm."
"It's fading away."
"It's totally gone."
    Moving his right arm, circling wrist
"It feels weak."
    Twisting both arms several times while straight and held in the air
"My left arm feels stronger than my right arm."
    Yawn
    Left hand in fist
    Arms stretched above head
    Yawn
    Wiping tears from left eye
"Now my arms feel similar."

...

At the beginning of the next session, Jerry told me that he had taken his tennis racquet out of the closet, and he was now playing tennis again. He started teaching tennis to a friend and some kids. He had been going dancing every night, and he was eating five small meals a day. He was sleeping solid for eight to ten hours each night, and he couldn't think of where his inhaler was located because he had not used it. He had had no asthma attacks. He was having a really good time playing Ultimate Frisbee. He asked to focus the session on a car accident. That was the last session in which he participated. He enrolled in a junior college for the next semester. I lost contact with him after that, but I learned twenty-some years later that he had graduated from college, earned a master's degree, and was working as a professional, conducting research.

These sessions with Jerry are good examples of how focusing on a few traumatic events can, within a few sessions, ameliorate symptoms and help a person. They also show how the energy associated with a couple of traumatic events in which injuries occurred to different parts of the body can appear in the same session. An interesting occurrence was the appearance of hunger during a session (my interpretation of this was that his digestive system was coming back online) and Jerry's subsequent improvement in eating. Jerry's sessions again show how the coordination of body parts and enjoyment in physical activities like tennis and Ultimate Frisbee can improve through participation in Somatic Experiencing Therapy. They also show how Jerry began to engage in social activities like dancing and teaching others to play tennis. Participating in new types of social engagement is a common improvement seen with many Somatic Experiencing clients.

CHAPTER 6
FALLS

Falls come in many shapes and sizes. Because they are an everyday occurrence, we often do not think of them as traumatizing. Nevertheless, they can have serious repercussions for the person who falls. Additionally, they are complicated by several factors associated with them. First, the speed with which a person is moving during a fall needs to be taken into consideration. Tripping on the sidewalk while running is a different fall than tripping while walking. A fall while slowly skiing down the bunny hill is a different fall than skiing down a black-diamond trail at top speed. Second, the height from which a person falls needs to be taken into consideration. A fall while walking along a trail is different from a fall from a roof. Third, the injuries sustained during a fall are important, too. A scraped knee resulting from a fall is different from a broken bone. Finally, whether the person has had a chance to use the protective reactions of outstretched arms during a fall is a factor. Often, after a fall, a person will lose the protective reaction of breaking a fall if the fall happens so quickly and unexpectedly that there is no time to extend the arms forward. Thus, recovering that protective reaction is an important part of therapy following a fall. In sum, all of these complications affect the amount of trauma energy stored, the time required to release that trauma energy, and the time required to restore protective reactions and the synchronization of body parts.

The Girl Who Tumbled Down a Slide

When I first met Julia, she was forty-two years old and married. She had a bachelor's degree and was working as a professional in her field. With regard to her symptoms, she reported having daily headaches. Every day, she was waking up with a headache. She reported waking up during the night and an inability to get back to sleep. She often felt "surges of energy" washing through her body during the night. Her eyes were twitching constantly and annoyingly. In addition, she said that she had no sensation in her cheeks, and the tear duct in her right eye did not work. Moreover, she felt like she could not speak. She said that she would "shut down" during conversations, especially during difficult or contentious interactions. Her overall feeling in these situations was that she was "overwhelmed" and "powerless." She also reported feeling sad and anxious. As a child, she "hated to be touched." Her only exercise was walking her dog.

When reporting the traumatic situations that she had experienced, Julia told me that she had fallen off a slide in the playground when she was eight years old in the third grade. When describing the incident, Julia said that she was playing on the school playground before school on a cold January day. The playground had a large jungle gym with a bridge, a slide platform, and a slide. The slide had no sides. She was engaged in a Star Wars pretend-play activity with a friend when she climbed to the top of the slide. She guessed that she had somehow tumbled down the slide instead of sliding down it on her butt. She landed on the pavement, face first on her right eye and the right side of her face. She stood up, climbed halfway up the hill to the school, and passed out. She came back to awareness as the school nurse was helping her walk up the hill to the school. She did not remember anything about the fall from the slide. She had cuts all over the right side of her face, and her right eye was swollen shut for a week. She had to have stitches above her lip and under her nose. She was diagnosed as having a concussion.

As a result of the fall, Julia was out of school for two weeks. The tear duct in her right eye no longer worked, and she had seizures until she was seventeen years old. Because of the seizures, she would walk into walls or objects. She had to take medication for the seizures. Before the accident, Julia remembered being a "top student." After the accident, she had difficulty learning. She said that her ability to process auditory information, such as oral instructions from a teacher, had been lost. In fact, her ability to learn was so hampered that she requested to repeat the fifth grade and was allowed to do so. She said that learning to play the flute during that fifth-grade year really helped her. She suggested that learning to read music, using her fingers in particular ways, and coordinating her breathing with her fingers had helped her. As a result, she had pursued music therapy as a career. Nevertheless, she still struggled to learn through her remaining school years. She recalled falling asleep in class and earning poor grades.

During the first few Somatic Experiencing sessions, Julia's body was frozen: she sat very still with her eyes closed, her hands on the arm rests of the chair, and her feet on the floor while reporting a variety of sensations to me. Occasionally, her head would move. Here are some excerpts from my notes from the first session when I asked her to think of the weather on the day when she fell off the slide.

"It was a cloudy, cool day. We were playing before school started."
   Deep breath
"I have a feeling of warmth in my R eye."
"The warmth is gone."
   Head tilted down a bit
"I have tension in my jaw."
"I have tingling in my throat."
"The tingling is gone."
   Deep breath
"I felt a flash across the front of my neck."
"I have an itch on the top of my right foot."
   Right head turn
"There's tension going up the back of my neck."
"The tightness in my neck went up in a wave across the top of my head."
"I have four or five itches (left eye, left arm, back, belly)."

Deep breath
"The tightness is gone."
Deep breath
Deep breath
Head turned back to center
...

In the fifth session, Julia's body started going through the first half of the Cobra Sequence (see Chapter 4 for a description). She went through this sequence five times. Here's an example of the sequence.

...
Head moving down to lap
"I feel heaviness and fatigue."
Deep breath
"I feel warmth on the right side of my face."
Left head turn while down on lap
"More tiredness"
Head coming upright and turning back to center
"The right side of my face feels numb."
"I feel a few tingles on the top of my head, right side."
Left head turn
Right head tilt
Deep breath
...

In the seventh session, Julia's body went through the whole Cobra Sequence for the first time. Here's an excerpt from my notes.

...
Head moving down to lap
Deep breath
"I have the sense of falling."
Deep breath
Deep breath
"I'm dizzy."
"The dizziness has passed."

Deep breath
Hands on the floor
Head moving up to sit upright
Right head circle
Head & body lean left
Head & body lean right
Head all the way back and back arched
Head upright
...

When she arrived at the eighth session, Julia reported having no more headaches or eye twitches. Between that session and the eleventh session, she reported that she had occasional headaches and eye twitches when stressful events occurred in her life (e.g., family disagreements). By the twelfth session, Julia had started attending ballet classes. She excitedly stated, "I want to move!" At the fifteenth session, she reported feeling sensation in her cheeks and that she was taking a speech course, called "Toastmaster." She said that she wanted to improve her public speaking and was thinking of enrolling in courses toward a master's degree.

During the eighteenth session, for the first time, Julia started feeling sensations in her arms while continuing to go through the Cobra Sequence. Here are some excerpts from my notes from that session, which started with her envisioning the playground where she fell.

...
"There's tension in the back of my throat."
"I do feel stuck."
"My arms feel stuck."
"There's a powerless quality to them."
"The word associated with this feeling is 'Collapse'."
　Deep breath
　Deep breath
"Other words are 'Powerlessness' and Helplessness'."
　Deep breath
　Deep breath

"It seems a little softer, not as stuck."
   Deep breath
"My arms are less heavy."
"My strong core and my weak arms don't feel like they are on the same
   body."
"It makes my head ache."
"I feel chills moving down both arms."
"I feel chills moving down the top of my right thigh."
   Yawn

. . .

"My arms feel a little warmer."
   Deep breath
"My torso is strong, reliable, steady."
"Spaciness is coming and going."
...
"I can count on the strength of my core but not in my arms. There's distrust."
"There's a sense of anger or frustration that I can't trust my arms and
   hands to be protective."
"My stomach feels queasy, and my arms are tingly."
"I'm reminding my arms that they are somehow attached to the solidity
   of my trunk."
"When I reminded my arms that they are attached to my trunk, that felt
   good and true."
"I have a sense that I am done now."
...

At the beginning of the twentieth session, Julia reported that
her arms did not feel connected to her body; instead, they felt frozen and inert. Here are some of my notes from that session during
which she started to move her arms. Again, the session started with
her envisioning the playground where she fell.

...
"My arms feel stuck and lifeless."
"A strip of intense sensation goes down the outside of each arm."
"There's a sense of solidarity with my legs: trustworthiness."

"That sense isn't present in my arms."

"They want to stay 'hidden'."

"My right wrist is burning."

    Moved left foot slightly

"When I moved my foot, I had the thought, 'My feet can do what they want'."

"I just got the picture of my feet just walking down the street."

"I'm seeing the back of someone's legs and someone just stepping, stepping, stepping."

    Her feet are stepping alternately

    More stepping

"There's now a sense that my arms are here and where they should be."

    Arms stretching straight forward with palms facing forward (repeated three times)

"I'm noticing my arms are less lifeless."

    Rubbing thighs with both hands

"I'm just reminding my arms that 'Your legs are here & you are, too'."

...

Julia continued to work on connecting her arms to her body in additional sessions through the twenty-fourth session; she reported no symptoms at the beginning of those additional sessions. When I caught up with Julia a few years after her last session, she looked bright-eyed and cheery, and she had a broad smile. She reported that she had finished her master's degree. She was continuing to dance weekly. She reported having no current symptoms. She said that her right tear duct was now working. She was not taking any medications and not having any seizures.

Her story illustrates how a fall on the playground at an early age can have lasting effects on a child's ability to do well in school. Although Julia recovered from most of the surface injuries to her face relatively quickly, the concussion resulted in long-term effects with regard to her ability to learn. Additionally, the protective reactions of her arms had disappeared, and she was not willing to engage in physical activities. During the course of therapy, she was able to participate in a sophisticated level of coursework in order to earn her master's degree. Exciting developments were her enrollment in classes to become a public speaker despite the traumatic injuries to her face and mouth, and her participation in dance classes.

When I asked Julia whether she wanted to comment on how Somatic Experiencing had helped her, she said, "I found it to be pivotable in helping me to embody a greater sense of groundedness and wholeness. The work also helped me to begin moving my body again in enjoyable ways. Once I started dancing, I began to create a community of friends, which has been supportive and meaningful for me. While I don't think that we necessarily addressed some relational challenges I was having with colleagues, I know we discussed them briefly during therapy sessions, and I felt our work helped me to be present and speak up for myself amidst complex office dynamics."

The Boy Who Nearly Swallowed a Ruler

Kiel made an appointment to meet with me in my university office. When we met, he introduced himself as a university student currently enrolled in a full load of courses. He explained that he wanted to talk with me because he understood that my specialty was learning disabilities. He asked me to determine whether he had a learning disability. He further explained that he had been an underachiever all his life. He said that he did extremely well on achievement tests and course exams, but he had trouble completing assignments. Despite the fact that he was a good reader and helped his friends write their papers, he could not complete his own work. As a result, his grades had been suffering, and he had eight "Incompletes" in college courses. He had been told all his life that he was not fulfilling his potential. The contrast between his achievement test scores and his academic performance had everyone puzzled.

As we chatted, Kiel told me that he had been a "sad person" since the fourth grade. That year, his family had moved from Ohio to Kansas, and he attributed his sadness to the move. He reported that he had been on and off antidepressants for years, felt dizzy, got sick often, was constantly in motion (e.g., cracked his neck and back, and his legs were jittery), had pain in his head, neck, and abdomen, had cut himself on fingers and arms, could not concentrate in lectures, felt extremely tired and froze when he was supposed to complete an assignment, and stayed in bed a lot.

When I contacted one of his professors with Kiel's permission, the professor told me that Kiel easily earned good grades (e.g., As, Bs, and Cs) on course exams. In fact, on an oral exam, he had earned a score of 100 percent, the top grade in the class. In comparison, when Kiel was asked to write, he would sit with a piece of paper in front of him, facing forward with a blank look on his face. He did not move. When the professor had called his name while Kiel was in this state, Kiel startled and "woke up." Kiel had not submitted a single writing assignment out of eight assignments. After receiving this report from Kiel's professor, I added "dissociation" to Kiel's list of symptoms because he was obviously dissociating when he was supposed to be working. ("Dissociation" is the term used for a state in which a person is consciously disconnected from events in the surrounding environment.)

After gathering this information from his professor, I explained to Kiel that I suspected that he did not have a learning disability; instead, he probably was feeling the effects of the traumatic experiences in his life. When I prompted him to talk about scary events in his past, he shared that he had some bad experiences in fourth grade. He described traveling down the hallway at school with a ruler in his hand. Somehow, he had tripped and fallen, and the end of the ruler had entered his mouth and cut the back of his throat. He had returned to his fourth-grade class after this fall. After a while, he had asked to go to the restroom and tried to see his extremely painful throat in the mirror. He opened his mouth over the sink and when blood poured out of his mouth, he thought that he was dying. Nevertheless, he did not tell the teacher about the injury; instead, he waited for school to be dismissed and got on the school bus, continuing to feel extreme pain in his throat. Here are excerpts from my notes taken during his second session, the first session where we directly addressed the fall with the ruler by starting with a few memories of the day when the fall occurred. After he stated a couple of sentences about the day, I asked him to describe the sensations in his body. These notes reveal the roots of the dissociation that Kiel was experiencing.

…

"My ears itch."
>Head all the way back
"My breathing is constricted."
>Mouth wide open while head is back
"My eyes want to open, but they can't."
>Head upright
>Deep breath
"I feel tingling itches on my face."
"I feel an itch on my right ear."
"I feel tingling itches on my chest and neck. Things are coming out to play on the surface of my skin."
>Deep breath
>Right head turn
"I feel tingling itches on my scalp."
>Deep breath
>Cracking knuckles
"My hands want to move but want someone else to move them."
>Right head tilt
"Oh wow! I'm thinking about the school bus."
"I have a thought about the school bus. I'm inside it and curled up on the floor of the school bus."
>Deep breath
"Now I'm outside the school bus. I'm floating above the school bus. I can see the street."
>Mouth opened wide
>Mouth closed
"The bus is stuck at one spot on Thirty-third Street. It won't move."
>[Go ahead and give it a push in your mind.]
>Head back
"There are two "me's" on the bus: One on the floor, one walking toward the bus door."
"Now I'm not on the bus anymore."

Deep breath
"I'm in Dr. Lee's office inside my body. It's late in the evening. We're
    waiting and waiting."
"I feel tingling above my eyebrows."
"I'm back in the back of my head."
"I feel tingling on the right side of my face."
    Deep breath
"I don't know where I am."
"My mom is acting impatient. She's saying, 'What's taking so long?!' My
    mom is mad."
    Right head circle
    Deep breath
"I'm in the examination room at the hospital."
"There's a male nurse with a hairnet on. His name is Reggie. I have my
    teddy bear. I don't know what's going on. I'm really scared. I'm focusing
    on the calming force of Reggie. I trust him."
"My head hurts in the back—it's a headache on the inside, the size of a
    tennis ball."
"There was pressure in my sinuses as it (the headache) left."
    Eyes are half open with white showing
    Deep breath
"This reminds me that I had a headache every day throughout fifth grade.
    It was a level '4' pain on a ten-point scale."
...
"My headache is a '2' or '3' now."
"It's hard to breathe."
"My headache is a '2' now."
    Deep breath
    Head moving back, whites of eyes showing
"My headache is gone."
...

At the end of this second session, Kiel explained that he had been
taken to the hospital in order for the cut in his throat to be sewn up.
At the beginning of the third session, Kiel reported that he had been
able to study for two hours after work, which he considered to be a
big accomplishment. He said this was very unusual for him. Also, he

noticed that he was not anxious when he took an oral test. He said that usually he would get very anxious before and during oral tests.

During the third session, he recalled an assignment given to him in fourth grade where he had to write one page on each of the fifty states. He could not complete the assignment and was told by his parents that he was "grounded" until he did the assignment. He was "grounded" for months. Here are a few excerpts from the session where he focused on that assignment.

...

"I felt the same kind of mental state then as I do now when I try to complete an assignment, I'm just staring at the book and not being able
to work. I just sat and did nothing."
"I feel no pain in my abdomen."
"I feel tension in my face."
"I had the sensation that my hands, face, and body are very large as I was
telling you that."
"I'm looking down over myself. I see myself sitting at a desk. I see the
desk light is on. It's the only light in the room. I'm definitely standing
behind myself, looking at myself, waiting for something to happen."
"I feel like I've been sitting at that desk forever."
Stretching arms up
Smile
Deep breath
"I feel tingling on the right side of my face."
...

"My right cheek and forehead are tingling now. Also, there's tingling on
my lip and back of my head."
Deep breath
"More tingling, but it's faint."
Deep breath
"Fainter tingling."
"The tingling is gone."
...

At the beginning of the fifth session, Kiel reported that he took one of his scheduled finals but did not take the other one. Here are some excerpts from my notes during that session that again touched on the roots of the dissociation that was interfering with Kiel's ability to study and complete assignments.

...

"I feel itches on my jaw."
    Deep breathing
    Head down and tilted left
"I'm thinking about curling up into a ball, like I did on the bus."
"If I don't want to be somewhere, I curl up."
    Tears running down cheeks
    [Are you on the bus?]
"I don't know if I'm ready to be there—on the bus."

...

"I see the two 'me's': one is on the floor of the bus, and one is above
    the bus."
"The one on the floor is my shell; the one above the bus is my spirit."
    [I have a suggestion for something you might try. If you're willing,
    please consider getting on the bus in your adult form and holding the
    "me" who is curled up on the floor.]
"I can see me holding me, but I also see me still on the floor."
    [You might consider gathering the two "me's" together in your arms
    and hugging them.]
    Deep breath
"I've got both parts now (the shell and the spirit). The spirit part is fine
    and happy. The shell part isn't."
    Mouth wide open and holding it open
    Mouth closed
Little smile, right side of mouth
"I'm having a conversation with the spirit part, not the shell part. There's
    nothing there. I'm telling the spirit part that they do their best work
    when they work together. They need each other."
"The spirit is receptive and smiling but has no face."
    Eyes blinking
    Left head turn

Right head turn
Deep breath
Left head jerk
"I was thinking of holding the shell part in my right hand and gently massaging the spirit part into it with my left hand."
[Please go ahead and do that if it feels like the right thing to do.]
Right head turn
Left head turn
Stretch with arms above head
"Good. He looks much better. The color is back. Fleshy glow as opposed to dark gray as he was before. Kind of smiling. He's not afraid."
Right head turn
Left head turn
"He's fine. He's tired of being on the bus. Time to get off."
Sitting up straighter
Stretching arms above head
"We got off the bus. We're skipping down the street."
Head upright and centered
Left head turn
Right head turn
Yawn
Stomach gurgling loudly

...

My notes at the beginning of the sixth session stated that Kiel looked great. He was smiling, and he had light in his eyes. He reported that he had studied for the organic chemistry final exam and took it. He also said that he noticed himself doing new things like reading and going to the library to research information. From this point on, Kiel's ability to study and complete work continued to improve. All in all, we worked together for 106 sessions on a variety of traumatic events. Over the next few years, he completed his bachelor's, master's, and doctoral degrees. Today, he is a researcher in a well-known research institute, and he has written several articles that were published in prestigious research journals. He is the father of two grown children.

Kiel's story shows how a simple fall in his school hallway had a tremendous effect on his life since thereafter he was not able to complete school assignments. An interesting complexity is that during the same fourth-grade year, Kiel fell off a trapeze in the school playground. As a result of that fall, he broke bones in both of his arms, which he had held out to break his fall from the trapeze. Certainly, although the fall with the ruler, subsequent ride on the school bus, and surgery to his throat were significant enough incidents to produce dissociation from academic assignments, his two broken arms added another layer of trauma to his "reservoir." His native intelligence had carried him through high school because he was able to remember information he had read or heard and do well on tests, but when he entered college, he was required to hand in papers and assignments to earn passing grades. He was no longer able to get by on his test grades. As an aside, Kiel mentioned one day after several sessions that he had found some roller blades in his closet, put them on, and started roller blading again that very day. He was thrilled to be physically active again.

The Girl Who Didn't Let Go

Lydia was a senior in high school when she began Somatic Experiencing work with me. She was an excellent student, and she'd also been an excellent athlete. She had unfortunately experienced several falls and other accidents. In one of them, when she was a teenager, she had been on a swing while holding her baby brother in her arms, and she had fallen backward onto the ground and onto her back. She said, "My wind had been knocked out of me." In addition, her baby brother had incurred serious injuries on his head, which required thirty-five stitches on his forehead and around his eye. Whether he would live and be mentally normal was unknown for about a week after the fall. In another fall, Lydia had "cracked her head open" in the second grade. In the eighth grade, a traumatic fall occurred when she was water skiing. Everyone who had skied that day had crossed the wake on their water skis, and she wanted to do so as well. Unfortunately, she fell trying to do it. Apparently, her resulting fall was pretty spectacular; she kept holding onto the tow rope even though she had lost her skis. Unfortunately, she felt paralyzed after the fall. She was in the water for an hour and a half as rescuers were summoned and came to help her. She had also ridden in an ambulance on the way to the hospital while she thought she was paralyzed.

Lydia was experiencing several symptoms as a result of this water-skiing fall and other traumatic events she had experienced. She had pain in her neck for which she took five pain pills per day. Her arms were constantly aching. Her lower back was also in pain regularly. Occasionally, she had a stabbing pain in her pelvis that would last one to two hours. She also had stomach aches that lasted for hours. She no longer engaged in sports activities or exercise.

Before we started addressing the water-skiing fall, Lydia participated in several earlier sessions where she focused on her tonsillectomy. (See Chapter 11 for the story related to those sessions.) At the beginning of the ninth session, she reported that her back was hurting in a band about four inches high across the width of her back. Below are some of her other statements as the energy related to her back was discharged.

"The pain next to my spine is the worst—It's at about the '1' or '2' level."
"If I just bend my spine, it will be ok."
    Bending torso
    Deep breath
    Deep breath
"There are streaks of pain in my back muscles."
"I sprained my back once when I was waterskiing."
"It was a hot day, and I had my hair in a ponytail. The water was cool and felt good."
    Swallow
"My feet are hot."
"My friends had been jumping the wake, and I wanted to do it, too."
"It was big deal to jump the wake."
"Both of my feet are really hot! Just the bottoms of my feet."
    Deep breath

"I was on two skis."

> Deep breath

"My back is getting better."

"My feet are still really hot."

"My back is better. Zero pain. There's a little shadow left."

"I made it over the wake!! Yea!!"

> Pulling her head down to her knees

"It feels good to stretch."

"I started to go over the wake again. I got one foot over. Then the wake from another boat came, and I lost my skis."

"My back feels so good."

"My back needs stretching."

> Pulling head down to knees, hands to floor

"I didn't let go of the rope until I was parallel to the water. My head and feet whipped back. My back kept arching. I couldn't make it stop arching. It was really dramatic arching."

"This makes me want to arch my back."

> Big back arch
>
> Deep breath

"My chest has pressure on it."

...

"My chest is almost normal."

"My feet are more hot."

> Deep breath

"My breathing is back to normal."

"My chest is normal now. The pressure is gone."

"When they put the stretcher under me, I couldn't feel my body."

> Breaths are short

"My arms are tingly, and my legs are a little tingly."

> Yawn

"Everybody was really helpful and supportive and worried. There were people all around me, paddling to shore. They were praying for me and touching my hands. It was nice to know they were concerned."

> [What was the moment you knew you'd be alright?]

"In the X-ray room. The lady kept going away and telling me not to move, but I could wiggle my hands and legs. I unstrapped myself."

> [Say "I'm okay. I survived."]

"I'm okay. I survived this."
    Deep breath
    Cough
"I feel relaxed and kinda tired."
...

In the tenth session, Lydia continued to notice some pain in her back. After that session, she did not report back pain or aching arms. She continued to participate in sessions and reported that she was experiencing some nightmares as she was preparing to leave for college. She continued to set up appointments during her freshman year of college at stressful times when she noticed that she was experiencing symptoms again. These times were times centered around midterm or final exams. The symptoms she started experiencing again related to infrequent sleeping and eating (which are typical symptoms for college students) and finger tapping (which was really typing—see Chapter 4 for more on this symptom and Lydia's story related to a tonsillectomy).

Lydia's case is important because it shows that although people might have experienced some traumatic incidents (e.g., falls, a tonsillectomy, parent divorce), these incidents need not result in poor academic work even though they are enrolled in the most difficult courses in high school (i.e., advanced placement courses). An important factor, though, is that Lydia is a highly intelligent person who had learned a great deal of skills and knowledge before her water-skiing accident. Subsequently, she was accepted at a top-tier college and graduated on time in four years.

The Girl Who Stopped Short

Susan was a thirty-four-year-old who was working as an educator with youth having issues related to depression and anxiety. At the top of her list of traumatic events was her mother's death when she was thirteen years old. Susan described her mother as free spirited, fun, funny, affectionate, and loving. She also reported that her mother was a recovering alcoholic and had been diagnosed with manic depression. As a result, there were times when she was not emotionally available to Susan. Nevertheless, they had a very close relationship.

Susan was born in a Cesarian-section birth. She was told by her father that the surgeon pulled and pulled on her head until she finally popped out. She had experienced typical childhood incidents like hitting her head on the corner of the coffee table, which required stitches. She had injured her right foot doing gymnastics. She had had her wisdom teeth taken out at age nineteen. As an adult, she had experienced two fender-bender accidents, but she had sustained no serious physical injuries from them.

With regard to symptoms, Susan reported that she felt tingling in her legs many nights as she was trying to go to sleep. As a result, she could not get to sleep for a long time, such as one and a half hours or more. She occasionally had nightmares. Sometimes, she had nausea with no appetite. Also occasionally, she experienced headaches and migraines. Starting when she was about twenty-eight years old, her periods were accompanied by such horrible cramps that she had to go to bed for a full day. She rated the pain at the "9½" to "10" level on a ten-point scale, with "10" being the most excruciating pain a person could endure. Besides the cramps she experienced with her period, she had daily pain in her neck and shoulder and occasional pain in her ribs, sternum, and jaw.

Susan's mother had grown up with and loved horses. As a result, Susan's family owned a horse for a few years, and they occasionally boarded other horses on their property. They often rode horses at a neighbor's home. Susan was enrolled in riding lessons when she was in elementary school. During those lessons, she learned to ride horses over fence jumps. In one of her lessons, the horse stopped, and Susan kept going, right over the horse's head. Below are a few excerpts from notes taken during her second session when Susan focused on riding lessons.

"I used to take horse riding lessons."
"I'm remembering a time when the horse stopped really hard, and I flew
    over the horse forward."
    Deep breath
"I feel split in half."
    Head tilt left and hold
    Head continuing in left tilt but also tilting forward
    Rubbing right eye
    Head still tilting left and forward
    Head tilt right
    Head down
    Pulling head down with both hands
    Head slowly moving down to her knees
    Turning head slowly left and right several times
    Hands holding onto toes tightly
    Hands flat on feet
    Head moving up to sitting
    Back arched with head turning left and right
    Arms stretching above head
    Mouth opened wide and then closed
    Head tilt left
    Head tilt right
    Rubbing both eyes

...

Susan then stopped focusing on the horse incident and went on during the same session to recall one of her car accidents in which her truck was hit by a car. Nevertheless, this first session about the horse incident was significant because it was the first time Susan did the Cobra Sequence (see Chapter 4 for more on this movement), which she repeated many more times during later sessions. It started with her pulling her head down forward to her knees and ended with a big back arch and stretch. Later, in her ninth session, she started talking about the horse accident again. She started by telling me that she had memories of working on a jumping course in an indoor horse arena, and the ninth session unfolded from there.

...
"There's tingling throughout my body."
>Yawn
>Head tilt left
>Head tilt right
>Arms up & arching back backward & hold
>Waving arms around
>Hugging self
>Arms out straight in front and making wrist circles
>Hugging self
>Head and torso tilt left
>Head and torso tilt right
>Torso lean left
>Torso lean right
>Torso lean left
>Torso lean right
>Head all the way down to knees
>Shaking head while down at knees

"When I fell off the horse, it was over the horse's head."
"I did a rolling somersault."
>Head moving up to sitting
>Head tilt right and left
>Arching back all the way
>Torso tilt right and then left
>Head moving down between knees
>Somersaulted body forward onto the floor
>Lying on the floor on her back

"I feel tightness in my neck."
>Moved back up into the chair
>Head tilt right
>Right arm held out straight

"My right hand was still holding the whip."
"I had a helmet on."
"I remember rolling on the dirt floor of the arena."
"I was told, 'You've gotta get right back on!'"
"My mom was proud, and I was proud that I got right back on."

...

This session is notable because, by somersaulting down onto the floor, Susan reenacted the fall in a controlled way. Then, in the tenth session which followed, Susan continued to process the fall by first doing the Cobra Sequence four more times. During the fourth Cobra Sequence, she somersaulted down to the floor, and I asked her to say, "I survived!," which she did. Then she continued to lie on the floor on her back and reported tingling all over her body. The session ended when the tingling had died away and Susan had returned to the chair.

Thus, the ninth and tenth sessions are significant because they show that, by completing the actions that her body could have taken to save herself from harm (i.e., by doing a large somersault instead of landing on her head), Susan discharged stored energy from her body. (i.e., the tingling throughout her body). This tingling throughout her body could have happened at the time of the accident if she had been given appropriate instructions to continue to lie on the ground and focus on the sensations in her body, but because she was told to get right back on the horse, she was not given the opportunity to discharge that energy. As a result, she had been experiencing symptoms in her body for years related to the fall. (See another story about Susan in Chapter 8.)

CHAPTER 7
VEHICLE ACCIDENTS

Vehicle accidents include any traumatic event involving a vehicle, including bikes, hoverboards, boats, cars, motorcycles, planes, and trains. Clearly, moving vehicles can be dangerous, and complications related to accidents with them involve the speed with which the vehicle was moving, where the person was in relation to the vehicle (e.g., inside or outside), who else was in the vehicle, and injuries that resulted from the accident. Another factor is whether the person was wearing a seat belt because different types of injuries occur with and without seat belts. Whiplash is almost always involved in auto accidents in which the person was inside the vehicle and wore a seat belt. Injuries can also occur when air bags release. Going through the Cobra Sequence (see Chapter 4 for an explanation) is typically involved in SE sessions related to whiplash incidents. A common situation often occurs when a person who has had few symptoms and then experiences a minor fender bender (like being hit from behind in a car), then experiences a whole host of symptoms.

The Boy Who Lost His Ear

Marcus was in middle school during his first session. He reported that he could take up to two hours to go to sleep. He said that he had a headache during six out of seven days of the week and often experienced migraines and cluster headaches. He had frequent asthma attacks and shaky hands. Although he had trouble concentrating on schoolwork (self-rated at the "4" level on a ten-point scale, with a "10" rating representing excellent concentration), he was able to concentrate on computer activities for four hours straight (self-rated at the "9" level on a ten-point scale). He ate a lot even when he was not hungry, and his mother had told him that he was overweight. He said that he didn't like to engage in most sports, even though he had tried many. He had a very nice bike, but he didn't ride it. I observed that he yawned constantly as he spoke with me, and he took a very deep breath every couple of minutes. He rated his level of depression at the "5" to "6" level on a ten-point scale, with "10" being most depressed/suicidal. His grades were As and Bs.

When I asked Marcus to tell me about the traumatic events in his life, he listed his parents' divorce and three bike wrecks. In one of those bike accidents, he had been hit by a car while riding his bike. These accidents had resulted in two ambulance rides and some surgeries, including plastic surgery on his right knee. He also reported a cracked jaw, cracked ribs, a cracked skull, a concussion, and a hematoma on the outside of his skull that was one and a half inches by three and a half inches in size. When he was three years old, he had eaten a bunch of Tylenol and was hospitalized. When he was four years old, he broke his right ankle while walking. In another incident, he was shot in the arm by a neighbor kid with a BB gun. After a couple of sessions, he shared with me that when he was two years old, his mother had put him in a little metal seat on the back of her bike. When she was riding over some gravel, her bike had slipped out of her control, and his body had hit the gravel hard. As a result, his left ear was torn off his head. His mother had recovered his ear, and a plastic surgeon had sewn it back in place. He had also eventually had plastic surgery on his upper lip and jaw.

During the first two sessions, Marcus was able to focus on and describe sensations that were occurring all over his body. They were mainly single itches in a specific location, like on his left knee or left forearm. During the third session in which he was standing, he reported sensations in areas specifically related to his injuries. Below are some notes from that session.

...

"My hip bones and forearm are aching."
"I have an itch on my upper lip."
"This reminds me of the plastic surgery on my upper lip."
 Stepping on one foot and then the other
 Swaying from foot to foot
"There's an itch on the right side of my jaw."
"I broke my jaw on the right side."
"The itch is a four-inch-long oval."
"The itch has moved down toward my chin. It's smaller now."
 Deep breath
"Little bubbles are moving in two spots on my chin on the left underside."
"There's an itch on the left top side of my head."
"The chin bubbles are totally gone."
"There's an itch on my head that is silver-dollar sized."
"Now the itch on my head is the size of a quarter."
"Now the itch on my head is gone."
"The chin bubbles are back on the left side."
"The jaw thing is pivoting around in place."
"The jaw thing is downsized."
 Swaying back and forth this whole time
"My nose is hurting."
"There's an itch above my left ankle that's half-dollar sized."
"The jaw thing is in a line two inches long and the width of a pencil line."
"The itch on my ankle is a racquet-ball size."
"Now the itch is a half-dollar size."
 Deep breath
 Blowing nose
"The itch on my left ankle is dime size."
"There's itching on my right foot under the ankle."
"My left ear is aching at the '6' level of pain."
"I often feel this pain in my ear."
"The right ankle itch is gone."

"The left ankle itch is half of a dime size."
"My earache is gone."
"The left ankle itch is a BB size."
"The left ankle itch is gone."
    (Tracking a few more random itches)
"Weird... Everything is normal now."
...

This session shows how a young person can matter-of-factly describe sensations related to vehicle injuries and surgeries. It is also an example of how trauma energy related to vehicle injuries can be resolved relatively quickly because Marcus only participated in two more sessions after the ones described above. The fourth session focused on a trampoline accident, which had occurred when he was four years old where he had fallen on the ground on his back. After that session, he started working a summer job, and I didn't see him all summer.

In October of the following school year, Marcus reported that he was sleeping well with no bad dreams, and that he had stopped taking asthma medication because he didn't have any more asthma attacks. He also hadn't been sick. He was no longer getting migraines and cluster headaches. He only had minor headaches in his father's presence. Since he didn't see his father very often, the headaches did not concern him. I didn't witness him taking deep breaths or yawning as we talked, but he reported still taking deep breaths. He said that he still didn't have much appetite, and he rated his depression at the "3" level on the ten-point scale, with a "10" rating being the most depressed a person can be (suicidal). He was earning As and Bs in school. During his fifth and final session, he focused on his throat and said that the sensation reminded him of the tube that was put down his throat when he had Tylenol poisoning. He said that he did not see the need for additional sessions after the fifth session.

When I tracked him many years later, I learned that he had graduated from high school and college. I was thrilled to find a magazine article extolling his career and his expertise.

The Girl Who Lost her "Mary Janes"

When I met Mia, she was a sixty-four-year-old married woman, mother of three, and grandmother to nine children. She had earned a PhD and was currently working as a psychologist in her own clinical practice. She had no plans to retire. When I asked her to specify some of her symptoms, she said that she was experiencing pain everywhere and that she had been diagnosed as having fibromyalgia. She told me that she could not feel the left side of her body when she was meditating and that she had been deaf in her left ear for many years. She said that she had stopped jogging, something she had enjoyed, but she continued to walk each day.

When I asked Mia about the traumatic events in her life, one of the events she named was being hit by a car. She said that the event happened when she was a little girl. One of her family's stories was that the impact of the car had knocked her "Mary Jane" shoes right off her feet. Here are some excerpts from my notes when we addressed that accident. She was standing during the session. I asked her to describe the day she was hit by a car in a sentence or two.

"I feel pain at the back of my right shoulder."
  Deep breath
"I'm nauseated."
"The pain is pulsing. It comes and goes at the '5' Level."
  Deep breath
"The pain has a core, and it radiates out. It's walnut sized at the core."
"My neck pain is a '6'."
  Tilting whole body left
"My neck pain starts and my shoulder pain stops."
"I had the thought that I'm not supposed to talk about this."
  Clearing throat
"I was three and a half years old at Sunday school. I came out of Sunday school."
"I feel frozen, sick."
"Pain shot up in my head."
"I'm feeling really sad in my throat and eyes."

"I feel angry."
> Deep breath

"My uncle came to pick me up. He's on the other side of the street. He got out of his car, and he's standing there."
> Deep breath
> Left head tilt

"My neck and shoulder are ok."
> Yawn
> Standing up straighter
> Hands on face
> Breathing fast and deep

"My heart rate is up."

"I'm really nauseated."

"My whole head is pulsating."

"I know what's going to happen, so I don't want to move."

"He's got his arms out for me to come to him, so I start running."
> Tears running down her face
> Hands on face

"I'm standing on the sidewalk. I can't move."

"I feel fear, shame, and all alone."

"My feet are like lead, and they hurt."

"In the hospital, my mother yelled at me for running across the street."

"I'm really hot."

"I'm most angry that my mom wasn't there (to pick me up)."

"I'm angry my uncle wasn't making it safe to do that."

"I'm angry that all the adults were so hysterical, which made me feel more lonely."
> Hands on knees

"I didn't feel like the world was a safe place."

"I'm starting to feel a little better."

"My throat feels like it's going to close in to keep me from talking. That's the rule: Don't talk, don't feel. I'm trembling inside."

"My tummy is a lot better."
> Big burp
> Picking up each foot and circling the ankle

"I'm shaky and cold."
> [I put a blanket around her]

"I'm laying on a metal table in a white round room. I'm really cold."
"I'm feeling sadness, fear, shame. I'm really pissed because I am all alone."
    [Say, "I survived. I'm okay."]
"I survived. I'm okay."
"I need to hear that it wasn't my fault."
    Tears running down cheeks
    [Imagine your uncle coming to you, saying it wasn't your fault, and
    apologizing.]
"That would be nice."
    Deep breath
"How about my mom?"
    [What do you want her to say to you?]
"You're okay. I'm so glad you're okay. I'm so sorry this happened to you."
    More tears
    Deep breath
"My tummy is okay."
"I have no pain anywhere."
    ...

We touched on this accident several more times in the time that Mia and I worked together. In various sessions, she referred to pain and the incident. Since the car had hit her on the right side of her body, and the left side of her head and body hit the ground, all of those areas experienced pain during sessions; nevertheless, the pain dissipated by the end of each session.

Mia continued to attend sessions regularly where we worked on her long list of traumatic events besides this car accident. Across the sessions, various parts of her body started to move until she was doing full Cobra Sequences (see Chapter 4 for a description) and fluidly running while seated during sessions. In the twenty-fourth session, she reported that she had begun running in her neighborhood daily and signing up for races. She said that she did not feel pain in the mornings when she woke up. In the fifty-seventh session, she said that she couldn't remember the last time she had a headache. In the sixty-first session, she reported that she could feel the left side of her body. She told me that she had read a 700-page book in two days.

She said, "This is some kind of a miracle for somebody my age to change like this after holding onto this stuff for so long!"

When I interviewed her twenty years after her last session, she was eighty-six years old and had just returned from a trip to Europe. Prior to that trip, she had recently visited her granddaughter and great-granddaughter in California. She had three great-grandchildren and was enjoying living in a retirement community. When I asked her to reflect on her treatment sessions with me, she said, "Somatic Experiencing gave me permission to accept what was going on with me and know that it was okay."

Mia's story is significant because it shows that an event that took place when she was three and a half years old was still stored in her body and memory. She remembered everything about the event with regard to what people said and did, and the repercussions for her body were consequential despite the fact that her physical injuries were minimal. For more than sixty years, she had dealt with pain related to the accident, but she did not realize that it was related to the accident. Further, she had been diagnosed with fibromyalgia, which disappeared after she had engaged in therapy.

The Toddler Whose Mother's Arms Served as Her Seat Belt

When I met Helen, she was fifty-five years old and an art professor at a university while also creating her own works of art. She had two grown children and five grandchildren. She described herself as having a flat affect. People had commented to her that they could not determine what her reactions to them were. She also said that she wears an "I'm fine" mask. She was having trouble concentrating, and she felt hypersensitive to criticism and a sharp tone of voice. Her digestion was problematic, and she felt "heavy" after eating meat. Her jaw was uncomfortable, and she felt like her bite was "off." She had high blood pressure and could not feel pain. (She reported, for example, that she did not feel pain while in labor and child birth.) She said she was fighting a "feeling of immobility" by filling up her life with lots of activities. When I asked her about the traumatic events in her life, she reported several, including a tonsillectomy and a dog attack at eight years old, a broken foot in basketball, wisdom-teeth removal at twenty-two years old, and an appendectomy and a miscarriage at twenty-six years old.

Helen also reported that her family was in a car accident when she was two years old. Her father was driving; her mother was holding her on her lap; and her brother was between her mother and father in the front seat. Her grandmother was in the back seat. During our initial SE sessions, she made head and neck movements and had begun moving her arms. Here are some notes from our thirteenth session. She had begun the session by recounting a few details about the car accident, like the position of everyone in the car. She was sitting on a large exercise ball in my office.

...

    Right head tilt
    Left head tilt
    Deep breath
    Right torso twist
    Deep breath
"I can see out the window."
    Her body is very still
"Huh..."
    Left head tilt
"Huh..."
    Right head tilt
"The car is all smashed on our side."
"We would have had to get out the driver's side."
"We walked around and picked up groceries."
"The windshield is smashed in."
    Hands on sides of chin
"Wow! There's no room for Mom and me."
"I wonder if Dad got pushed out of the car."
"It's so closed in and tight."
    Head down
"How scary and tight it feels."

"I have the feeling of being trapped."

"Now I have the feeling of being lifted out of it."

"The right side of my face feels smashed."

>Scratching right cheek

"I don't remember being held or cuddled like I'd like to be now. I want a complete feeling of being safe. Mom used to rock me, but I'm not sure who was rocking whom. Not a safe place."

>Deep breath

"The person who should do it is me."

"Nobody is taking care of anybody. Everybody is busy picking up groceries. They needed care, too."

>Holding her chest tightly and rocking on the ball

>Smiling

>Scratching the back of her neck

"I'm still smashed in on the right side of my jaw."

"My body wants to be held."

>Mouth opening in surprise all of a sudden

"OH!!"

"The guy who hit us went through the windshield!!"

>Hands over her eyes

"Mom was keeping me busy, so I wouldn't be so focused on that."

"The car is all ugh... The man is all bloody on the ground. People in the house on the corner came to help. My dad was really preoccupied because he had grandma and that guy. My mom and grandma had broken pelvises."

>Her arms are hugging herself

"I still need some cuddling, a feeling of warmth and comfort, and a safe place."

>[Say, "I survived."]

"I survived. We ALL survived."

"That accident took away my feeling of security. I needed that feeling."

"Hmmm..."

>Shoulders relaxed downward

>Hands on cheeks

"It's a feeling of feeling secure in myself that I'm really wanting. Making it okay in here."

>Placed both hands on center of chest

"That's something I'm not familiar with except when I'm alone out in
    nature."
    Shoulders are jiggling downward
    Right head tilt
    Left head tilt
    Hands with palms up on thighs
"Everything got all jangled and broken."
"Nothing helped me settle back in."
    Hands on face and turning face right
"It wasn't just the cars and windshield that got shattered, was it?"
"It's not about putting the pieces in place. It's letting them settle into
    their right place."
"I can do this!"
    Deep breath
"I can do this! It's really scary to take care of myself."
    Hands in center of chest
    Deep breath
    Rocking on the ball continues
"I can do this slowly."
    Smile

...

After that session, Helen stated that her body felt more aligned
and "unkinked." She said, "My body feels good!" When we worked
on the accident again, she said that she had no memory of flying
through the air during the accident but remembered being held
tightly by her mother. Thus, her mother's arms had served as her seat
belt. She reported pain in her right arm, and she asked to focus the
session on her arms. Here are excerpts from my notes taken during
the session. She started by stating a few memories about the accident.
The session notes start with the initial impact of the accident after
her description.

...

    Huge shudder in torso with body falling forward
    Head turning right

  Head moving up
  Head continuing to turn right more
  Held up her right arm and moved it to the right
  Tears
  Pulled right arm back to her body
  Torso turn left, and head and right arm are hanging over the left arm rest
"The gear shift is right here, and I can feel it."
"Mom wants me off of her."
"Dad reaches over to get me."
"That car must have come in a lot further than I thought."
"I have to get around the gear shift to get out."
"My right arm feels useless and trapped."
  Holding upper right arm in left hand
  Left torso lean over left arm rest
  Right arm is starting to move when she leans left; it's reaching out left
  Left torso lean over left arm rest
  Sitting upright
  (Whole sequence with arms again)
  (And again)
"My jaw and the right side of my neck really hurt."
"I can see the interaction between my mom and dad. They really loved each other. What a wonderful thing!"
"The feeling is, 'If I lock my jaw, everything is ok.'"
"Because I can't cry. The feeling is that I have to take care of Mom by not crying. It will upset her. I want to be ok for Mom."
Tears running down her cheeks
"If I don't take a deep breath, Mom won't know I'm not ok."
"I'm out of the car, and my body wants to twist and stretch."
Standing up and moving right arm in a big circle several times
Moving right arm in a variety of directions
  "There's warmth in my arm!"
"It feels like that's what my body wanted to do. It feels like a completely different neck and shoulder. There's an ease there that I don't think I've ever felt."

  ...

At the beginning of the next session, Helen reported that her right arm was much better. She had given her arm a massage and enjoyed every minute of it. She found that she could lift objects at arm's length, which was something that she had not been able to do. She exclaimed that her jaw was now matching up with a coordinated bite. We did several more sessions on a variety of issues, completing twenty-two sessions in all.

This session on the car accident illustrates that trauma energy stored as a two-year-old child can continue to cause pain and discomfort in an adult's body. It also illustrates how vibrant a two-year-old's memories can be when they are tied into memories of a traumatic incident. Helen literally "saw" the accident scene and described it to me in living color, putting her hands over her eyes because of the horror she felt as her adult self. When I asked Helen how participating in SE sessions had helped her, she said, "It has given me confidence that my body 'knows.' I now listen to my body. I take time to sense what my body is telling me." Today, Helen is enjoying retirement in a new home and visiting her children and grandchildren.

The Girl Who Was Hit by a Train

Rachel was a forty-five-year-old woman working in the nursing profession during the Covid-19 pandemic when we began to work together. She was married with three natural-born children and two stepchildren, four of whom were grown and out of the house. She reported a long list of symptoms, including depression, nightmares, self-loathing, panic attacks, anxiety, and pain in her neck, shoulders, and joints. She said that she was "terrified of people." She reported that she did not like to eat because her stomach did not feel good with food in it. Even though she ate very little, she could not lose weight. During her childhood, she had had many visits to the principal's office because of rule-breaking behavior. She also had been "thrown out" of the gifted program for her disobedience. Thus, although she was very intelligent, her experience with some teachers, especially authoritative ones, had not been pleasant.

She also told me about a number of traumatic events that had occurred in her childhood and adulthood. She had had several surgeries, including an anterior cruciate ligament (ACL) surgery (see Chapter 11 for that story) and a recent sinus surgery. She had been a first responder as well as a nurse. Thus, she had witnessed numerous deaths and the results of catastrophic accidents. In her first few sessions, though, Rachel had focused on the sinus surgery, her most recent traumatic event.

At the end of the tenth session, after Rachel's body had done six full Cobra Sequences (see Chapter 4 for an explanation), I had started wondering whether she had experienced some car accidents. I asked Rachel whether she had had any car accidents. She replied by asking whether she had told me that she had been hit by a train. (She hadn't!) She reported that, when she was eight years old, her dad was driving her to school in their Volkswagen bus. They lived out in the country, relying on a wood-burning stove for heat. As a result, their well water froze regularly. That day, they were traveling on a country road in a snowstorm. Rachel was in the front passenger seat; her younger sister was in the back seat. Neither girl had utilized a seat belt. Both girls saw the lights of the train coming in the snowy darkness on the left side of the car, but they said nothing to their dad. He told Rachel years later that he never saw the train approaching. The train hit their vehicle on the driver's side. After the impact, Rachel opened her eyes and found that she was on the floor of the vehicle in front of her seat in the fetal position.

In the eleventh session, we addressed the train accident directly by starting with a couple of sentences about Rachel's memory of that snowy morning. Below are excerpts from my notes.

"It was snowing really hard, and it was very cold."
 Yawn
"Everything feels heavy, like a weight pulling me down."
 Yawn
 Left head circle
 Right head circle

Left torso turn and left head turn
Right torso turn and right head turn
Yawn
Full Cobra Sequence #1
Left head tilt
Right head tilt
Head tilted back
Head upright
Yawn
Full Cobra Sequence #2
Left head tilt
Right head tilt
Yawn
"The weight is better."
"My insides are now moving."
Yawn
"I was like a statue."
"I am so scared."
Full Cobra Sequence #3
"My neck is not as stiff as last week. It's been stiff my whole life."
"The weight is much better. I can feel myself, my core. I'm engaged."
Yawn
Full Cobra Sequence #4

...

Full Cobra Sequence #5

...

Full Cobra Sequence #6
"There's no weight now."

...

"I feel like when my head goes down, it was like when I was thrown down to
    the floor in contraction, and when I come back up, it's like expansion."
"Going down is like going into a ball, and coming up is expansion."

...

"I feel more lifted up, not as heavy, not as dead."
    [Say, "I survived!"]
"I survived." (Said with no expression.)
    [Say, "I survived!" again with expression this time.]

"I survived."
"I survived!!"
"I feel kinda sad."
    Deep breath
    Yawn
    Deep breath
"What a relief!"
"I'm alive!"
    Deep breath
"It's hard. I don't deserve to be alive."
"It's hard to take up space."
"It's good that I'm alive."
"It's okay for me to be here."
"Oh…"
"Yeah…"
    Deep breath
"It's hard for me to take up space."
"I don't know where that thought comes from."
    Yawn
    Deep breath
    Wiping tears from cheeks

…

The next few sessions were very similar, with Rachel going through the Cobra Sequence several times in each session. During the fifteenth session, as she went through the Cobra Sequence a few times, her body went entirely down to the floor and curled up in the fetal position before coming back upward and returning to her chair. Her whole body started to tremble, and she remembered being very cold and shivering after the accident. As she warmed up during the session and the trembling continued, she remembered being in the policeman's car and how warm it was. She recalled that she had a bump on the right side of her forehead as a result of the accident and that she had experienced daily headaches for a long time. She also recalled a classmate bringing a newspaper clipping to school about the accident and gleefully announcing how Rachel's dad had wrecked their car. She reported that she got in trouble with the teacher for how she had reacted to the boy.

During the sixteenth session, we focused on Rachel's head and the bump on the right side of her forehead. That was the first and last time we worked on that head injury. She did not complain about pain in that part of her head again. We worked together weekly for a few years and continue working together when Rachel needs a session. Meanwhile, she earned a doctoral degree, she became certified as a Somatic Experiencing Practitioner, and she began doing clinical work in a mental health clinic. She is a brilliant woman who cares deeply about helping others.

LIGHT-BULB MOMENTS

While you were reading the stories about childhood trauma related to common events like injuries, falls, and vehicle accidents, what are some "Light-bulb moments" that you have had?

CONCLUSIONS

CONCERNS

FUTURE PLANS

CHAPTER 8

LOSS

Loss due to death can be a very traumatizing and debilitating event. Loss of a parent can be especially traumatizing to a child. The circumstances and the environment surrounding the child can exacerbate the situation. The younger the child, the more likely that the loss will result in symptoms. The key concept to remember related to child loss of a parent is that children are biologically programmed to stay close to their parents, especially their mothers who can ensure their survival through breast feeding and other types of care. When children lose that connection, they can feel as if death is imminent. Losing a loved one after a long illness can be debilitating as well. Fighting a potentially terminal disease keeps everyone surrounding the patient in flight or fight mode, sometimes for months or even years. Experiencing the loss of a loved one due to suicide, accident, or overdose is also traumatizing because of the sudden nature of the event and the lack of opportunity to gain closure in the relationship. Individuals who work in environments where people are dying regularly can also be affected by each loss. For example, workers in Neonatal Intensive Care Units and Adult Intensive Care Units can become emotionally attached to the babies or people in their care and can be affected over time by the sheer volume of the losses they experience. A wide variety of symptoms can result from all these types of loss. The most common symptom is grief, where the person is overcome with emotion and frequent tears. Sometimes, the person's eyes are itchy or affected in some other way. Children may not be able to function in school; adults might not be able to be productive at work. Energy discharge during SE sessions tends to be centered in the chest or upper torso and eyes.

The Girl Who Wanted to Say More

Susan was experiencing serious grief symptoms when she was thirty-four years old. Her mother had died when she was thirteen years old, but she continued to miss her mother immensely. Susan started having menstrual periods while her mother was on life support in the hospital. From the time she was in her late twenties, every month, she had experienced horribly painful cramps at the "9 ½" to "10" level of pain (on a ten-point scale, with ten representing the most excruciating pain imaginable). Each time, she had to stay home from work for a day or two to recover from the cramps.

After her mother died, Susan was often alone with friends because her father was working or at his girlfriend's house, and her sister had left for college. Her father eventually married a woman who had two daughters. As a result, a blended family was formed when Susan was seventeen years old. Unfortunately, Susan's stepmother favored her younger daughter and was very critical of Susan and the older daughter. She discouraged Susan (or anyone else) from talking about Susan's mother and from reminiscing about the times before her mother had died. Nevertheless, Susan wanted to talk about her mother and reminisce about her. She was very artistic and had made several portraits of her mother, some of which she kept in her apartment.

In the initial sessions, we worked on Susan's injuries and accidents. (See Chapter 6 for the work she did related to a fall from a horse.) During her sixth session, I asked Susan to envision her mother in the hospital when her mother was on life support. Below are some of my notes from that session.

"There's a band of tingling across my torso—It's dark."
"There's tingling on the right side of my face."

"I feel fear. It's very scary."
"They had taken her off all meds."
"She was already a different version of herself."
"I feel pressure on my chest."
"I feel pressure on my lower abdomen."
"The pressure on my chest is more spread out now."
"There's tingling in my lower abdomen."
  Tears running down cheeks
"I feel sadness. It's a cone of energy moving upward from my abdomen."
"I'm having a kind of out-of-body experience."
"Now the tingling is getting stronger as it moves upward. It's crawling up."
"The pressure on my chest is gone."
  Deep breath
  Deep breath
"The tingling in my abdomen is lighter."
"There's a tight feeling in my throat."
"I feel this same tightness when I'm stressed out."
  Deep breath
  Toes of both feet are moving up and down in unison
"I'm thinking about choices that were made."
"I'm thinking about being left out of decisions."
  Tears continue
"I wanted to be in the room when they took her off life support."
"I didn't advocate for myself."
"My jaw is tightening."
"The throat tightness is stronger, pretty strong."
"I have a headache in my forehead at the '3' level."
"The throat feeling is on both sides of my neck and throat."
  Jaw is opening and closing, two times
  Wiping tears from her face with handkerchief
"My headache is gone."
"The throat tightness is not as intense."
"I'm imagining myself voicing more."
"I feel a strong swirling in my torso."
"It's icy hot—really cold at the top of my abdomen."
  Wiping tears away
  Wiping tears

"Being left out is like being complicit. I wish I would have voiced what I
    wanted."
"I want to be in the room."
"Why can't I be in there?"
"It's not fair!"
"I'm still feeling that swirling. It's expanding upward and out."
"The temperature is an interesting part of it—it's so cold!"
    Wiping tears
    Wiping tears
"The tightness in my throat is pulsing."
"The headache has moved to the sides of my forehead at the '2' level."
...
"My throat feels good."
"The headache is faint."
"My throat is better."
"The headache is gone."
"I have a feeling of elation in my chest."
...

This session was important for Susan because it not only enabled
her to discharge some of the trauma energy associated with seeing
her mother in the hospital on life support, but it also enabled her
to address her discomfort with not feeling free to speak and feeling
"left out." She made some of the statements that she had wanted
to say for years. The energy she felt in her chest and swirling in her
abdomen was likely associated with her grief. From my experience,
grief trauma energy tends to be stored in the heart and chest area.
Additionally, I tell people that one tear shed in an SE session is worth
a few buckets of tears in real life. I encourage them to allow tears to
fall. Trauma energy associated with not being able to speak is usually
stored in the throat area. After this session and others, I observed
that Susan was able to speak about her feelings more freely, and she
reported being able to speak up in difficult or contentious situations.
The cramps she experienced with her periods became less and less
painful over time, until she reported that she sometimes has to take
life a bit easy on the first day of her period, but she engages in a full

schedule of activities thereafter. During the time that we worked together, Susan took coursework and became QuickBooks certified so that she could work as a bookkeeper. Additionally, she completed all the requirements to become a certified Somatic Experiencing Practitioner. She currently operates a private practice, providing trauma therapy to people who have experienced traumatic events.

The Girl Whose Eyes Itched

Lily was a freshman in high school when we met. She had had a tumultuous childhood until then. She was born in an emergency Cesarian-section birth. Her mother and father were divorced when she was two years old and had initially shared custody of Lily. Her mother was a drug addict and did not follow through on her promises and responsibilities. For example, she would leave Lily at a friend's house and not come back for her for days. Other times, she would say that she would pick Lily up shortly after 8:00 a.m. and not show up until 10:00 p.m. Eventually, her mother became homeless. She died of congestive heart failure when Lily was ten years old. Thereafter, Lily lived with her grandparents in California for a time, and she called her grandma her "second mom." She was living with her father when I met her. Her dad had remarried, and Lily, her dad, and her brother had moved in with her dad's new wife and her children. Lily and her stepmother did not get along. The stepmother called Lily names, like "Slut," "Crybaby," and "The girl who can't remember anything."

With regard to other traumatic events in her life, Lily had witnessed her mother and her mother's boyfriend fighting. The boyfriend had hit and tried to choke her mother, and Lily had tried to defend her mother during the fights. She remembered always being hungry with only bologna or pizza in the house if any food was present at all. She couldn't remember her mother ever cooking a meal. Her mother's boyfriend died of a drug overdose. The boyfriend's dog had bit Lily on her hand and her right eye. Lily had had a couple of accidents requiring stitches on her chin. One involved another child falling on her from above. Lily remembered being in several earthquakes in California that scared her, but she was not injured during them.

With regard to symptoms, Lily reported that she required an hour or two to go to sleep. She had no appetite. She often skipped breakfast and lunch. She had a surprised look on her face, with very wide-open eyes. As she spoke to me, she rubbed one of her eyes constantly. She was also very fidgety, popping her knuckles, popping her neck, and swinging her legs often. She said that she used to bite her nails; currently, she just picked at them and would tear them off. She complained of pain on her hip bones, like being pricked by a needle. She reported crying at least once a week. She said that she had trouble with her balance when rollerblading and walking. Each time she stood up, her vision blacked out, and she heard ringing in her ears constantly. Her father reported to me that she frequently touched and poked other people in annoying ways. Although she had some acquaintances, she felt she had no real friends. She rated her depression level as varying between "3" and "7" on a ten-point scale (with ten being suicidal). She rated her happiness level as varying between "10" at school and "3" at home. She felt like she was in agony when she was supposed to do her homework. She knew that her attention span was short, and her memory was poor. She could earn As, Bs, and Cs on tests, but she did not complete her homework.

When Lily and I initially did some Walk-Up Activities, she was unable to stand up by herself for more than a few seconds. She had to lean up against the wall for balance. She could not close her eyes for more than a few seconds. By the third session, she reported that she did not cry in the previous week. Below are some of my notes from the first Walk-Up Activity in the third session where she felt sensations in her eyes. She stopped me at the four-foot distance, but still couldn't close her eyes or stand up without help.

...

"I feel stinging in my eyes."
    She leaned against the wall
    Yawn

"My eyes just feel tired now—they aren't stinging."
"There's tingling along my lashes."
"My eyelashes feel like they are going into my eye."
    Yawn
    Her eyes are watering
"My right knee wants to give out."
"My right knee is okay now."
    [I asked her to try closing her eyes.]
"My eyes want to be open."
    Yawn
    Both shoulders are leaning against the wall
...

By the twelfth session, Lily was taking about thirty minutes to go to sleep. She was earning better grades and rated her level of depression at "2" on the ten-point scale. She was able to sit in a chair with her eyes closed and concentrate continuously during the session. She appeared very calm and still. During the session, she experienced sensations in her eyes as well as other parts of her body. Here are some of my notes from the session.

...
"My right ear tickles inside."
    Yawn
    Scratching her right ear
    Yawn
    Rubbing her left eye
    Rubbing her right eye
"I just got a picture of my mom from the shoulders up."
    Yawn
    Right foot moving a tad
"It feels like there's an eyelash in my right eye."
"I have a burning feeling in my right eye on the lower eyelid."
"The burning feels like Bactine on a cut."
    Rubbing left eye
    Rubbing left eye
    Opened eyes

"There's a lot of moisture in my right eye when my eyes are closed."
  Yawn
  Closed eyes
  Eyes watering
  Tears running down cheeks
  Rubbing eyes
"My right eye is okay except my eyelashes are stuck together."
  Opened eyes
  ...

By the fifteenth session, Lily reported that she had finished reading a novel. She had started a job as a grocery bagger. She had passed all her courses. She was taking fifteen minutes to go to sleep. She reported having a couple of good friends. By the eighteenth session, Lily reported that she was no longer blacking out when she stood up.

In the twenty-fourth session, Lily directly addressed her mother's death. She was sitting in a chair with her legs on a big exercise ball. I had asked her to think about the day she heard her mom was in the hospital. Here are some notes I took during that session.

  ...
  Yawn
  Yawn
  Lips taut over teeth
  Head turn left and down
  Yawn
  Rubbing and squeezing eyes
"I was in school."
"My dad told me she was in the hospital and might have died, and he
  started to cry."
  Hands over her face
  Yawn
  Yawn
"I started to cry."
  Yawn
  Head upright
  Facing forward

"My dad and I went into the office and asked them to page my brother."
"My dad signed us out, and we went out to the car. My dad told my
    brother about my mom."
    Yawn
"My dad and I were both crying."
"My brother didn't cry."
"We got to the hospital."
"We went into the waiting area. There were two people there who knew
    my mom."
    Loud stomach gurgles
"I was crying some, but it was drying up."
"The doctor came out and talked to my dad."
    Arms up straight above head and big stretch
    Yawn
"The doctor came over to me and my brother."
"I started crying my eyes out."
    Legs bouncing alternately on the ball
    Left leg bouncing on the ball
"After the doctor told us she was dead, he asked if we wanted to see her
    body. My dad did."
    Yawn
"My dad did not let me go see her."
    Yawn

...

In total, Lily completed fifty-one sessions. We continued to work
through that summer and the next school year. Unfortunately, her
family life was not stress free, so her symptoms increased each time
some traumatic event occurred. For example, her dad was temporarily
blinded and was diagnosed with diabetes. Her dad and stepmother
had frequent fights, and, after one of them, her stepmother called
the police. Consequently, her dad was arrested, went to jail, and
had to face a court case. One of her stepbrothers moved back into
the home and caused problems. Her parents started talking about
filing for bankruptcy and later about moving. Her boyfriend moved
to another town. Thus, her future was uncertain in a lot of respects.

Nevertheless, she continued participating in regularly scheduled sessions. During the summer after her sophomore year in high school, I lost touch with her.

When I caught up with Lily, twenty-three years later, I learned that she had graduated from high school. She went to nursing school and became certified as a licensed practical nurse (LPN). She had worked for a time as a nurse, but because her schedule needed more flexibility (she eventually had four children), she searched for other jobs that would work. Since she likes being outside, she currently works in construction. She still loves to read, and she told me that she has read the Bible three times as well as many other substantial books, including the whole *Harry Potter* series and the *Dune* series.

This story illustrates how slow progress in treatment might be if the person is living within a chaotic situation in which traumatic events are frequently occurring. It also shows how slow progress can be when a child is living with a predator—her stepmother was continually attacking her verbally. Lily was making slow but steady progress while her life was relatively stable. She was sleeping and eating, she was earning better grades in school, and she was no longer experiencing poor concentration, blackouts, and imbalance. In fact, she frequently reported earning an A on a test or a science lab report. She read several novels. Her body was calm. Unfortunately, as time went on, and the frequency of strife in her home-life increased, she started experiencing symptoms again. With each new threat, her capacity to deal with trauma energy was challenged. Under these circumstances, she was not able to complete assignments and produce consistently high grades in her high-school courses.

CHAPTER 9
PARENTAL ABUSE

Parental abuse can be physical, sexual, and psychological, and each of these types has various dimensions. Children have no recourse against an attacker who is bigger, stronger, and smarter than they are. Thus, they are likely to freeze when a parent attacks them, and trauma energy is likely to be stored. Children also have no recourse when a parent abandons them. Some parents take their children to someone's home, say they will be back soon, and do not return when they are supposed to return. They may say that they will pick a child up after school, and then they do not show up for hours. They leave children in places where children do not belong, and they put children in isolation for hours and even days. All of these incidents are examples of abuse, and they can lead to stored trauma energy that results in symptoms.

The Boy Who Could Not Speak

Robert was my friend; we had met through the community of healers in my town. We had enjoyed many conversations together, and he often shared vegetables with me that he had grown in his garden. One day, when we were chatting, I noticed that he was having a hard time speaking. He tried to speak and ended up coughing uncontrollably. When I expressed concern about whether he had asthma, he indicated in writing that he was dealing with an emotional issue related to his childhood. When I volunteered my help, he agreed to meet with me to do some sessions. He was fifty-four years old at the time.

In our first session, I explained the reservoir analogy to Robert. During the next week, he wrote me a letter that gave me a history of the traumatic events in his childhood. The letter explained that when he was a baby, family "lore" held that the family doctor told his parents not to pick him up when he was crying. As a result, he cried and cried and eventually held his breath until he passed out. After he passed out, he started breathing again. This happened many times before his parents learned to calm him when he was crying. Then, as a little child, Robert did not learn to speak fluently. Because of his speech difficulties, no one understood what he was saying except his mother. Although he had speech therapy in school, he had a lot of difficulty communicating with others. He had tantrums when people did not understand what he was saying, and, as a result, he spent a lot of time in the hall at school.

When he was nine years old, his mother became abusive. She often hit him and his siblings on their backs and thighs with coat hangers, spoons, a broom, and a hairbrush. Once, she hit him so hard on his arm that she broke her hairbrush. During his eighth-grade year, he was hospitalized because he had become withdrawn and self-destructive. He was the "identified patient." The choice given to the family was to hospitalize him or his mother, and they had chosen him. When he had tantrums in the hospital, where he was surrounded by children who had been diagnosed as schizophrenic or autistic, he was over-powered by the staff and drugged. He was eventually diagnosed as "schizophrenic" and "catatonic schizophrenic." After several months, he was released from the hospital to complete the eighth grade and progress to high school, where he would scream out in frustration and withdraw if he could not get people to understand what he was trying to say. In college, he worked hard to learn to speak clearly, and he became an articulate speaker. Indeed, I had always known him as an articulate speaker.

As I mentioned above, I witnessed that Robert was no longer able to speak without coughing uncontrollably before he began SE Therapy with me. After his first SE session, he reported that his cough was better. He reported no coughing in the first week and that he coughed ten times in the second week. He came back for a second session since his rate of coughing seemed to be increasing. Below are some notes from that second session after I asked him to think of how it feels inside his body when someone is not listening to him or understanding what he is saying.

"I feel a tickle in my throat. It's pea sized, at the '2' level, and it's moving
   around in my throat, touching me like a feather."
   Deep breath
   Wiping mouth with hand
"It wants me to cough it up and out."
   Cough
"The pressure to cough went away."
"The tickle is still there."
"My heart is beating hard inside my chest and head."
"I feel heat in my face and my whole head."
"The pulsing is filling my whole head."
   Moving his head around in a variety of ways
"The heat is better. My face is still warm."
   Deep breath
"The tickle is at the '1.5' level."
"The pulsing continues lightly in my chest. There's hardly any pulsing in
   my head."
   Yawn
"My feet are tingly."
....
"The tickling sensation is gone."
   Deep breath
"My feet are okay."
"The tickle came back a little."
"The pulsing continues."
   Deep breath

...

"There's no tickle."

"There's no heat or pulsing."

...

During the remainder of this session, Robert released numerous huge burps, saying that he felt pressure in his chest and abdomen after I asked him again to visualize someone not understanding what he was saying. After releasing a really huge burp, he said, "I've been waiting fifty years to release that burp!" We did two more SE sessions together, after which he went on with his life and continued to speak fluently with no more uncontrollable coughing and no stomach problems. He lived a productive life, continually and generously giving to all the people he knew. He also helped many people through his profession. Sadly, he died when he was sixty-seven years old from congestive heart failure.

Robert's story is significant because it shows how a few therapy sessions can eliminate a very troublesome symptom that was interfering in his personal and professional life. It also shows how gentle a therapy session can be even though the initiating traumas were quite serious. Sadly, his hospitalization as a boy illustrates how the medical system can make mistakes with regard to identifying and diagnosing abusive parents. Instead, Robert was the identified patient and misdiagnosed as schizophrenic.

The Girl Who Spent an Evening by Herself in NYC

I met Mia when she was sixty-four years old. (See additional stories about her in Chapters 7 and 11.) She reported fainting and vomiting a lot when she was a child. As an adult, her right eye was constantly twitching, and she was experiencing pain in her neck and shoulders. She had a history of frequent panic attacks and was so anxious and fearful that she refused to sit in a chair in my presence. As a result, we were both standing during her fourth session. I was standing about ten feet away from her and took one step forward toward her, when she suddenly began remembering an incident when she had been taken by her parents to New York City. She had not mentioned this incident previously, and she did not remember it until the middle of the session. Below are some notes that I wrote during the portion of the session that occurred after she started remembering the incident.

...
    Breathing deeply and slowly
"My heart hurts."
"I have tears in my eyes."
"I have nausea in my stomach."
"It's the size of a small child's ball. It's in the center and moving up."
    Torso tilt left
    Torso tilt right

...
"I feel frozen in my chest, feet, & legs."
"There's nausea in my throat now, too."
"The ball is golf-ball sized & right below my breasts in the center."
"I feel very vulnerable and scared. I want to curl up in a ball."
"I feel alone."
"I have the memory of lying on the floor of a car. I could hardly breathe
    because it was so hot."
    Deep breath
"It's August. My parents and their friends took me to New York City and
    left me locked in the car by myself for hours. They went bar hopping.
    It's hot and dark. I was ten or eleven years old."

...
    Hands at sides
    Bending knees
"I want to scream. I want to tell them how scared I am, and they shouldn't
    have left me there."
    [Please say what you want to say to them.]
"I'm really scared!"
"It helped to say that. I can't even fathom why they would do such a thing."
    Fingers moving
    Fists opening and closing
    Tears continue
"I can't really say that, though. I wasn't permitted to tell them I was afraid."

"When I'm in New York now, I am terrified. I see the connection now."
"The nausea is gone."
"My shoulders are okay."
"My neck is okay."
    Tears continue
    Bending knees
"My right eye continues to twitch."
...

    Turning whole body in a circle
"I feel wobbly and tingly."
"My feet are heavy, but they aren't rubber or concrete anymore."
    Stepping in place
"My feet are tingly."
...

    Walking around the room
"I feel pissed now!"
"That is disgusting that they left their little girl in a car at night in NYC
    in the middle of August!"
    She continued walking around until the end of the session

...

This session is significant because it is the second session where Mia started moving her feet and the first session where she started walking. As she was walking around and around the room, she started looking more and more alive, with color appearing in her face and her arms swinging. Up until these moments of walking, she had been reporting that her feet felt like they were in concrete. A continuing theme throughout her sessions was that her mother told her not to move or speak. She reported being terrified of doing so.

When I tracked Mia to ask her to read the stories I had written about her, she was eighty-six years old, living in a retirement community, and enjoying riding her three-wheeled bike after having a hip replaced. She travels widely, visiting her grandchildren and great-grandchildren. She continues her private practice as a psychologist and generously gives to others in many ways.

The Girl Who Hid Her Mother's Riding Crop

I first became aware of Chelsea when her stepmother (who is one of my friends) spoke with me about her. She was wondering whether Chelsea might have a learning disability. She mentioned that Chelsea, who was ten years old and in the fifth grade, was very shy and fearful. She was concerned because Chelsea was not doing well in school. After asking some questions, I tentatively concluded that Chelsea did not have a learning disability, and I suggested that my friend and her husband consider a small private school where the staff would be able to work with Chelsea in very small classes and analyze the problem. After that, my friend reported that Chelsea had adjusted to the new school, and things were going well.

Several years later, when Chelsea was sixteen years old and in high school, my friend and her husband (Chelsea's biological father) reported that Chelsea and her younger sister had experienced some traumatic events involving their biological mother. They asked me to speak with the girls. In our first meeting, I learned that their mother was drinking heavily, and the girls had witnessed numerous violent fights between her and a series of boyfriends. At different times, their mother had locked herself and the girls in a room and barricaded the door with furniture while their mother and the boyfriend yelled at each other through the door. One of the boyfriends had threatened to kill the girls.

Chelsea also reported that their mother had beaten them numerous times with a riding crop on their butts and on the fronts and backs of their legs. She told me that she did all she could to protect her younger sister from the beatings (e.g., by lying to her mother, doing her sister's chores, covering for her, making excuses for her, and standing between her and their mother to act as a shield), and she reported that she eventually had hidden the riding crop. The beatings had stopped. When I said that I was concerned that her mother might find the riding crop, she told me that would not be possible since they had moved out of the home where she had hidden it.

After I had reported the abuse, the girls' father initiated custody proceedings so that the girls could live at his home full time. The girls' mother was ordered by the court to have supervised visits with the girls for one hour each week. I volunteered to provide trauma therapy to the girls. Chelsea agreed to work with me, and she eventually chose to live with her father.

When I first started working with Chelsea, she was so frightened that she would not sit in a chair for a session; she would only stand near the door to the room. She was so afraid of my dog that she inched along the wall as far away as possible from my dog when she was walking through the same room in which my dog was resting on the floor. She reported a whole list of symptoms, which I compiled over time. They included taking two hours to go to sleep, feeling safe only at home, nightmares, aches and pains, digestive issues, depression, anxiety, irritability, and inability to concentrate.

We started with the Walk-Up Activity (see Chapter 4 for a description), with me standing about fifteen feet away from her and walking slowly toward her. I found that she became aware of sensations in her body when I walked to a point eight feet away from her. This meant that the space within which she felt safe had an eight-foot radius. We also worked on her defensive reactions with her arms, with Chelsea pushing me away from her with each arm in turn and allowing the tingling to dissipate each time. After two sessions, she reported that she was no longer depressed, and after three sessions, she said that she was falling asleep faster, within thirty minutes. She stated, "I feel normal" and reported having no anxiety and no nightmares.

By the eleventh session, Chelsea was comfortable enough with me that she was sitting in a chair during sessions and describing sensations continuously, tracking twitches, itches, spots of tension, and pain as they moved around her body. She was able to concentrate constantly for about thirty minutes. By the thirteenth session, Chelsea reported that she had earned all As and Bs for her quarterly grades, and had no worrisome thoughts, anxiety, or nightmares. During the fourteenth session, she had some inflection and excitement in her voice as she spoke with me, and she did not react fearfully to my dog.

She had gone to a party and reported, "I like crowds." Thereafter, she discontinued participating in sessions. She continued to earn good grades in high school and was awarded a substantial scholarship for college. She made the President's List in college, was selected for the Honors Program, earned her college degree, and became a designer on the West Coast.

Chelsea's story is important because it shows that the combination of SE Therapy and living in a safe environment (her father's home) can significantly reduce symptoms and help an abused child live a productive life. (For more details on her symptoms and her life during the years when Chelsea was in college, see Chapter 13.)

The Girl Who Hated to Bathe

Brianna was referred to me by her school counselor when she was thirteen years old. She had experienced a long list of traumatic situations, including sexual molestation by her father from age three to nine, rape by her uncle who was fifteen years old when she was eight, her mother leaving the home when she was seven years old, domestic violence between her parents, verbal and physical abuse from her parents, her parents' divorce, falling out of a second-story window after someone sat her on the windowsill, and other childhood accidents (e.g., biking, rollerblading, and skateboarding accidents, and a collision inside a water slide). She reported a list of eighty-two symptoms, the most serious of which included failing grades in school, poor memory and concentration, infrequent attendance in school, frequent illnesses, no appetite, not eating for days, depression, and a suicide attempt. In the current school quarter, she had dropped all her courses except math. She and her parents reported that she couldn't complete the simplest of tasks and spent hours and hours on homework.

She looked ghostly pale with dark circles under her eyes, and she was wearing all dark clothing covering every inch of her body, except her face. She said that she wore her clothing to "disguise who she was." She reported that she hated to take showers and never took baths because she hated to get undressed and see her body. She said, "I feel so bare because I don't have anything to hide behind. I don't want to leave my safe prison." Despite being a very cute teenager, she said that she cried anytime she saw herself in a mirror.

Brianna was currently living with her mother, her stepfather, and two younger siblings. When we met for sessions, Brianna was constantly in motion, with her hands fidgeting with her hair or face and her feet and legs moving around or bouncing up and down. She was very frightened and wanted to stand instead of sit in my therapy room. When I did an exercise by walking up to her very slowly, she started to notice sensations when I was about twelve feet away from her. After only two sessions, she reported that she finished her math homework in record time and got an A+ on a math test. She also reported sleeping through the night and showering every day. She was no longer experiencing nightmares. She had put on make-up and nail polish.

By the fourth session, Brianna was wearing a no-sleeve blouse; by the fifth session, she was wearing shorts. By the sixth session, she reported that she was eating "like crazy." She was craving meat, and eating meat was not making her sick to her stomach anymore. For the next few sessions, she continued to report a decrease in symptoms and improvements in her behavior like waking up early, no asthma, weighing 110 pounds (a good weight for her height), not fighting with her mother, and not crying daily. During the twelfth session, we started the session with me walking up to her. She started noticing sensations when I was six feet away from her. Below are some notes from that session.

...

    Her eyes are closed
"My knees feel weak."
"My arms feel heavy."
    Biting her lower lip
"There's a heaviness in my abdomen."
    Yawn

"I feel lightheaded."

    Moving and shaking her hands

    Stepping up and down

    Sat down in the chair

"When my dad messed with me, I'd feel this same light-headed feeling. I'd feel scared, sick to my stomach, and trembling in my hands."

"The scared feeling is in the bottom of my abdomen."

"The sick-to-my-stomach feeling is in my stomach."

"My hands are trembling."

"I'm focusing on my hands."

"The shakiness went away from my hands."

"The lightheadedness has gone away."

"The nausea went away."

"The 'Oh-oh scared feeling' is still there."

"It's the size of an apple but a flat splotch—a big black spot, but now it's really red."

"It's slowly fading away like vanishing ink."

    Her fingers are tightly intertwined

"It's gone for now, but I have a sense that there's a lot more there."

"I now feel a constant flow of energy from my waist down to my feet."

"I feel that I no longer belong to my father. I was a belonging to him, like a sweater or a coat.

    Now my mother is my connection through love. I'm not a belonging to her."

"The flow has stopped."

"I'm feeling peaceful and relaxed."

"I'm feeling relaxed and soothed—almost empty."

    Yawn

...

This session was significant because it was the first session where Brianna spoke about her father's sexual abuse and released trauma energy directly related to it. In the following sessions, she reported an increase in symptoms at first, like having a nightmare about her father, being afraid to go to sleep, and feet moving constantly. Nevertheless, she reported that her neck didn't ache anymore, she'd had no asthma attacks, she'd had no headaches, and she hadn't been sick. By the fifteenth session, she was reporting more and more improvements, with only occasional asthma. Thereafter, her grades continued to improve, and she was completing courses with mostly As and Bs. I continued to work with her until she went to the prom wearing a lovely sleeveless dress and had graduated from the ninth grade. (See Chapter 13 for more of Brianna's story.)

The Girl Who Was Determined to Get Better

My office manager at the university received several phone calls from Edie, who asked her to convince me to provide treatment sessions for her. Edie had gotten my name from her aunt who had "studied with" Peter Levine, my mentor and the developer of Somatic Experiencing. When I called her, Edie told me that she was determined to seek a better life for herself, and she convinced me to help her. When I met with Edie, she told me that she had experienced physical and sexual abuse by her father when she was two to nine years old. When she told her mother about the abuse, her parents divorced. Her brothers were angry with Edie for telling their mother about the abuse. Additional traumatic events in her childhood included a broken right femur, a horse stepping on her right foot when she was eight years old, a right wrist injury from gymnastics, a jammed elbow in a basketball game, and four concussions, all of which knocked her unconscious. The most recent concussion occurred when she was sixteen years old.

Edie was currently nineteen years old, and she had been experiencing symptoms for many years. She had trouble going to sleep and staying asleep for more than six hours. She had frequent night terrors where she dreamed of being held down by one or more males and could not scream. She hated being touched, and she was having difficulty interacting with men her age. She was having frequent headaches and could not concentrate long enough to read a page of text, even though she was a good reader and previously enjoyed reading. She had been enrolled in an alternative high school because she needed a self-paced curriculum, which helped her earn a B grade-point average. Eating meat made her nauseated. She described herself as withdrawn from other people and not participating in exercise or fun activities with others. She said that she was not able to speak up when others were being abusive or insensitive to her. She felt powerless. She described herself as experiencing a "paralysis thing" three times per week as she was going to sleep. When it happened, she felt like her whole body was immobilized or frozen.

Edie started doing sessions on average about twice a month. By the third session, she said that she did not experience headaches during the previous week. By the sixth session, she reported that she was reading the novel *Ishmael* and enjoying it immensely for one and a half hours straight per day. By the eighth session, she had finished the book and had been bike riding with a friend. She had gone camping with friends. By the tenth session, she announced that she "had met a guy" and was seeing him occasionally. Across these and other additional sessions, Edie focused on a variety of traumatic incidents in her life, such as her broken leg, hurt wrist, and concussions.

Edie reported distancing herself from the guy she had been seeing; she had met another guy. She said that she was frustrated with herself because she was so afraid of being close to these men. She continued to have terrible dreams. She said that she did not want to talk about or work on her father's abuse, so we started a session where she agreed to imagine herself holding a guy's hand. Below are some of my notes from that session.

[Please take a moment to visualize yourself walking down a sidewalk holding your date's hand.]
    Yawn
"My right arm got sore like there's a broken bone inside."
"The pain is at the '2' level."
"The pain is throbbing in a circular pattern."
"Now it's a bubble that is stationary."
    Mini-yawn
    Left head turn
    Both thumbs twitching

"My right arm is okay."
      Both thumbs still twitching
"There's a pulse in my left arm in the same spot. No soreness, though."
      Yawn
      Head down
"My left arm is okay."
      Yawn
      [Think of walking together in a chummy way.]
"My head hurts behind both eyes at the '2' level."
"My stomach feels heavy."
      Head is still down
"The pain in my head is gone."
"The stomach stuff is gone."
"My neck is sore on the left side."
      Yawn
      Arms stretched out straight forward
      Hands in fists
"The soreness in my neck is a vertical band."

...

"Hello..."
"The pain in my neck shot up to my eye."
"Now it's in my cheek at the '3' level."
      Both arms are stretched above her head
"There's a line of pain shooting in my chest on the left side."
"It's no longer in my cheek."
      Yawn
      Sitting up straighter
      Both hands open
      Arms braced on armrests
"There are strands of pain throughout my torso."
"The strands are three inches long."
"Feels like it's a random arrangement, out of control."
      Yawn

...

"My belly feels lighter and like I can breathe."
      Stretching arms above head
      Whole torso twist left

Whole torso twist right
Sat up straight
Yawn

...

This session illustrates that the original trauma, her father's abuse, does not have to be the direct focus of a session. Indeed, trauma energy can still discharge after the person imagines a similar but distant event. Edie completed several more sessions after this one. She reported kissing and holding the hand of the young man she was dating. She said she was in love with him. In addition to reporting that she had increased her social engagement with friends, she proudly shared that she had submitted an application for college. In her last session, she reported an incident where her boss had become enraged and threw a chair. She had told him that she could not tolerate his behavior and had asked for a transfer to another job. She was given the transfer. I saw Edie in the grocery store several years after her last session. She happily reported that she was married. If my memory serves me correctly, she had two beautiful little towheads in her grocery cart, whom she proudly and joyfully introduced as her children.

CONSEQUENCES FOR VICTIMS

Now that you have read several stories about victims of childhood abuse throughout this book, please list the consequences (symptoms) that these children face.

CONSEQUENCES

Given these consequences, what consequences do you believe their abusers should face?

CONSEQUENCES FOR ABUSERS

CHAPTER 10

INESCAPABLE ATTACK

An inescapable attack involves facing an opponent that cannot be challenged in a meaningful way. The opponent is perhaps larger, stronger, faster, more numerous, or in possession of more weapons than the victim. The opponent is determined to harm the victim, and the victim is intent on survival.

The Boy Who Was Attacked on the Playground

Michael was a fifty-one-year-old father of three when I met him. He was adopted when he was six months old. Prior to that, he was cared for by a nun. His adoptive dad was a professional at the top of his field and an alcoholic. He paid little to no attention to Michael. His adoptive mom had been diagnosed as bi-polar. When he was in high school, Michael was given the choice of going to a boarding school or public school, and he chose the boarding school. At heart, Michael was an artist and a free spirit, but he completed his bachelor's degree in a professional field. He loved to ride his motorcycle and to snowboard. He was divorced, and he had remarried.

When we met, Michael told me that he was getting four hours of sleep per night if he was lucky. He was waking up three or four times per night. He was diagnosed with sleep apnea and was using a C-pap mask at night. He didn't eat breakfast in the morning; he just drank coffee. He was eating two meals a day at the most; two or three days per week he was eating one meal a day. He was easily concentrating during three-hour time blocks. He rated his energy at the "5" level, his happiness at the "7" level, and his depression at the "3" level on the ten-point scale. He had chronic pain in his right knee where he had had arthroscopic surgery. He was not exercising. He didn't like being in crowds. He said, "I'm burned out, and I've had enough. I'm questioning what my life is for."

When I asked him about traumatic events he had experienced, he mentioned that he had had three car accidents and a motorcycle accident. He had had at least six snowboarding accidents. He had not suffered any broken bones as a result of these accidents, but he had broken a finger and a toe in softball games as an adult. A girlfriend had tried to stab him with a knife when he was breaking up with her. During that incident, his finger had been cut and required seven stitches.

Fourteen years after I first met Michael and had worked with him relating to several traumatic incidents, he would call me to make an appointment when he felt he needed a session. When he came to his next session, he reported that he had been feeling anxious. He said that a feeling of anxiety would come over him all of a sudden, and he had to stop what he was doing and breathe deeply until it went away. As it turned out, he was dealing with the repercussions of an incident that had occurred on the playground, when he was a child, but he had never mentioned the incident to me previously, and we had not addressed it in previous sessions. I knew he was afraid of dogs because he never had "made friends" with my dog and avoided her. He had told me that he did not remember any incident that had caused that fear. His memory of the incident became clear in the middle of this session. He was sitting in a chair with his feet on a large exercise ball. Below are my notes from the session.

[Just take a moment to think of the feeling you get when you suddenly feel anxious.]
Knees are gradually bending up toward his chest

Head back on cushion
Head upright
Head back on cushion and up, two more times
Head back and lying in chair on back
Arms are moving in a running motion
Legs are running alternating
Arms are punching upward
Feet and legs are running very fast in synchrony
Body is shaking very fast
Arms are still punching
"My arms have a crazy amount of force, like two magnets trying to come together."
Arms and legs continue to punch and kick in the air for several minutes
Body is still and relaxed
[I asked him, "Were you attacked?"]
"Yes, I was attacked by a dog at age eight or nine."
"I was at school on the playground."
"It was a 'no-jacket' day."
"A group of kids started chasing the dog."
"I got close to them."
"My heart rate just increased."
"My heart rate has slowed."
"The dog singled me out and started to chase me."
"He overtook me."
"I was on the ground."
"I balled up."
"My knee got chewed on."
Deep breath
"My heart rate is up."
"My heart rate is better."
"I'm just relaxing."
"I'm seeing yellows, oranges, reds, violet."
"Now, it's like I'm lying on the beach and relaxing."

...

This session provides an example of an inescapable attack for which the person needed to complete the actions that were not completed during the incident. By balling up during the actual incident, he was able to protect himself somewhat, but he was not able to run or punch. By completing the actions during this session by punching, kicking, and running, he was able to discharge the stored trauma energy, and the symptom of anxiety was relieved. In future sessions, Michael reported that the anxiety episodes had disappeared. This session also illustrates how a traumatic event that occurred years in the past can suddenly show up during an SE session even without the person speaking about it or calling it to memory at the beginning of the session. Finally, the session's ending shows how the body can provide a sense of peace and renewal after the intense discharge of energy that had lasted close to thirty minutes. (See Chapter 11 for another of Michael's stories.)

The Girl Who Got Arrested AND Kidnapped the Same Night

Sally was forty-three years old when I met her. She was in a managerial position in a large office. Her husband had recently died in a tragic accident, and she had told me that she was depressed. She had stopped running for exercise, which she missed. I offered to help her, and she agreed to participate in SE sessions with me.

Sally shared with me a handwritten list of the traumatic events that she had experienced. Her father was an alcoholic and always acted like he didn't want to have anything to do with his children. Her grandfather was killed by her uncle when she was four years old. Her parents divorced when she was twelve years old, and she also broke her arm that year. She had her appendix removed when she was sixteen years old. She was arrested and kidnapped when she was eighteen years old, all on the same night. When she was twenty-two and twenty-four years old, respectively, she had her wisdom teeth taken out, and her appendix operation had to be redone.

In the first few sessions, we did some Walk-Up Activities, and I found that Sally's boundaries were set at about five feet. By the third session, Sally said she was feeling better and had begun running again. During the fifth session, when her shoulders were moving forward,

Sally said that the movement reminded her of when "I leaped out of a car when I was kidnapped." Her heart started beating fast and other body movement occurred, but no additional information was shared during that session about the kidnapping.

Sally started sharing information about the night of the kidnapping during the eighth session. She said that she was studying at a friend's house. Jimmy was helping her write a paper. There was a knock on the door, and the police arrived, stating that they had warrants for Jimmy's and her arrest. Below are some of my notes about the session after I asked Sally to think about the police entering the house unexpectedly and to check into how her body was feeling.

"My stomach is in a knot."
"My shoulder has pain."
"My shoulder is ok now."
"I just thought of something else I didn't tell you about."
"My stomach feels normal now."
"My foot is pressing hard into the floor."
"My foot is pressing less now."
"The police put me in a car. I was arrested for being in a 'house of common nuisance'."
"I'm feeling shame—it's a tightness in my stomach."
"We got fingerprinted, mug shots taken, and strip-searched."
"My arms are heavy."
"My stomach is tight."
"There's tension in my neck at the base of my head."
"Very embarrassing."
"I feel anger in my back on the right side. It's a pain."
"It was ridiculous!"
...
"I was put in a cell with five girls I didn't know."
"It was scary."
"There's tension in my shoulders."
    Breathing deeply
"I was talking with the other girls."
"My arms are digging into the chair."
"That's gone now."

...

"About 11:00 p.m., a deputy came to the cell and said we were released."
"He didn't let me call for a ride. He put me out on the street."

...

We stopped the session here and continued the narrative in the ninth session. Below are excerpts from my notes from that session after I asked Sally to think about being released from jail.

"I was walking away from the jail."
"My left leg is tense."
"A car came along—an older car, a Rambler."
"The driver asked if I wanted a ride. I said, 'No,' and he took off."
"There's tension in my stomach and my whole left leg."
"Tension in my left leg is just on the top of my thigh now."
"Tension in my stomach is gone."
"Tension in my leg is gone."
    Swallow
"The guy went around the block and came back and asked again. I said,
    'No.' He took off again."
"Tension in my left leg again."
    Moving left foot
"The tension is gone."
"The guy came back again; he asked again. I said, 'No.' That's when he
    pulled out a gun."
"My chest, left leg, and left side of my stomach are tight."
"The tension is draining away now."
"He said to get into the car. I was thinking I was in trouble, and I didn't
    know how to get out of this trouble."
"I have a sinking feeling in my stomach."
"My right leg was tense, but now it's okay."
"I'm okay now."
    [I asked her to fast forward the video recording of her memory to
    walking into her dorm, and I asked her to say, "I'm alive." "I survived."]
"I'm alive."
"I survived."
"I feel pulsing in my stomach."

"The pulsing is gone."
"I feel happy."
...

During the tenth session, we resumed the narrative. Below are some of my notes from that session. The session began when I asked Sally to think of walking down the street after she was released from jail. My notes start when Sally mentions that the man in the car is pointing a gun at her and telling her to get into the car.

...

"I don't know how to get away."
"Both of my legs are tense."
"The tension ran around in circles and then went out my feet."
    Deep breath
"My legs are okay now."
"I thought he would shoot me in the back if I ran, so I chose to get in the car—a strategy I'm not advocating."
"My stomach is tight."
"My legs are tight."
"The stomach tightness drained into my left leg and now it's going out my heel."
"My left leg is okay."
"My right leg is slightly tense."
"I sat down. He put the gun under the seat. I told him about the bad night I was having. He wasn't big. He didn't scare me. He didn't try to touch me, but he could've made it much worse."

...

"I didn't have a seat belt on. He wasn't driving crazy."
"My body tensed up."
"My body is okay now."

...

During the eleventh session, we revisited the kidnapping incident one more time. Below are excerpts from my notes. We began in the middle of the incident when I asked Sally what she saw when she got into the car.

"I'm getting into the car."

"There's blue shag carpet, and blue and white dice."

> Hands pressing each other at finger tips
> Head up a bit
> Hands in fists
> Head is rising

"My shoulders are tense by my neck."

"I'm wondering whether I can get away."

"The left side of my neck is tense."

"My head wants to turn right, but it isn't turning."

"I have pain in the left side of my neck (at the '1' or '2' level). It wants to turn away, but I have to keep an eye on him."

....

"The pain in my neck is gone."

"The feeling that I want to turn right is gone."

"We talked for two hours and drove around the whole time."

"I started thinking that he isn't going to do anything."

"Then he says, 'It's time.'"

"I got angry. I thought we'd become friends."

"I feel that anger as tension in my arms, shoulders, and fingers."

> Deep breath

"I opened the car door. There was enough space between us that he couldn't grab me."

"I'm feeling tension everywhere in my body."

"I'm ready to jump, but he speeds up the car."

"I don't want to jump. I closed the door."

> Head jerked
> Left leg rolled outward

"The tension is gone."

"He slowed down, and I opened the car door again."

"I'm looking at the ground and how fast it's going by and what kind of ground it is."

"My hands are digging into my legs."

...

"Three times, and I jumped on the fourth, or two times and I jumped on the third. I rolled out onto the ground."

"I feel like twisting to the right."
Body twist right

...

"My body isn't tense now, but my shoulders are still tense."
Deep breath
Head is shaky
"That breath released everything."
"The decision is made. You're going!"
"My right leg is twitching."
"I feel strangely relaxed. I'm going to end this, and I'm going to be alright."
Head still shaky
"My teeth were clenched, but now they're okay."
"I don't feel that flight response anymore."
"I saw the wheels go by. I don't want him to run over my legs. Then I would really be helpless."
"My legs are tense."
"I got up."
"He stopped the car and came running back to me."
"I cried a bunch."
"He wanted to give me a ride back. I declined."
"He got in the car and left."
"He didn't ever touch me."

...

Then Sally told me that she walked all the way home to her dorm at 1:30 a.m. Her head continued shaking through the rest of her story and eventually stopped shaking. We ended the session when the shaking had stopped. We began each subsequent session a bit before the last segments of narrative in the previous session. In all, we did seventeen sessions together (four of them on the kidnapping incident), and then Sally went off to experience the rest of her life. She continued to work and participate in a variety of activities. She especially enjoyed dancing, and she eventually found a dancing partner. Today, she is retired, and she is seriously involved in animal rescue and adoption efforts. She has seventeen pets of her own, a true menagerie!

The best way to thank an author is to post a review online. If you are benefiting from reading this book, your review on Amazon would be greatly appreciated.

CHAPTER 11
MEDICAL PROCEDURES

Medical procedures include anything that is done to a person's body related to medical purposes. Most often, the medical procedures that cause trauma energy to be stored in the body involve the invasion of the body in some way (e.g., surgery, invasive testing methods). They can also include procedures that involve restraining a person in some way, such as a brace, a cast, tying the person down, quarantine, or general anesthesia. The cases included here involve a variety of medical procedures that children and teenagers experienced during the normal course of events related to illnesses and other medical ailments. Although they may be considered to be necessary procedures by the medical world and our culture, and, in some cases, actually may have saved a child's life or the lives of others around the child, they resulted in definite repercussions for individuals in terms of life-long symptoms.

The Boy Whose Brain Exploded

I had known Paul since the time he was about four years old until he had graduated from high school because his mother was my friend. Throughout his growing years, I knew him to be a very normal and attractive youngster who was active in a variety of sports activities and very physically fit. He was on the tennis and cross-country teams in high school, had lots of friends, and did well in school. He had been accepted into college and had planned a fun summer after his high-school graduation.

Partway through that post-graduation summer, Paul's mother called me to report that the two of them had traveled out of state to visit friends. While there, an arteriovenous malformation (AVM) in Paul's brain had suddenly burst. (An AVM is a group of blood vessels that are tangled together. As a result, the arteries and veins in the tangled mass do not connect with each other properly and do not function as they normally should. In fact, they can weaken and burst, which is what happened to Paul.) Paul's mother reported that a brain surgeon had conducted surgery to stop the bleeding on the left side of Paul's brain and that another surgery had been required to remove the AVM from his brain. Both surgeries were successful, but Paul was currently in a coma in an intensive care unit. It was too early to determine what amount of damage had been done to his brain by the internal bleeding. His future was unclear. I asked Paul's mother to keep me informed about his progress, and I offered my help.

Several weeks later, Paul was released from the hospital and came home. His mother had kept me informed that he was having difficulty speaking and that he had lost most of his ability to read and write. I suggested that the effects of the surgery and anesthesia might be adding to his difficulties and offered to provide him some trauma therapy.

When I first met with Paul weeks after he returned home, he reported that he was experiencing the following symptoms. He had constant pain on the left side of his head that was at the "3" or "4" level (out of ten) when he was just sitting still, regardless of the pain killers he was taking. (The left side of his head was the site of the brain surgery.) When he touched his head, the pain increased to level "5" or "6." If he got cold, the pain also increased to level "5" or "6." His feet hurt, and he found running to be difficult. He had not been able to exercise like he had in the past. (He used to run for forty minutes each day.) He was very frustrated that he wasn't allowed to drive, based on the doctor's orders. His peripheral vision had not recovered to normal levels, and he hadn't adjusted to having very little peripheral vision. He understood that he really couldn't see well enough to drive. He wanted his vision to improve. He stated that his other goals were to be able to speak, read, and write fluently again.

During Paul's first and second sessions, his body remained relatively still. He reported the pain in his head at the "3" level as coming and going. He felt itches on his head. He also reported tingling in his hands, arms, legs, and feet. He called this discharging energy "electric currents" or "electric vibrations" at different times during the sessions. At one point, he said that he didn't have enough strength to hold up his head, so he let it fall back on the back of the chair.

During the third session, Paul's body started to come out of the freeze state. His head started to move around, as did his legs, feet, arms, and hands. Below are some notes from that session. I had simply asked him to report any sensations he was feeling in his body.

...

    Eyes closed and blinking fast
"My right wrist hurts."
"My nose is itching."
    Head tilted up
    Head upright
    Deep breath
    Toes moving randomly
    Feet moving randomly
    Head down
    Knees swaying in and out four times

...

"My forearms are electric and tingling."
"My right eye has tears."
    Head all the way back
    Head upright
    Head down a bit
    Head upright

...

Yawn
   Rotating wrists & moving fingers
"My right cheek is itchy."
"The right side of my neck is itchy."
   Right eye is still watery

...

   Right head circles (3)
   Left head circles (3)
   Head back all the way
   Head down
   Right head turn
   Left head turn
   Stretching arms forward
   Arms stretched out to sides
   Arms relaxed on arm rests

...

   Fingers twitching
   Toes moving
   Right eye watering
"No tingling in my arms."
"No pain in my head."

...

By the fifth session, Paul reported that his tennis coach said that Paul was playing tennis as well as he did before the surgery. Paul reported that his running was getting easier and that he had no pain in his head during the previous week. I noted that his conversation was flowing nicely, and although he was using relatively simple words, he was no longer pausing and searching for words. During the fifth session, Paul's body, especially his neck, was continuing to emerge from the frozen state. He was exhibiting a full range of motion in his neck. He showed the first sign of running in place during the fifth session when his heels started to bounce on the floor.

By the sixth session, Paul reported that he was working out with weights. I wrote in my notes that he was using sarcasm and joking with me appropriately. By the seventh and eighth sessions, he was using words like "introspective" and phrases like "just peachy," and his social skills were very appropriate as he conversed with me. He was asking me questions and responding to my stories. He reported feeling good while running two miles daily. He also reported reading the first chapter of a Harry Potter book and had started a part-time job. He said, "I'm way less stressed today. My neck is looser." His heels continued to bounce up and down in alternation during these sessions.

By the ninth and tenth sessions, Paul had registered for a couple of courses at the university and had passed the state driver's test. He had started to drive by himself, even from one town to another. By the twelfth session, he reported that his old friends were treating him like they used to treat him, and they were having good times together. He continued to report no pain in his head and body. After the twelfth session, Paul went off to college and chose to discontinue treatment.

When I caught up with Paul a few years later in order to show him what I had written about him, he was enrolled in college courses and reported that he had learned to speak Spanish fluently. During the pandemic, he had been required to take several courses online, but he had done well. He said that he was not experiencing any symptoms. In fact, he reported that he had had no head pain since he had stopped working with me. He also reported continuing to run daily, as much as eight miles at a time, but usually two to three miles. His peripheral vision had not improved much, but a doctor had told him that the part of the brain that controls peripheral vision has no neuroplasticity; that is, it cannot grow new brain cells. He did not expect it to change, but he had adjusted to the situation. He had plans for studying abroad in Spain for the next school year since he had been awarded a grant to study there. After that, he would have one more semester of college courses to complete before he could graduate. He texted back and forth with me, appropriately writing me messages. He proudly announced that he was reading *The Grapes of Wrath*. I later learned from his mother that he was named to the

Dean's List based on his grades, had graduated, and was taking a post-graduation trip to South America.

Paul's case is an example of how, within a few sessions, a person can recover from symptoms such as pain, lack of coordination, and inability to concentrate on academic tasks (like reading) that arose after a surgery. His case was complicated by the fact that he suffered some brain damage (as evidenced by his loss of speaking, reading, and writing skills), and his brain needed time to produce new neural pathways. Of necessity, he was relearning skills and adapting as needed; nonetheless, these changes occurred across the next couple of years as a result of his perseverance and determination.

The Girl Who Was Constantly Typing

When I met Lydia, she was a senior in high school and an excellent student. She had been accepted to a top-tier university, and her future seemed assured. (See another story about her in Chapter 6.) Unfortunately, she was experiencing a wide range of symptoms that threatened to derail her. She was sleeping six hours per night and had to go to sleep exactly on the hour or half hour. She had been constantly dizzy and nauseous since the tenth grade, and her vision "blacked out" for several seconds each time she stood up from a sitting position. She took big gulps of air frequently (about every five breaths), and she had been diagnosed with stress-induced asthma. Also, since the tenth grade, her fingers had been constantly moving; she explained that she was "typing" what she said and what anyone else said to her. To keep herself from typing, she sat on her hands. She picked at the acne on her face, and her face was red and blotched as a result.

In addition, Lydia constantly had a severe sore throat that felt like a strep throat, but the tests had all come back negative. Her stomach hurt when her throat hurt. She had pain across the front of her neck, for which she took pain killers every day. She was constantly feeling exhausted. Her arms ached all the time. Her periods were accompanied by severe cramps and lasted fourteen to eighteen days. She was irritable and couldn't stop herself from lashing out at others and being critical. She wasn't hungry. She said that she hated her body and wasn't interested in taking care of her hair and wearing make-up. She didn't want anyone to touch her.

Lydia had a long list of traumatic experiences to report. When she was three or four years old, she was nipped on the face by a dog. Her dad had rolled her neck up in a car window when she was in the second grade. As a result, she had to have stitches on the cuts made by the window and to wear a brace on her neck. She was shot with a BB gun by a neighbor kid when she was in the fourth grade and had to testify in court. She had her tonsils and adenoids taken out when she was in tenth grade. Her parents had divorced, and each had remarried.

In her very first session, Lydia reported sensations in her throat and neck. Below are some of my notes from the session after I asked her to describe those sensations.

"It feels like two cotton balls are inside my throat. They are stuck in there and taking up space."
"Something is puffing out on the inside of my throat—a swollenness."
"There's throbbing in my neck."
    Deep breath
"My eyes feel heavy."
"There's a throbbing on top of my head. It's one inch in diameter."
"It's moved to the back of my head."
"Now it's a plate of pain and covers the whole back of my head. Those areas throb and hurt all the time."
    Deep breath
"Now the plate of pain is a crescent shape at the base of my skull."
    Cough
"Now the pain is on the right side."
"The throat pain is moving up toward my ears, but it's still in my throat. It's at the '3' level."
    Cough
"Now the back of my head is fine."
    Deep breath

"I'm very dizzy."
"The throat pain has moved up to a band near my ears. It's in the form of
    a strap down from my ears and covering my ears like a helmet strap."
...

    Deep breath
"The dizziness is somewhat better but not gone."
"The pain is back on the left side of my throat."
"The back of my head is ok."
...

"The straps are almost gone."
"The throbbing is less."
"The straps are coming together at the front of my neck."
...

"The puffed balls are still inside my throat."
"The pain in my throat continues."
"The pain is gone."
...

In the second session, Lydia continued to describe sensations in her head and neck. By the third session, Lydia reported that she was sleeping seven or eight hours per night. She was still dizzy, though. By the fourth session, she reported that her throat and stomach hadn't been hurting, her cramps hadn't been as bad, and her period was lasting seven to ten days. She was able to go to bed and go to sleep at a variety of times. By the fifth and sixth sessions, she reported that her arms had not ached for two weeks. She was not sitting on her hands, and she didn't feel as driven to "type." She could feel parts of her body; they weren't numb anymore. She wasn't taking deep breaths as we talked. Below are some of her reports during the sixth session after I asked her to describe the sensations in her throat.

"I can't feel my throat."
"The feeling is coming back in layers."
...
"It's mainly where my tonsils used to be that feels weird."
    Fingers are moving

Wrist circles with hands as fists
"I can't feel my throat. It feels non-existent."
"It's like my throat is in outer space or something."
…
"I can feel my throat some on both sides."
"My throat is coming back."
"There's nausea in my throat."
Deep breath
"This is how I felt in the mornings in eleventh grade. I woke up feeling dizzy, faint, and needed to throw up."
…
"There's a weird feeling. I can feel my throat where my tonsils were."
"There's pain around my right wrist."
…
"My throat is still unpleasant. It aches a little."
Swallow
"When I swallow, there's pain."
…
"There are itches all over my face."
…
"My face isn't itching."
…

By the tenth session, several of her symptoms had decreased in frequency and intensity. Her vision was blacking out only once a day or every other day, for example. By the thirteenth session, her periods were lasting six or seven days and were starting on the same day each month. In additional sessions, she continued to discharge energy associated with her tonsillectomy and other traumatic events until she left for college. Thereafter, she scheduled phone sessions about once a month. She experienced increased symptoms at the end of semesters when she wasn't able to sleep regularly, projects were due, and exams were imminent. She completed her bachelor's degree and a master's degree, and she moved into a professional career.

Lydia's case is important because it shows that a surgical procedure considered "common" in our culture (a tonsillectomy) can result in severe symptoms, especially if it is combined with other traumatic events related to the same body part (the neck and throat). It also shows that such symptoms can be eliminated through the use of SE Therapy, as long as other extremely stressful events are not present. Because Lydia jumped out of the frying pan and into the fire, by going to an upper-tier college where the level of coursework was high and the stress level was even higher, she occasionally required additional sessions during exam periods and times when projects and papers were due.

The Boy Who Tried to Jump Out of a Moving Car

My friend and I were exchanging our news one day when he told me that he was extremely worried about his son, Graham, who was a high-school senior. I had watched this young man grow up throughout his childhood, so I immediately became concerned and volunteered my help. My friend shared that Graham had been diagnosed as suffering from "Psychotic Depression" and despite being prescribed medication, he did not seem to be improving. He was barely able to speak or answer simple questions, and he was very confused, depressed, and suicidal. He was so claustrophobic that he tried to jump out of a moving car. He was having trouble sleeping. Needless to say, he was not able to be productive in school or participate in sports. He had no appetite, and as a result, he was losing weight.

When my friend brought Graham to his first session, I was surprised by Graham's physical appearance and state. He was very disheveled, with his hair and clothing askew. He looked frightened and uncomfortable. His eyes were glassy and half closed, his face was expressionless, and he could barely speak in one-word utterances. When he did not answer my questions and I gave him choices among two simple options, he had trouble choosing. I wondered whether we would be able to even *do* a session. I decided to try the Walk-Up Activity (see Chapter 4 for a description), and I found that he was able to follow my instructions about putting his hands up to stop me when he felt a change in his body as I was walking toward him.

He stopped me when I stepped within eight feet of him. He was able to point or say a couple of one-word utterances to indicate where he felt the energy discharge.

In the second session, Graham again stopped me at the eight-foot distance when he felt swaying in his body. Then his legs started to shake. After a few minutes, he sat down, and his head started to turn. His legs started to shake again, and then I could see twitches occurring all over his body, including both legs, both arms, his back, shoulders, neck, and head.

By the third session, Graham had gone back to school. He reported that he felt more involved in class. He could understand what the teachers were saying. His appearance had improved and his eyes were clear and fully open. He spoke to me in phrases and sentences. He shared with me that he had had nine surgical operations to fix his cleft palate: seven as an infant, one as an eleven-year-old, and one as a seventeen-year-old. The most recent surgery had involved restructuring his nose, which required transplanting cartilage from his ear to his nose and wearing two painful shunts in his nose for a month after surgery.

During the third session, he stopped me again at the eight-foot distance, but he was able to concentrate for a longer period of time and to complete several exchanges. Below are a few of my notes from this session, which we started in the standing position. I had simply asked him to report the sensations he was feeling in his body after he had raised his hands and stopped my approach.

    Eyes shifted right
"Heat in my head."
"Heat is gone."
    Swaying torso forward and back
    Fingers fidgeting
    Sat down in chair
    Legs and feet running in place, alternating
    Legs and feet slowing
    Legs and feet still
    Toes tapping in unison

Legs and feet running alternately
Twisting ankles while running
Now just running
Left hand continues to fidget
Both hands fidgeting
Legs continue to run
Shoulders are joining in with the running movement
Legs crossed at ankles and quiet
Arms swinging as if running
Arms quiet

...

Similar types of movements occurred in the fourth session. By the fifth session, Graham rated his depression at the "1" or "2" level on a ten-point scale. He was smiling and laughing as we chatted. He reported sleeping solidly for seven hours, and he was taking about twenty-five minutes to go to sleep. He said that he could concentrate to read and do his homework. He was no longer thinking that teachers were "making stuff up" in class, and now that he could believe them, he was much more able to focus on the information they were delivering in class.

Despite these improvements, Graham's level of depression went up and down over time. He reported that he was no longer disbelieving street signs and that his tendency to misperceive happenings was going away. He wasn't constantly asking himself, "What's going on here?" By the seventh session, he was going to sleep right away and sleeping well. He was no longer shaking all over when he woke up in the morning. By the eighth session, he reported having *real* conversations with classmates and participating in class.

By the tenth session, Graham reported that he was passing all of his classes. Moreover, he was earning some A's on assignments and papers. Although he was still choosing not to eat much meat, he was eating regular amounts of food and enjoying a good appetite. In fact, by the eleventh session, he had gained twenty pounds (165 pounds at six foot one). He was looking thin but well-proportioned for his height. By the thirteenth session, Graham had rejoined his sports team, and he reported that he scored the game-winning goal in the most recent game.

By the eighteenth session, Graham had stopped taking any medication for his condition. He reported feeling really good and that he was chosen as the Most Valuable Player, and he was the leading scorer for his team. By the nineteenth session, he reported that he was easily able to memorize information. He was going out with friends to lunch and to the movies. He continued participating in a few more sessions until he graduated from high school and went off to college.

A few years later, Graham called me and asked for an appointment for an SE session. He explained that he had experienced a traumatic situation involving his younger sister, and he was experiencing symptoms again. He said that his sister had called him at three a.m. one night and asked him to extricate her from a party situation where she had been attacked. He and his brother went to the house and encountered some physical altercations while helping their sister exit the situation.

As a result of this event, Graham couldn't sleep, and his brain was foggy. He had lost all motivation to go to college and had stopped going to class. Subsequently, he had earned three F's and one D during the last semester and had to change majors. He had stopped participating in his sport. He also reported a poor memory, test-taking anxiety, poor concentration, chronic pain in his back, neck, and shoulders, and frequent illnesses.

When I met with Graham and asked him to report any other traumatic events of his life that had occurred since I last saw him, he told me that he had experienced a spider bite that caused him to be hospitalized. He had broken his left wrist and also had a head injury that had required stitches.

In the following sessions, Graham focused on each of these traumatic events in turn. He also recalled memories from some of the surgeries that he had experienced to correct his cleft palate. Below are some of my notes taken after I asked him to describe something he remembered from the surgery when he was eleven years old.

"I remember an operation when I was eleven years old. They took cartilage
     out of my right hip and used it in my nose and mouth."
"I was in a room with another kid who talked a lot."
"I feel warm in a nice way, like when you're laughing—the feeling you get
     in your chest and arms."
     Moving his jaw back and forth
"The warmth has changed to tingling."
"The tingling is fading away."
"The tingling is gone."
     Hands up and moving his fingers
     Yawn
"I have that warm feeling again."
"I was in the hospital for several days after the surgery."
...

     Tear under right eye
     Right head tilt and hold

...

     Yawn
"My dad took me to a professional game while I was in the hospital. I had
     bandages on my head."
"The ushers gave us seats in the 'GOLD' section."
...

"I tried to walk. I was holding the IV stand. I wanted to go to the bathroom."
     Yawn
"I was crying because it hurt so bad, and I couldn't move my right leg."
...

"My mom said, 'It'll be ok. You can make it. It's good for your hip to walk
     on it.'"
"I didn't want to do it."
     Two fists
     Feet flat on floor
     Yawn
"My jaw is really much looser."
     His mouth opens much wider with each yawn

...

     Right leg out straight
"There was a pop in my right leg when I moved it."

Left leg moved forward a bit
"My right leg wants to move."
Pulled right foot back to chair
"My right knee feels weird, like a bubble that needs to be popped."
Yawn
Two fists continue
Stretching out right leg straight
Turning right foot left and right
Yawn
"My right knee feels better now. It's just like the left knee."
Hands open on the arm rests
Left leg out straight
Yawn—the biggest yet
Head upright
Yawn

...

This session is a good example of how the body alternates between discharging trauma energy and "taking a break" by reviewing pleasant times (attending the professional game and sitting in the gold seats) or feeling pleasant sensations (the feeling of warmth). The situation was obviously complicated by the fact that the surgeons used healthy parts of his body (in this case, cartilage from his right hip) to repair his cleft palate. This meant that there were two wounds that had to heal and two parts of the body that were traumatized. Also, in another surgery, the surgeon scratched Graham's eyeball, so Graham had to deal with the pain of the eye injury, plus the pain of the surgery, plus the inconvenience of having a bandage over one eye until it healed.

Graham has continued to work with me over the course of about sixteen years, usually scheduling a session once a month or every other month, but especially when he has experienced a traumatic situation and an increase in symptoms. Today, Graham is a college graduate, married, and has four children. He continues to participate in his sport, and he enjoys playing a guitar and singing with a band. He is an executive who works for an NGO that provides education, activities, and food to thousands of children in the US. (For more of Graham's story, see Chapter 13.)

The Boy Who Took Some Scary Showers (as a Man)

Michael was fifty-one years old when we met. I would describe him as something of a renaissance man because he had a wide variety of talents and enjoyed a wide range of activities. For example, he was an artist who produced two- and three-dimensional pieces. He had earned a professional degree in the medical realm and was working in his chosen profession. He liked to swim, water ski, ski, snowboard, play softball, and ride his motorcycles. He owned and managed several rental properties. When he no longer had rental property work to perform, he started building a new house or bought a new property on which he could work. He was married and raising three children. (For more on his story and a description of his initial symptoms, see Chapter 10.)

Michael participated in many SE sessions with me over the course of fourteen years. During some of those years, he did not request sessions or only requested an infrequent session, and, at other times, we did weekly sessions, depending on whether he had experienced an accident or other traumatic event. During the thirteenth session, he reported that when he was taking a shower, he felt like a strand of pearls was coming out of his penis. It was a painful experience, and the pain lasted about twenty minutes after completing his shower. In the eighteenth session, he reported that when he was taking a shower, he felt like a long piece of rope was being pulled out of his penis. This time the pain lasted for one hour after the shower. At the time, I wondered (silently) whether this symptom might have something to do with his circumcision surgery, but we were working on other traumatic events at the time, and he didn't report the symptom again.

It wasn't until the ninetieth session that Michael's body started discharging energy in a way that made me think it was related to a circumcision surgery. At the beginning of that session, he was seated in a chair with his feet up on an exercise ball. Below are some of my notes from the session. I had asked him to take a "tour" of his body and notice any sensations that jumped out at him. After he reported a few painful sensations in his back, his head started to move.

...

> Head moving back all the way and resting on chair back
> Butt has raised off the seat cushion
> Back is arched
> Arms are "spread eagled" with fingers splayed
> Elbows are on arm rests (all weight of torso is on elbows and head)
> Whole body is stiff as a plank, and body is bracing
> Legs are stiff and spread eagled
> Breath is being held
> Arms are still spread eagled and rotating on axes
> Body relaxed so butt is now on chair seat
> Knees bending slowly, heels moving toward butt
> Legs straightening
> Legs bouncing on ball simultaneously
> Legs bouncing (running) on ball alternately
> Butt raised off seat cushion
> Back arched
> Body is stiff as a plank again, body is bracing
> Arms are spread eagled and rotating, fingers splayed
> Legs are spread eagled and rotating on axes on ball
> Butt in seat, arms relaxed, legs relaxed

...

From this point on, Michael moved his arms in a variety of ways. Individually, he struck the air with them, hit the chair with them, made circles with them, swung down to the floor with them, raised them above his head, and waved them in the air. Next, he was lying on his back in the chair. His legs were up in the air and pumping the pedals of a bicycle, and his hands and arms were simultaneously circling around each other. All parts of his body were synchronized. Finally, his legs were running very fast on the ball while his whole body was shaking.

From session ninety-two until the 130th session, Michael's body discharged energy by going into this "plank" position one or more times. In between those times, his arms and legs became active and moved in a variety of ways. He had no visual memories of any event associated with these sessions. My interpretation of these sessions is that they were related to when Michael was tied down in a spread-eagle position for the circumcision. As each session progressed, he was able to move more and more until his body parts became synchronized, and each body part eventually exhibited a full range of motion. These sessions illustrate that although a person has experienced a traumatic event prior to learning to speak, the body remembers the body position as well as the traumatic event.

Across these sessions, Michael reported that he was feeling better and happier. He became well-groomed, his coloring was healthy, and his eyes were bright and sparkling. He had lots of energy that he could use to participate in all his favorite pursuits. He has put his children through college, constructed a couple of houses and renovated others, and made several trips on his motorcycle. He continues to maintain a professional degree in a medical field and is licensed to practice now in dozens of states after studying for and passing all the required tests in those states. He is currently creating beautiful collages and displaying them in galleries.

The Girl Who Got Left Out in the Cold

Rachel was a forty-five-year-old woman when I met her, and she continued to work with me over several years. (See another story about her in Chapter 7 for her symptoms, traumas, and many accomplishments.) When listing her trauma history, she reported to me that she had injured her left anterior cruciate ligament (ACL) when she was fifteen years old. She remembered the incident as occurring when she was playing a game of pick-up football outside her church during the after-school meeting of the teen church group. During the game, a very large boy tackled her, fell on top of her, and her left knee was injured. She was on the ground, crying, and she was not able to stand up. At that point, the group leader called the teenagers to come inside. She was told that she wasn't really hurt: "It's not a big deal. You just sprained it or something." Everyone left her outside in the cold while darkness fell. No one came to find her or check on how she was feeling. Eventually, she partly crawled and hopped to the church door. For years, she kept telling her parents that her knee hurt, and they kept minimizing the situation, telling her to stop being so melodramatic. At one point, they took her to a doctor who said that the knee was sprained and that it would gradually improve over time. At first, she refrained from participating in sports and any physical activities. Then, as a senior in high school, she ran cross country. In college, she was on the rowing team. She told me that she was determined not to be "a baby." Finally, when she was twenty-two years old, she went to an orthopedic surgeon who declared that her ACL had been severed. Thus, she had been limping around for seven years on a leg that was seriously injured.

During one of her SE sessions, Rachel started feeling discharge from her legs after focusing on the sadness she was feeling. She was sitting in a chair with her legs on a stool. Here are some excerpts from that session.

...

Yawn

Yawn

"I just went to the feeling of wishing I was dead."

Crying

Yawn

"I'm always anxious."

"I see a big sad frown in my torso."

She outlined the frown on her torso with her hand

Deep breath

Yawn

"Half of the frown has disappeared."

"Now, it's just on the left side."

Yawn

....

"My legs are tingling on the top."
"A wave of energy went down my legs."
"My left knee hurts."
"It's been bugging me more lately."
...
"It's a level '3' pain."
"It feels injured."
    Yawn
    Pointing at the top of her left knee
    Holding her left knee with both hands
"There's pulsing in my knee."
"When I take my hands away, there's buzzing in my knee."
"The sadness was gone, but now it's back."
...
    Crying while holding left knee
...
"These are big fat tears."
    Blowing nose
...
    Still crying while holding left knee
"There's no throbbing in my knee now."
...
    Right leg kicked up
    Left leg kicked up (3 times)
...
    Yawn
"The sadness in my chest is gone."
...
"The feeling that I should die is gone."
"I can feel my feet."
    Yawn
"I'm aware of my body, my ears, my nose."
...

In a subsequent session, Rachel recalled the knee surgery itself. Since her career had been in the medical field, she reported that she felt very comfortable in the hospital and operating room initially. I had asked her to share a brief memory from that day with me.

"I remember being in pre-op."
"A guy scrubbed my leg with iodine."
     Left head tilt
"An IV was put into my left arm."
     Yawn
"I was excited because my knee had been hurting for a long time."
"Whoa! My knee has some really sharp pains in it now."
"Those pains are jabbing me!!"
"It's very weird."
...
"I was waiting, waiting, waiting."
...
"Getting the Versed was the first time the pain left."
"I was not afraid. I was looking forward to it being good."
...
They put the mask on for oxygen, and I went out immediately."
     Rubbing left eye
...
"I'm aware of both of my legs and the rest of me."
     Yawn
"There's a dull ache in my left knee."
     Eyes blinking
"My left knee hurts more than my right knee. It was a 'masked' level '4'
     pain. Now it's an 'open' level '4' pain."
"My right knee has a level '2' pain."
"The pain is moving up and down my left leg—it's at level '2' now."
     Yawn
"I'm bracing around it."
     Feet moving a bit
"I feel a warm glow on the left side of my body."
     Yawn
"My left knee pain is at '0.5.'"
"My right knee pain is at zero."

"My left knee was having a sharp pain from the front and then from the
    side. It comes and goes."
    Yawn

...

"There's no pain in my left knee."
    Head back on cushion
"I can feel my fingers finally."
Yawn
"I threw up so many times."
    (Talking about how sick she was from the anesthesia.)

...

At the beginning of the next session, I asked Rachel to describe
the sensations she was feeling in her body.

    Yawn
"I can feel the soft inside of my sweatshirt, my favorite sweatshirt."
    Yawn
"My left leg feels bigger than my right leg, and it's heavier."
    Yawn
"My left leg is warmer than my right leg, in the inside part of my knee
    especially."
"Both legs have intermittent buzzing—it's like a flickering light."
    Swallow
"I'm totally still focusing on the buzzing."
"Once in a while, the buzzing changes and feels better. It's blue instead
    of brown and fuzzy."

...

    Swallow
"It's more peaceful."
"My left leg is the same size as my right leg now."
    Swallow
"Now there's just a faint buzzing on the soles of my feet."
    Breath

...

"I can feel my jeans touching my left knee."

"It's a burning sensation."
"I'm far away from my knee & my body."
"I can't move."
"I don't want to know what's going on with my left knee."
"My heart is flip-flopping."
"My left knee is burning in spots."
"I feel like I'm stuck."

....

"There's no burning in my left knee."
"There's a level '1' pain in my left knee."
"I'm afraid to move it."
"My legs are the same size."
"I'm all here."

...

"My left knee is okay now."

...

    Looking at her right hand
"I had a pain button in my right hand."

...

"I just kept hitting that pain button."
    Deep breath
"I just wanted to sleep all the time."
    Huge burp
    Huge burp
    Yawn
"I was terrified of the pain."
"I was not happy when I woke up."
"The nausea is gone, but I have that memory of throwing up. I vomited
    a lot."

...

"My legs feel good. They're not so heavy."

...

Rachel's sessions related to her knee are instructive because of the emotional overlay associated with the original injury, where she was left by herself out in the cold and then not heard for years when she expressed her pain. Eventually, we spent as many sessions on her feelings of being left out and not allowed to speak about her pain as we did on the actual knee surgery. Feeling that one part of the body is bigger than a comparable part of the body is typical in a session where that part has been injured or is the target of surgery. Feeling frozen, unable to move, and far away from the body is also a common occurrence during a session focused on a surgery where general anesthesia was used. The burping is a sign that her digestive system was affected during the surgery and was coming back online during the session. Likewise, the yawns are a sign that her lungs were affected, and her respiratory system was coming back online.

The Girl Who Was Trapped in Concrete

When Mia came to her first session, she was sixty-four years old, a professional woman in the helping professions, and she was determined to improve her health. She had earned a PhD in her field, and she was a working woman with three adult children and three grandchildren. I had asked her to make me a list of her symptoms and another list of her traumatic events. Her list of symptoms was one typed page, and her list of traumatic events was four typed pages. All of these pages were single spaced, and all of the events were legitimate traumatic situations. To summarize a few of her symptoms, she was experiencing extreme anxiety and panic attacks, chronic pain, and high blood pressure. In the past, she had spent years in bed and additional years isolated in her home. At one point, she had been diagnosed as agoraphobic. She was currently taking an anxiety medication, a medication to help her go to sleep, and a medication to lower her blood pressure. She said that she did not trust anyone, nor did she feel safe anywhere. She attributed her ability to earn her degrees and continue to work to her strong internal drive and motivation. (See other stories about Mia in Chapters 7 and 9.) She stated that she always wanted to help others.

One of the traumatic events that Mia described to me occurred when she became ill with meningitis. She was eight years old, had a fever of 106 degrees for ten days, had an intense headache, and her eyes experienced extreme sensitivity to light. She was taken to the hospital during a "terrifying" ambulance ride, complete with red lights flashing and sirens blaring, and she was put into an isolation ward. She went into a coma for five days and was hospitalized for thirty days. She was not allowed to get out of bed during that whole time. She complained that the nurses tucked her sheets in so tightly that she could not move. She received a shot from the nurses every three hours. At the time, her mother was taking care of her six-year-old twin brothers in their home, so her mother never visited Mia in the hospital.

In our initial meetings, Mia was so anxious that she remained standing throughout each session, and she did not want me to approach her within eight feet. Thus, we both stood during sessions, and I tried not to move much. Here are some excerpts from our second session in which the first trauma energy associated with her meningitis was discharged. I had walked toward her, and she had stopped me at the eight-foot distance. I prompted her to think for a moment about being in the hospital when she had meningitis.

"My hands are tingling."
"I have a marble-sized lump in my throat."
"I feel pressure on the front of my lower pelvis."
    Left hand on belly
    Both hands on belly
"I have a sensation like I want to cry behind my eyes and in my throat."
"My throat is more intense."
    Deep breath
"I have pain in my left hip—level '4' to '6'."
...
    Stepping in place
    Walking around a few steps
"It feels like I need to walk to get the pain to go away."
"The pain in my left hip is like a spike going in there."
    Burp
"My belly is better."
    Deep breath
"The marble in my throat is like a bubble."

"I want to run out the door and leave."
    Deep breath

...

"The pressure in my pelvis is gone."
"The hip pain is gone."
    Deep breath
    Deep breath

...

    Standing still
"I'm curled up in bed."
    Both hands on belly

....

"I have the sensation that I'm not supposed to move or make a sound."
"I feel a tear on my cheek."
"There's a vise holding my chest and shoulders in."
    A few tears are running down her cheeks
"It feels like I might get hurt if I move or make a sound."
"It's like I'm not supposed to breathe even."
"There's a bubble is at the base of my throat."

...

"My abdomen is nervous, like it's filled with bumble bees."
"I'm opening my mouth for the bumble bees to come out, like in the
    movie, *The Green Mile*."
    Holding her mouth open

...

"The bumble bees have settled down."
"The main thing I feel is this gully washer that needs to come out—all
    these tears."
    [Please give yourself permission to cry.]
    Chin on chest
    Lower lip quivering
    Lots of tears flowing
"The bubble in my throat is gone."
    Crying stopped
    Blowing her nose
"I feel like I can't move. She's in isolation. I can see her all alone, curled
    up in bed. The only time someone came in was when I got a shot."

...

Throughout this session, except for the brief period of walking, Mia remained standing in place. She barely moved except to put her hands on her belly. This is typical of someone who is in the freeze state. She referred to her frozen state in the coma in the hospital in other sessions, too. Here is an excerpt from the next session after I walked toward her, and she stopped me at the eight-foot distance.

...

"I feel real frozen like I'm not supposed to move or talk. I'm most frozen from the waist down."

...

"My whole body feels like concrete. I hear your words, but they don't come in."
"I need not to move, not to talk, not to bother anyone."
    Deep breath
"My hip is okay; my neck is okay."
"I feel heavy from the knees down."
    Left head tilt
"I want to scream out, 'There's somebody in here!!'"

...

In the tenth session, Mia referred to sensations related to the coma again.

...

"I feel like a block of concrete that nothing will penetrate. I can't get out and nothing can get in."
    Head down to chest
    Hands on belly
"It felt good to move my hands and arms just then."
"Life is going on all around me, but I can't be a part of it."
    Cough
    Cough

"Seems like I was laying on my left side when I was in the coma. I hated having those people walk around me and talk about me like I'm not a person."

...

"People need touch when someone is in a coma. I needed someone to touch me, hold my hand, or rub my back."

...

At the beginning of the twelfth session, Mia reported that she was feeling "an incredible peace and calmness." Her blood pressure was normal, and her friends were telling her how much she had improved. This was the session when she did her first head circle and started moving her ankles. Nevertheless, she was still making statements like the following during her session: "I feel frozen in my arms and legs," and "My mother used to tell me to be still and not utter a sound. It feels like that's what I'm supposed to do right now." Mia also said, "Somebody should have sat down next to me and talked to me and held my hand. Instead, they looked at me, talked about me, and poked me."

In all, Mia participated in eighty-seven sessions. Over time, all parts of her body started to move and became synchronized. Her sessions spanned three years, during which many events took place in her life. Some of these events (e.g., falling off a ladder, severe illnesses of her husband and her brother) were traumatizing, and we continued to do therapy as they occurred. All in all, I was truly impressed with her intelligence, her determination to become healthy, and her compassion. By the end of her treatment, she had taken part in the New York City Marathon, and was fully involved with her family. She cared for her grandchildren regularly and took them on wonderful trips. She continued her work as a therapist, reporting that she was "much more able to be present" for her clients. When I met with her years later, she was eighty-six years old, and she reported that she was still seeing clients, working as a life coach, and leading a grief group at her retirement community. She is still very much involved in helping people around her.

PART III
CONCLUSIONS

CHAPTER 12
LESSONS LEARNED

The stories of the people spotlighted in this book, plus the many others with whom I have worked, have several themes woven throughout them. From those themes, I have derived several lessons. The patterns and commonalities are as follows, and they are summarized in Appendix B.

Traumatic events come in lots of shapes and sizes

I have grouped the stories in this book into seven categories. These categories are not "set in stone," nor are they meant to cover all types of traumatic events. Some of the traumatic events described in the stories can be included in other categories. For example, many injuries can be considered falls. Further, since everyone had experienced more than one traumatic event, each person could have been included in more than one category. A boy who had an injury to his ankle also had been beaten by his father. The categories I chose simply are categories related to the people and stories I have encountered and that I wanted to share in this book. Another important consideration is that the stories related to each type of traumatic event are very different. For example, the stories in the Medical Procedures section vary considerably, from a girl who was quarantined while in a coma to a boy who experienced nine surgeries. Additionally, I've learned that people often experience numerous traumatic events that they don't even think of as traumatic events. Sometimes they are reluctant to share their stories, they experienced the events at a very young age before they were verbal, or they have forgotten the events. I sometimes find out about events that occurred after providing SE Therapy to a person for years.

Common events can result in stored trauma energy

As a culture, we think of injuries on the sports field and surgeries as common and relatively benign events. Because they are so common, they can accumulate. People can experience several traumatic events without becoming alarmed or concerned. Nevertheless, these events can result in stored trauma energy, which may have serious repercussions in the future.

The number of symptoms that people experience has no end

Likewise, people are often suffering from several symptoms. Often, as the stories in this book attest, many of the same symptoms occur across people who have experienced traumatic events (e.g., sleep disturbances, pain, digestion issues, cognitive issues, poor coordination, social isolation). Because our culture encourages self-medication through over-the-counter medications, alcohol, and recreational drugs, many of these symptoms are not considered serious or even worth mentioning. For example, headaches are considered common occurrences by some people and for which people take a variety of pain killers, but they are a symptom that can be alleviated through trauma therapy.

Stored trauma energy has no expiration date

Based on the stories provided by Michael (Chapter 11) and Helen (Chapter 7) about traumatic events in their lives, we know that trauma energy stored near birth and prior to being able to speak is still present and can be discharged. Michael's body stored memories possibly associated with his circumcision, and Helen had vivid memories of a car accident she experienced when she was two years old. Additionally, Mia (Chapter 7) had vivid memories of an accident when she was hit by a car as a three-year-old. All three spent several sessions discharging the energy associated with those early events in their lives. Mia was sixty-four years old; thus, there was a sixty-one-year gap between her accident and her therapy. In other words, Somatic Experiencing Therapy can work regardless of how long the gap is between the traumatic incident and the therapy, and regardless of how old the client is at the time of the incident and at the time of the therapy.

Trauma has no prejudice

Trauma is ageless, classless, and color blind. People of all occupations, interests, and ideas can become traumatized. Clearly, some occupations and activities are more dangerous than others, and people who engage in dangerous activities have a higher probability of storing trauma energy and experiencing symptoms than others. Nevertheless, based on my experience, there does not seem to be a pattern related to those who experience trauma symptoms and those who do not.

Symptoms are not permanent

All of the stories in this book chronicle the reduction of symptoms in individuals who have participated in SE Therapy. Symptoms that are typically considered permanent such as pain, asthma, or other chronic conditions can be alleviated. Symptoms related to an inability to learn, work, and perform can also be alleviated. Indeed, all of the individuals with whom I have had experience have shown a similar reduction in symptoms, with one type of exception. As I explained in my Preface to this book, I have told people that I would not work with them if they were involved in self-medicating with alcohol or recreational drugs. Thus, my conclusions are limited to a group of people who did not use these substances regularly.

Trauma symptoms cannot be cognitively controlled

Although people experiencing trauma symptoms may be told to control their symptoms, they cannot do so voluntarily. They are not able to start or stop engaging in symptomatic behaviors, even though they sincerely express the wish to do so. These symptoms can only be controlled through the release of trauma energy. The parts of the brain that control these symptoms must be engaged in the release. of the trauma energy associated with the symptoms. These parts of the brain are not under voluntary control. (See Appendix A for an explanation.)

Individuals have their unique trauma-symptom profiles

Each person presents not only a unique history of traumatic events but also a unique profile of trauma symptoms. Although different people might share certain symptoms, their total profile will vary, and the order in which the symptoms may dissipate will also vary.

Trauma symptoms can be mitigated at any age

My experience has taught me that people as young as elementary students and as old as senior citizens can transcend trauma by participating in Somatic Experiencing Therapy sessions. The stories in this book illustrate that many different kinds of symptoms can be alleviated at any age. In other words, it's never too late to heal from trauma.

Symptoms can return after additional traumatic situations

Although people can heal as a result of trauma therapy, they live in an unpredictable world and can experience additional traumatic events. When they do, based on my limited experience of working with several clients across several years, I've learned that clients experience some of the same symptoms as the symptoms they reported in their first therapy session when they experience a new traumatic situation. However, they experience fewer symptoms than those reported in their first therapy session, and even fewer symptoms as additional traumatic situations occur. A few therapy sessions are likely to remedy the situation each time an additional traumatic situation occurs.

Stored trauma energy can exceed people's capacity for storage, and they can become dysfunctional

Numerous stories in this book have focused on how individuals have become unable to function in their daily lives after experiencing traumatic events. They no longer were able to leave their homes, go to school, work at a job, or take part in social events. If they were enrolled in school, they were often earning failing or barely passing grades. In most cases, several traumatic events preceded that dysfunction. Typically, in cases involving more than one traumatic event, the last traumatic event, which may not even be an event involving an injury (e.g., a minor fender bender), can serve as the "last straw" that pushes the person into dysfunctionality. Additionally, a series of relatively "minor" traumatic events can wreak as much havoc in a person's life as a single major event. Fortunately, I have not encountered many people who have become dysfunctional after one traumatic event.

Energy discharge occurs in distinct body parts that have been injured

If a person has been injured, and an SE session focuses on the incident in which that body part got injured, energy is likely to discharge from that body part in the form of sensations and body movements. For example, a person might feel tingling on the skin of an area of the head that was injured in a fall. In the case of a surgery, a person might feel heat or tingling in the area of the incision made during surgery.

Energy discharge in particular body parts slows down across SE sessions and stops

For the most part, if a person has injured a particular body part such as a leg bone, the discharge associated with that body part is strong at first and can last most of a given session. The discharge will be weaker and will last less time over successive sessions until no discharge appears in that body part in future sessions. When this occurs, the symptoms associated with the body part are likely to have disappeared.

Energy discharge occurs in certain patterns across people

For the most part, during SE sessions, people complete the actions that they might have completed during a traumatic event if they had not frozen. For example, they begin to run when focusing on situations where they might have run away. They begin to punch or push away with their hands when focusing on situations where they might have fought off an attacker. They go through the Cobra Sequence many times (see Chapter 4 for a description) if they were in a car accident.

Involuntary functions can be disrupted after traumatic events

Imbedded in all the stories in this book are reports of symptoms related to involuntary functions in our bodies. These functions sometimes are related to timing. For example, our bodies alert us when we are hungry by giving us hunger pangs. We normally eat a variety of foods three times in a day. We normally sleep about seven or eight hours at night. We fall asleep a few minutes after our heads hit the pillow and stay asleep all night. Women's menstrual cycles average about twenty-eight days in length, and their periods begin about once a month. After traumatic events, all these timed functions can become disrupted in some way. People can stop eating entirely or stop eating certain foods. They can start eating everything or engage in binge eating. Their digestive systems can have all sorts of symptoms such as stomach aches, acid reflux, heartburn, diarrhea, gas, and constipation. They can experience insomnia, nightmares, screaming dreams, and other sleep disruptions. They can have no menstrual periods or have heavy periods with severe cramping.

Involuntary functions can be restored through Somatic Experiencing Therapy

In all the cases that I have witnessed, I have seen the improvement of involuntary functions after SE Therapy. People who previously reported that they have no appetite have reported that they are eating again and have gained weight. People who previously reported that they could only sleep about two or three hours per night report that they have slept four, or five, or even six hours per night. Women who reported that they had to take a day off work because of severe cramping on the first day of their cycle, now report that they stayed at work and felt okay. The one major exception to these improvements is related to eating meat. Some people have reported to me that they continue to avoid eating meat. Otherwise, they eat a variety of foods more often.

Physical coordination can be disrupted after traumatic events

In some of the stories in this book, people have reported that they no longer engage in physical activities that they used to enjoy after experiencing traumatic events. They reported that they put their sports equipment (e.g., tennis racquet, Frisbees, roller blades) away in a closet, and they no longer used it. They say that they used to run, workout, or swim, but they no longer do it. In some cases, they simply have not engaged in physical activities their whole lives after an early traumatic event.

Physical coordination can be restored through Somatic Experiencing Therapy

When people spontaneously report to me that they went out for a run for the first time in years or they took their tennis racquet out of the closet and played tennis, I know that they are healing. People who have not engaged in physical activity for years often say that they signed up for the first time for a dance course or a cave-exploration course. Sometimes, they rejoin their sports team. This is wonderful news to my ears because these reports indicate that different parts of their bodies are coming out of the freeze response and are becoming synchronized enough that they can comfortably engage in vigorous physical activities.

Cognitive functions can be disrupted after traumatic events

Throughout the stories presented herein are reports of impaired cognitive functioning. Adults and children have reported that their cognitive functioning was greatly impaired after the traumatic events of their childhoods. In all cases, they reported that their memory, concentration, and motivation to learn were reduced. They could no longer complete learning tasks. Although they knew how to read and enjoyed reading before the traumatic events, they no longer were reading. Despite their parents isolating them for days in their rooms or basements until they completed their schoolwork, they still could not complete their homework assignments.

Cognitive functions can be restored through Somatic Experiencing Therapy

Throughout the stories in this book are reports of individuals becoming capable of engaging in learning tasks again and enjoying their learning pursuits. Many of these people were failing or barely passing their school or college courses, and some of them have now completed master's and doctoral degrees. Most of them have reported enjoying reading for pleasure again. Thus, a key lesson is that their brains were not affected in a permanent way. Despite them not receiving special tutoring or educational programs, they gradually became more and more productive as learners while participating in Somatic Experiencing Therapy.

Social engagement can be interrupted after traumatic events

Individuals who have experienced traumatic events can become more and more socially isolated over time, and they can limit their environment to their home or even to one room. They complain that they feel uncomfortable in "crowded" places like stores, restaurants, school cafeterias, hallways, and classrooms. They are extremely uncomfortable in truly crowded places like a sports arena or a sold-out theatre.

Social engagement can be reinstated through Somatic Experiencing Therapy

As shown in many of the stories in this book, people can reengage with the world after taking part in SE Therapy. They report making new friends, reengaging with old friends, being included in activities by friends, and their friends treating them more positively over time. They begin attending events out in the community that they have avoided in the past.

Physical health can be negatively affected after traumatic events

Many of the clients with whom I've worked were experiencing physical health problems when I started working with them. They had numerous colds, bronchitis, strep throat, pneumonia, and other ailments, including high blood pressure, asthma, fibromyalgia, and racing heart beats. At times, keeping a weekly schedule with them was difficult because they were often calling me to report that they were sick. (See Appendix A for the causes of this increase in physical health issues.)

Physical health can improve after Somatic Experiencing Therapy

Fortunately, over time and across sessions, I witnessed a reduction of physical health problems. Students began attending school regularly. Adults reported that they no longer had to take a certain medication, like blood pressure medicine or acid-reflux medication. Mia (see Chapters 7 and 11 for her stories) reported that her fibromyalgia symptoms had dropped away. Several teens reported that they no longer experienced asthma. People stopped cancelling sessions because of illness. These changes happened gradually over a series of sessions.

Symptoms associated with the term "mental illness" can appear after traumatic events

In many of the stories in this book, people reported experiencing symptoms that are typically associated with "mental illness." They complained about feelings of anxiety, panic attacks, depression, manic behavior, and invasive thoughts.

Symptoms associated with the term "mental illness" can disappear after Somatic Experiencing Therapy

Based on my experience, the symptoms typically associated with what our culture calls "mental illness" can disappear as a person engages in Somatic Experiencing Therapy. Many times, people have reported to me that they are no longer depressed after a few sessions. Other times, people have slowly reported gradual decreases in depression across sessions by using a rating scale. Similar phenomena have occurred with other symptoms like anxiety, panic attacks, invasive thoughts, and repetitive thinking.

LESSONS LEARNED

Please scan through the "Lessons Learned," and list the ones that most pertain to you, a loved one, or someone you know.

Lessons that Connect	To whom?

CHAPTER 13

SOME CAVEATS

In addition to the basic lessons described above, my observations require the addition of three caveats. These caveats involve complicating factors that might temper the key lessons specified above.

Caveat #1: The storage and discharge of trauma energy is a dynamic phenomenon

Based on my observations, I've come to fully respect the idea that the storage and discharge of trauma energy is a dynamic phenomenon. That is, once trauma energy has been discharged from the body and symptoms have decreased, a person's capacity to store new, additional trauma energy can be restored. This capacity can be overwhelmed again as the result of additional traumatic events. That is, symptoms can increase again. For example, if a person participates in trauma therapy and no longer has symptoms and then has a car accident or a surgery, that person might experience some symptoms again, and these symptoms can be serious. Fortunately, through Somatic Experiencing Therapy, a new sense of equilibrium can be restored, and symptoms can disappear again.

Chelsea, the girl who hid her mother's riding crop and whose story was told in Chapter 9, presents a good example of this phenomenon. She had her ups and downs during therapy, but for the most part, her trajectory was positive, with fewer and fewer symptoms being reported over time. After sixteen sessions, she discontinued therapy, completed high school, and went off to college, reporting that she was no longer experiencing symptoms. Her parents concurred with her reports. All of her accomplishments were evidence that she was doing well in high school and during her initial time in college. Nevertheless, a more longitudinal look at her whole course of treatment over several years paints an informative picture.

The graphs in Figures 16 and 17 (pp. 179-180) show how, across that whole course of treatment, her symptoms increased and decreased over time related to traumatic events in her life. The bottom half of the graph (with the dark bars) shows the number of symptoms that she reported or which I observed in each session; the top half (with the gray bars) shows the number of improvements she reported (or I observed) in each session. For example, if she told me that she hated being around people and especially disliked crowds, that was counted as a symptom. Likewise, if I saw her inch along the wall to stay away from my dog, that was also counted as a symptom. If she told me "I went dancing," that was counted as an improvement. If I saw her walking smoothly and moving freely in the presence of my dog, that was also counted as an improvement.

All of the improvements that were tallied were related to the original twenty-seven symptoms that Chelsea reported in her first session. That is, any time she made a statement to me that indicated that a symptom was no longer present, it was counted as an improvement. Any time she made a statement to me that indicated that a symptom continued, it was counted as a continuing symptom. At the beginning of treatment, she reported the twenty-seven symptoms shown in Table 1 (p. 181). Thus, the dark bar in the bottom half of the graph in Figure 16 (p. 179) in the space above the "1" (for Session #1) shows twenty-seven symptoms for the first session.

Figure 16: Chelsea's symptoms and improvements in Sessions #1 - 23.

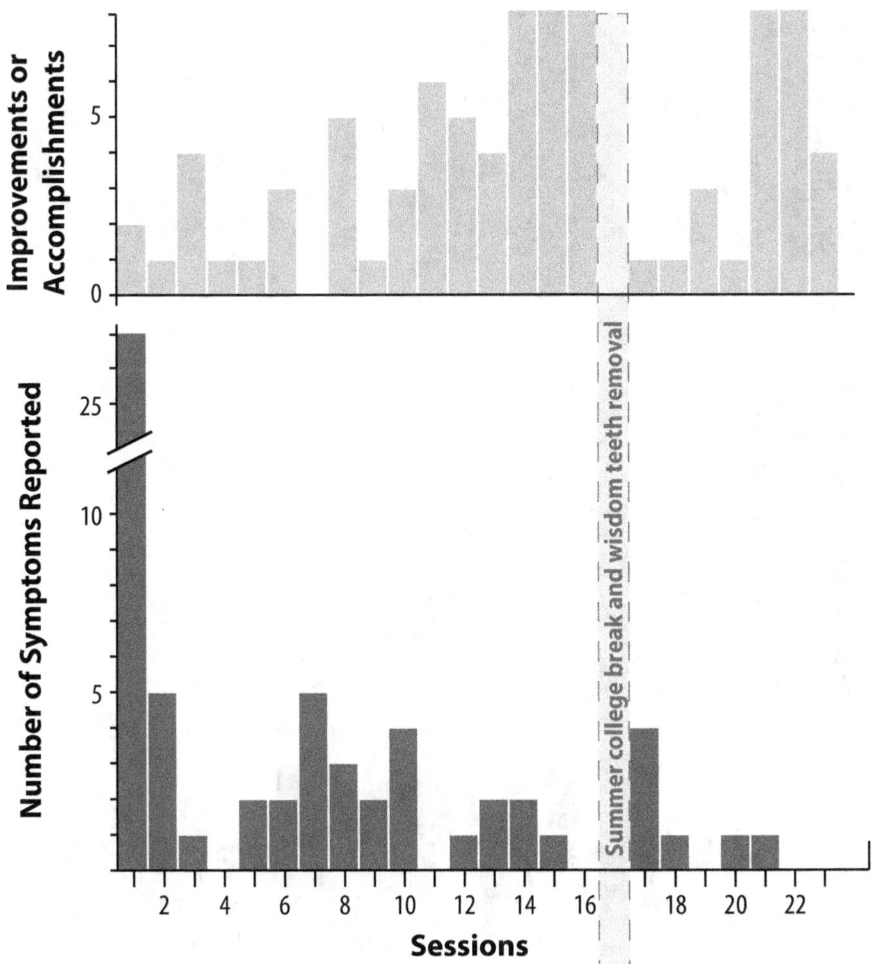

Figure 17: Chelsea's symptoms and improvements in Sessions #24 - 43.

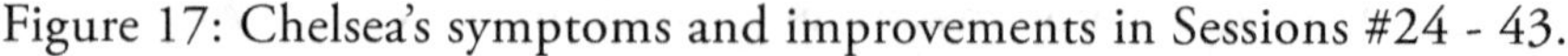

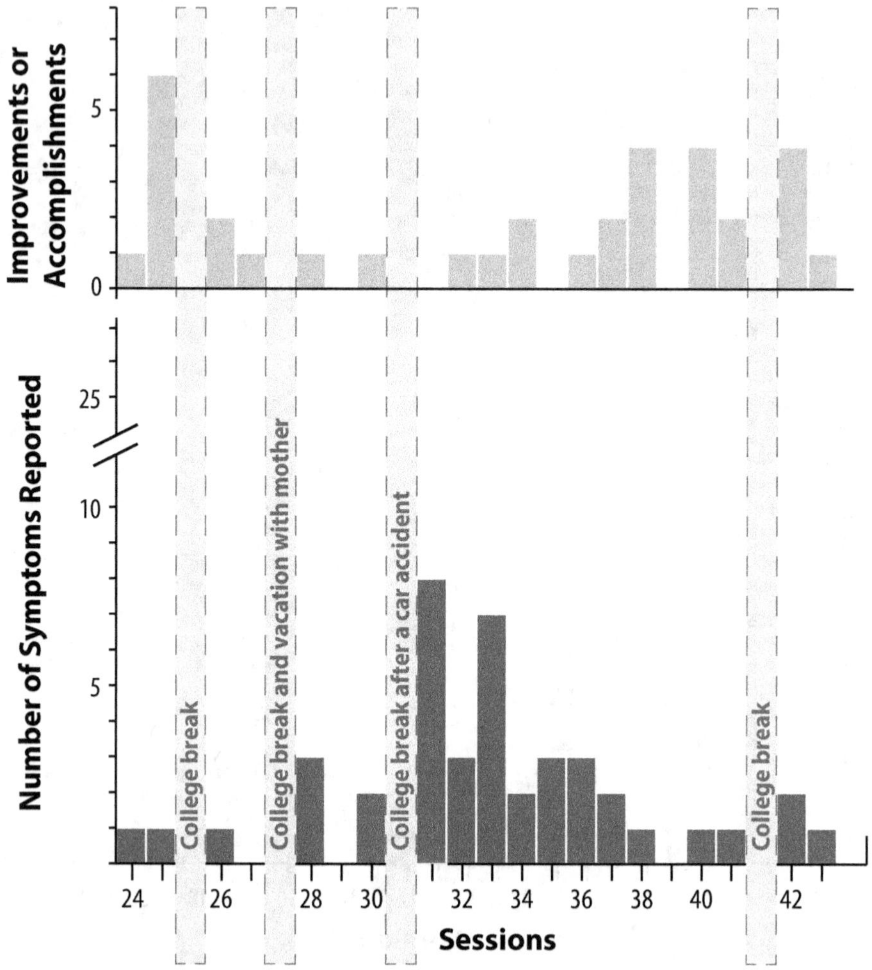

Table 1
Chelsea's Symptoms

Has daily stomach aches
Wants to be in her home all the time
Takes two hours to go to sleep
Has scary dreams
Feels depressed
Is irritable
Can't concentrate
Earns poor grades
Feels anxious
Has dog phobia
Has no appetite
Feels nauseated and vomits often
Is afraid of germs
Has a poor memory
Gets sick often (e.g., colds, flu)
Has either constipation or diarrhea
Has a stiff neck
Is teary/cries/overreacts emotionally
Has test-taking phobia
Holds a pillow in front of her
Feels bad/achy when wakes up
Has an overactive startle reflex
Fears someone seated or standing behind her
Has an eight-foot boundary around her
Has trouble breathing when exercising
Feels cold all the time
Isolates herself

Below is an accounting of the story of how Chelsea's symptoms increased and decreased over time, based on my notes.

Session Number	Description
2	In the second session, Chelsea said she was not depressed (for one improvement illustrated by the gray bar above the "2"), but she was still taking two hours to go to sleep, was worrying a lot, was irritable, couldn't concentrate, and was uncomfortable around friends (for five symptoms illustrated by the dark bar above the "2" for Session #2).
7	Chelsea made some gradual improvement until the seventh session. Up until this time, she had been living with her dad and wasn't spending much time with her mother (who had beaten her). Once she was participating in supervised and unsupervised visits with her mother around the seventh session, she reported increased symptoms. Her mother kept pressuring her to resume living with her half of the time.
11	Once the judge allowed Chelsea to choose to live with her father and have infrequent visits with her mother, Chelsea's symptoms decreased, she stabilized, and her improvements increased, with her earning excellent grades and being awarded a substantial scholarship to college.
16	Chelsea went to an out-of-state college for her freshman year after Session #16. During that session, she reported no symptoms and several improvements. She reported that she might have her wisdom teeth removed over a break from college, so I cautioned her and her parents that she would likely need some SE sessions after that surgery.

17	Chelsea did have her wisdom teeth removed during the summer break from college, so we started SE treatment right away after the surgery. She reported four symptoms during the seventeenth session.
18-25	The few symptoms Chelsea reported between Sessions #18 to #25 focused on sleep issues, like having trouble waking up, or feeling weak when she woke up. After Session #25, Chelsea went back to college for her sophomore year.
26-27	Sessions #26 and #27 occurred in the summer after her sophomore year. They were basically sessions where she reported making the President's List again and being accepted into the Honors Program. She was doing well. After Session #27, she left for her junior year of college.
28-30	These sessions occurred during the Christmas break of her junior year. She spent a week with her mother in Jamaica during that vacation, and she experienced an increase in symptoms. After Session #30, she went back to college for the remainder of her junior year.
31-41	During her junior year, Chelsea experienced a car accident. Although she was not seriously injured, she began to experience a host of symptoms, including frequent vomiting, anxiety, trouble going to sleep and staying asleep, and irritability. When she came home for summer break, we did a series of sessions. Her symptoms gradually decreased across the sessions, and improvements increased. She went to college for her senior year after smiling and laughing in her forty-first session.

42-43   At Christmas break during her senior year, Chelsea participated in two more sessions and reported doing well. She went back to college for her final semester, graduated from college, and moved to another state for work.

In summary, Figures 16 and 17 show that the increase and decrease of symptoms can be a dynamic phenomenon related to traumatic events in a person's life and participation in trauma therapy. In essence, they show that once a person participates in trauma therapy, the number of reported and observed symptoms can decrease. They also show that, when that person has surgery or experiences a car accident, the number of symptoms can increase (and then decrease again associated with additional therapy). When experiencing exposure to the perpetrator of past abuse, symptoms can also increase. Thus, individuals who experience trauma therapy need to be cautioned to monitor their symptoms and their choices regarding the activities in which they choose to engage so that they can avoid unknowingly increasing their load of trauma energy and can seek additional trauma sessions when needed.

Caveat #2: The body's reactivity to traumatic events appears to decrease over time, with fewer symptoms arising over years

The second caveat is obviously based on my limited experience as a therapist regarding work with people over a number of years. Based on what I've seen, the number of symptoms experienced after subsequent traumatic incidents is fewer than the number of symptoms that were reported originally in the first session, and that number of symptoms seems to decrease across additional traumatic events.

This phenomenon is illustrated by Graham, the boy who tried to jump out of a moving car and whose story was initially told in Chapter 11. I have worked with him across several years, and I noticed that his case illustrates not only the dynamic phenomenon of trauma energy but also how the number of symptoms can decrease across time. When I first met him, he was experiencing several serious symptoms, including not being able to speak. After about twenty sessions, he finished high school and went off to college. He was reporting no symptoms.

I heard from Graham again several years later when his symptoms became so serious that he was no longer functioning in college. He had earned failing grades in three courses during the previous semester, and he was no longer going to class. When he listed the traumatic events that had occurred in the intervening years, they included a serious crisis involving his sister, a head injury that required stitches, a spider bite that required hospitalization, and a broken left wrist. He was also playing his sport again. His sport is probably among the two or three most violent sports, and he was getting injured regularly while participating in it. We started therapy sessions again, and over the ensuing years, Graham has continued to request sessions (which have been conducted over the phone), despite Graham being an international traveler and worker.

In order to provide a picture of the dynamic phenomenon that was at work in Graham's life, Figure 18 depicts Graham's major traumatic events and symptom increases across the first sixteen years of our work together. The black boxes along the horizontal axis show where major traumatic events occurred. The white number inside each box is the number of sessions we had completed at that time. The sixteen symptoms that Graham and his parents reported in his first few sessions are listed in Table 2 and are shown in Figure 18 with the bar above Year 1. The number of those same symptoms that recurred after major traumatic events are shown in the bars in the graph. (No new symptoms were reported by Graham across the years.)

Table 2
Graham's Symptoms

Can't stay asleep for long
Takes a long time to go to sleep
Can't complete tasks
Has confused thinking
Can't concentrate on tasks
Is depressed
Has digestive system issues
Feels dizzy constantly
Does not exercise
Has shaking/tingling/electric feelings in his torso
Engages in manic behavior
Feels chronic pain
Is disorganized
Can't speak fluently
Has no facial affect or social engagement
Engages in perseverative thinking

Figure 18: Number of Graham's symptoms reported over the years and sessions.

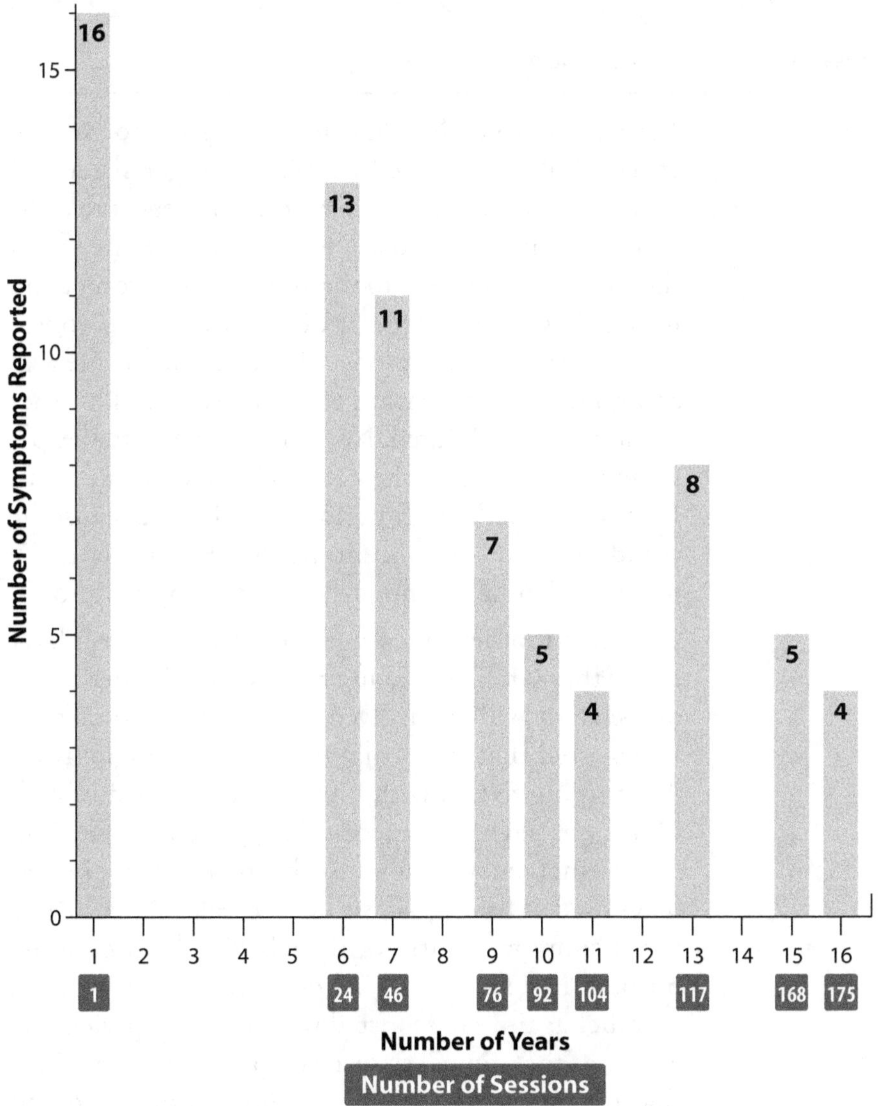

Below is an account of what was happening in Graham's life across the years. The session numbers refer to the white session numbers on the graph in the dark boxes in Figure 18.

Session No.	Description
24	After going to college and not seeing me for several years, Graham reported that his younger sister had called him at three a.m. one morning to report that she had been raped and to ask him to extricate her from the situation. He went to the site with his brother and found that getting her out of the situation involved some physical altercations with other men. He was able to leave the situation with his sister and brother without getting injured. Nevertheless, he started experiencing thirteen of the original sixteen symptoms. He was not able to function in college because he could not sleep or concentrate. Six sessions later, he reported that he was not experiencing any symptoms.
46	Graham's mother called me one morning a year later to say that Graham was in crisis. When she described his behavior, which involved constant and fast talking, I suggested that she bring him to see me right away. After trying to talk with him and start a session with him, I was having no success. I suggested we take him to the emergency room of the hospital. There, he was diagnosed as having a "psychotic break." After he was given some medication, his behavior became more normal. In a few days, we were able to start working together again. He reported that he was experiencing eleven of the original sixteen symptoms. He explained that his girlfriend was in a foreign country and had become ill with a life-threatening disease. Meanwhile, he was in the process of completing his college work

and sleeping few hours in the process. He was working as a coach of a college team, traveling with the team, and missing a lot of classes as a result. He was also trying to make decisions about what he was going to do with the rest of his life. After eighteen more sessions, he reported that he was "100 percent back" to normal.

76   About a year later, Graham was mugged by three men. He managed to get away from them, but he said that he had shut down all activity for about a week. He didn't go to work and reported experiencing seven of the original symptoms, including sleep disturbances and an inability to do work or concentrate. After five sessions, he reported that he was symptom free.

92   Another year later, Graham was in a motorcycle accident with his sister. The motorcycles slid on gravel, and they each had one leg pinned under their respective motorcycle. He was able to pull his leg out, but his sister couldn't, and he had to pull the motorcycle off of her. Her leg was broken. He reported experiencing five symptoms after this incident. Within two SE sessions, he no longer was reporting symptoms.

104   Still another year later, Graham's first child was born. Graham was present at the birth. As with any new dad, he reported having trouble with sleeping. He also felt jittery and had some manic episodes. Again, though, within a couple of sessions, he reported that he was symptom free.

117   Two years later, Graham's second child was born. Again, Graham was present during the birth. The baby did not breathe right away, so emergency procedures were implemented until the baby breathed. Graham again had difficulty adjusting to sleeplessness, and he had a manic episode a week after the birth. He

	reported eight symptoms. He took a leave of absence for two weeks from work to recover. A month later, he was doing well.
168	Three years later, Graham's wife was pregnant. After she experienced serious and life-threatening complications with the pregnancy, Graham reported having five of the original symptoms. After three SE sessions, he became symptom free.
175	A few months later, Graham's fraternal twins were born. Naturally, as a result of caring for them, he did not get much sleep. Again, he reported that he was a "little manic" the day after the birth, plus he was experiencing confused thinking and difficulty concentrating. Nonetheless, after two sessions, he had no symptoms to report.

This list of events and symptoms does not mean that Graham did not experience other traumatic events and symptoms in between these heightened periods of symptoms. Indeed, whenever circumstances didn't allow him to sleep much, he experienced some tingling or electric sensations in his torso. Also, he experienced additional traumatic events, including a bike accident, a bus accident, car accidents, sports accidents, the deaths of children and adults associated with his job, a fall on a steep hill, threatening wildfires on a mountain he was climbing, a few attempted muggings, a burglar entering his home and stealing money and belongings, and arson on his land that caused a very large fire that he fought to control. Each time, Graham immediately accessed treatment after experiencing one or two symptoms, and he recovered quickly. In fact, in the last nine years, he has not had a major shut down or onset of multiple symptoms.

The overall pattern shown in Figure 18 is interesting and instructive. First, some of Graham's original symptoms recurred over time after every major event. The most frequently experienced symptom was some type of sleep disturbance. The second and third most frequently experienced symptoms were a jittery electric feeling in his torso and some sort of manic behavior. He never mentioned depression again after the first few SE sessions, and his poor appetite, stomach issues, and dizziness faded away.

Second, the number of symptoms that Graham experienced as a result of a major traumatic event decreased over the years from sixteen symptoms after an event in the first year to four symptoms after an event in the sixteenth year. The reason for this is unknown. Perhaps Graham and his wife became more sensitive to behaviors that indicate when he needs to access a treatment session and thus have prevented major shutdowns. Perhaps Graham has learned to keep his life relatively stress free over recent years in comparison to the college years and the years where he was building his career. He is now able to lead a very busy and productive life raising four children and working in a professional job in a large, bustling city.

Caveat #3: People can reenact previous traumatic events

"Reenactment" is the acting out of a previous event in some way. In the case of traumatic events, victims often engage in reenactments of the events. Based on my experiences working with traumatized people, the likelihood that reenactment of their traumatic experiences will occur is high. For example, people who have had a surgery might engage in a series of additional surgeries. A frequent story that we hear is about people who continually seek out more and more elective plastic surgeries. For another example, people who have been abused in one relationship might engage in a series of additional abusive relationships or might engage in self-abuse or self-mutilation. They might also be attacked by random others in their environment. They might continue to interact with their abuser. Across several of the stories in this book, individuals reenacted their traumatic events in some way. For example, Mia (see Chapter 11) had a history of agoraphobia where she had spent three years isolated in her house as an adult after being in a hospital isolation ward in her childhood. Brianna (Chapter 9) and Lawrence (Chapter 5) were attacked by their peers in school after their fathers had abused them. Thus, the task of trauma therapy is to discharge not only stored trauma energy, which is related to the initial traumatic event, but it is also to reduce the likelihood that the event will be repeated. In other words, the task is not necessarily complete when the trauma energy related to the initial event appears to be discharged and when associated symptoms have initially disappeared. There is often more work to be done, and people need to be made aware to watch for certain signals.

The story about Brianna is instructive in relation to this phenomenon. She was thirteen years old when I met her. (See another part of her story in Chapter 9.) She had been sexually molested by her dad between the ages of three and nine years old and raped by her uncle when eight years old. In other words, she had a long history of being abused for her short life. One of her initially reported symptoms was that she often chose not to eat. As I was getting to know Brianna and I was gathering details about this symptom, she complained to me that she rarely got to eat lunch at school because another girl stole her lunch every day. The girl who was taking her lunch was very tall and very large, and Brianna reported that she was afraid of the girl who was stealing her lunch. The other girl would walk up to Brianna after Brianna had gone through the cafeteria line and simply grab her whole tray and take it away. Brianna hadn't complained to anyone at the school in fear of retaliation from the other girl who was known to beat up other students. We initially resolved this situation by communicating with school personnel about it, and a staff member started interfering each time the situation occurred.

Nevertheless, I soon realized that this was not the end of Brianna's problems with other students. A pattern soon emerged whereby Brianna was being bullied, taken advantage of, or was actually physically attacked by other students. She and I started referring to this phenomenon as the "door mat" phenomenon. Similar to being the target of her father and her uncle's abuse, Brianna also became the target of bad actors, and this interfered with her ability to get well. She made excellent progress and had stabilized well until around the twenty-fourth session, when a girl made an attempt to break up

Brianna's relationship with her boyfriend. This continued for almost a month, with the other girl spreading rumors and creating drama in relation to the boyfriend. Meanwhile, Brianna's boyfriend (another predator?) began pressuring her to have sex with him. Brianna finally broke up with him, but not before she became pregnant. Thereafter, her symptoms increased to the point where she couldn't eat until after 11:30 a.m., couldn't sleep, refused to bathe, and was having nightmares. Brianna made a decision to have an abortion and stopped going to school for a few weeks around the time of Christmas break.

Meanwhile, Brianna continued to participate in trauma therapy, almost weekly. She began to sleep well, eat well, take showers, and went back to school. She finished the first semester of eighth grade with grades of C or above. Nevertheless, other students started to call her names and to use racial slurs about her in her presence. Then her ex-boyfriend overdosed on a recreational drug and was in critical condition in the hospital. Her symptoms increased for a few weeks, and after a few therapy sessions, the symptoms decreased until she was stable again.

Next, around the forty-ninth session, she was physically attacked after school by the same girl who had been stealing her lunches. The girl jumped on her back, pulled her hair out, bruised her behind her ear, hurt her neck, and tried to push her to the ground. The attacker was arrested. The next day, two other girls started threatening bodily harm to Brianna if she testified against the attacker. Brianna's symptoms increased to the point where she couldn't concentrate in school and eventually refused to go to school. Brianna participated in several trauma sessions about the attack. She reported several improvements and started to go to school again. School personnel escorted the threatening girls to class and around the school, and Brianna started to feel safer in school. She finished her eighth-grade year with continuing good grades.

Throughout the next summer, Brianna continued to participate in trauma therapy sessions, reporting few symptoms and preparing to testify in court against her attacker. Her court appearance went well. She started her ninth-grade year reporting that she was doing well.

She said, "I went from this person who used to be slapped around to someone who says, 'No you don't!'" She reported that her grades in the first quarter were six A's and one C, and that she was enjoying her friends. Then suddenly she did not participate in sessions for a few weeks, and she stayed home from school one day and had sex with a boy, another predator. When I asked her why she was doing so well and then decided to skip school, she said that she got scared because she was doing so well. "I was on enemy ground, and I didn't know what to do next." Thereafter, she continued to attend therapy sessions, and her symptoms decreased.

Later in the fall, Brianna's mother had a serious physical condition and surgery, and Brianna became symptomatic again. She was worried about losing her mother. Despite experiencing a raft of symptoms again, Brianna participated in therapy sessions and took part in the school play. She became the manager of the basketball team. She was invited to the Winter Formal, and she spoke regularly to me about doing activities with friends. Suddenly, though, when all seemed to be going well, she reported that she was being stalked by someone in a car after school. Again, she became very fearful and frightened. Fortunately, that situation passed without incident. Then a girl in school started to act meanly toward Brianna. Brianna reported to me that she had concluded on her own that she was participating in a "door mat" situation, and she had acted on it. She reported that the girl had stopped being a problem.

In summary, this constant "back and forth" between having few symptoms and experiencing several symptoms is typical of a person who has experienced abuse and has a high likelihood of experiencing abuse again. In the case of Brianna, the recurring symptoms were dramatic enough that they threatened her ability to stay in school and complete her coursework to earn high-school credits. Once she understood the behavioral pattern of being vulnerable to bad actors, she began to act on it and help herself avoid more trouble.

Another person who illustrates the reenactment phenomenon is a boy I met when he was thirteen years old. He was a talented and skilled athlete, competing on a varsity high-school team while he was still in junior-high school. Although Nathan was somewhat shorter than the other athletes, he was handsome, perfectly proportioned, and had a muscular physique. I learned that Nathan was a star in his sport, and, as a result, he competed at the regional and national levels in it.

Despite all this success, Nathan was struggling. He had experienced a variety of traumatic situations in his earlier years. When Nate was three years old, he had been sexually molested by his dad. (A subsequent restraining order had prevented Nate from seeing his dad until he was sixteen years old.) Additionally, Nate had witnessed domestic violence in the home. His parents divorced, and his mother sought treatment for alcoholism. He had tubes put into his ears as a one-year-old. He also had a number of childhood accidents and injuries, including a sledding accident when he ran into a tree and a skiing accident when he broke his nose.

Nathan was known for his inappropriate behavior in junior high. He was disrespectful, quick to react in negative ways, argumentative, got into fights, and expressed sexual innuendos toward girls. He was often in the principal's office because of these and other behaviors. He was diagnosed as having ADHD, was in constant motion, and was taking medication for the ADHD. He was earning failing or very poor grades in school. He reported that he got stomach aches if he ate meat. He also reported that he was frightened and did not trust anyone. He lamented that he had no friends in junior high. (He was spending all his after-school and weekend hours with the high-school students on his team, but they ignored him because he was so young.) Despite all these issues, he was credited with saving another youth's life and with acting responsibly and maturely when his mother had a medical emergency. He also had success with his own paper route, which required him to deliver daily papers each morning before school.

Nathan started participating in sessions with me at the beginning of his seventh-grade year. He said his goals were to improve his grades (he had a 1.25 GPA), and to improve the way he was acting. In the first few sessions, we did the Walk-Up Activities. (See Chapter 4 for a description.) I found that he stopped my forward progress when I was about six feet away from him. At the beginning of the third session, he reported that he had cut his leg. I could also see that he had two black eyes, which he reported were the result of his sport activity. Nevertheless, he was able to concentrate well enough to describe sensations occurring throughout his body for thirty minutes at a time.

I soon learned over the course of several sessions that Nathan was constantly getting injured, sometimes related to his sport, sometimes just because accidents continued to happen, and sometimes because he was attacked by other youths. On his way to the fourth session, for example, he fell off his bike. By the fifth session, Nathan reported "Everything is good" and that he was passing all his courses. In the next two weeks, though, he got into two fights in school and spent time in detention. He reported that he was the target of bullying that had resulted in the fights. During the eighth, ninth, and tenth sessions, he reported additional injuries in his sport, all of which were significant. He arrived at the eleventh session with a broken fibula and a sprained ankle. Another student had fallen on his leg. His pain was at level "8" on the ten-point scale.

This pattern of experiencing injuries and getting into fights and other kinds of trouble continued throughout the first semester of his seventh-grade year. He was also sick a lot with respiratory infections and a strep throat. He was the target of predators who called him names and attacked him in school and on the bus. Nevertheless, he started to make friends and to get lots of phone calls from them. In the nineteenth session, he reported, "I have a best friend now." He also mentioned two other friends and a girlfriend. When we discussed the frequent attacks in his life, he said, "It's because I'm vulnerable." He named his size and reputation as the key factors related to his vulnerability. In my mind, his history as an abuse victim was probably the most important factor related to his vulnerability.

During the second semester of his seventh-grade year, Nathan struggled with his grades as they went up and down. Happily, he was not sent to the principal's office, and he had no suspensions. He had one detention for arguing. He continued getting along with friends. In the thirty-third session, his legs started running, which was a key indicator of his healing. Unfortunately, soon after this, he got caught with pot in his backpack in school, and he started receiving death threats related to identifying the drug seller. These events as well as a broken hand and a bike accident were the focus of subsequent sessions. He finished the second semester of the seventh-grade year by passing all his courses.

For eighth grade, Nathan transferred to a new junior-high school after he and his parents decided that he needed a new school community. He continued to participate in weekly sessions. He reported that he was making lots of friends and enjoying activities with them. Although he got sent to the principal's office once for engaging in a "pencil fight" on the bus, he didn't get in trouble during class, and he didn't have any detentions. He was pleased to report that he was now accepted by the "popular group" (which he had stated spontaneously as one of his goals). He had no illnesses to report.

For the most part, Nathan's eighth-grade year went well except for a few incidents. In one, another student spread the rumor that Nathan hated Black people. Soon thereafter, a Black student jumped Nathan and started choking and kicking him. There were a few other bullying incidents, too. He had a couple of random injuries related to ice skating and his sport that were not serious. Most of his weekly reports to me were related to his successes in his sport's activities and his passing grades. He stopped participating in therapy sessions the summer after his eighth-grade year when he started working a full-time job. He proceeded to high school at the beginning of the next fall semester, and I did not hear from him again.

Nathan's story is typical of someone who has had a history of being abused. He continued to be abused wherever he went. For years, he had difficulty interacting with others, and he was the object of others' attacks and bullying. He also engaged in a sport that resulted in many injuries, which might be considered self-abuse by some. Nevertheless, he eventually was able to interact with peers in a way that led to their positive responses, and he had success within the academic setting with regard to behavioral requirements and academic work. His sports injuries became less frequent and less serious over time.

Years later, when I tried to trace Nathan's whereabouts, I found two announcements on the internet. The first was a wedding announcement. The other was an obituary, which reported that Nathan had passed away when he was thirty-four years old. He had graduated from high school and was a military veteran. He had married, and he had one child. I was not able to learn additional information.

Summary

These stories about how trauma is a dynamic phenomenon and how reenactment is a real factor in the healing process are instructive and important. First, they are important because people need to be aware of them. Although accidents can be random, people need to be aware that they need to protect themselves from further trauma. They need to adopt ways of taking care of themselves and reducing risk in their lives because they have learned the consequences associated with overwhelming their capacity to store trauma energy. They need to adopt ways that reduce the stress in their lives so that their capacity to deal with symptoms is not overwhelmed. Additionally, they need to be aware to watch for initial signals that they are becoming overwhelmed. Also, they need to be cautioned about reenactment. When a pattern of reenactment occurs, they need to become aware of the pattern, how to recognize it by watching for key behaviors in themselves and others, and how to avoid the reenactment.

One further note is important here. In the stories related above, the individuals continued to come to treatment sessions over long periods of time. Certainly, one factor associated with the length of their treatment was the fact that they were not paying for sessions. Another factor was that they wanted to address as many traumatic incidents in their past as possible, and they had many. A further factor was that they had experienced a successful reduction in symptoms in previous sessions, and they wanted to experience that reduction again when another traumatic incident had occurred. In the cases of Brianna and Nathan, they were attending school where abuse kept happening, so the termination of treatment did not seem feasible until they were succeeding in that environment. In the case of Graham, he made a decision that he did not want to experience another psychotic break, so he has continued treatment on a monthly basis, and I have been willing to provide it.

This does not mean that everyone requires years of treatment. What it does mean is that people who have "maxed out" their capacity to store trauma energy typically need to release trauma energy over time and for several traumatic incidents. All the people represented in the stories in this book had experienced numerous traumatic incidents, and they reported numerous symptoms. In most cases, the large majority of their symptoms dissipated in a few sessions. Perhaps, if they had had treatment after their first major traumatic incident, they would not have experienced additional serious symptoms when additional incidents occurred. Indeed, if treatment were readily and cheaply available and accessible, their capacity to store trauma energy might not have been overwhelmed, and they might not have experienced such serious symptoms that jeopardized their ability to be successful in their daily lives.

REENACTMENT

Now that you are familiar with the term "reenactment," please list the events in your life (or someone else's life) that indicate that reenactment might be occurring.

EVENTS

SYMPTOMS

Consider how the symptoms that you are (or someone else is) experiencing have changed over time. Plot out that change below.

SYMPTOM	CHANGE

PART IV

RECOMMENDATIONS

CHAPTER 14
RECOMMENDATIONS FOR YOU!

I'm guessing that if you've read this book up to this point, chances are high that you and others in your life have experienced some traumatic events and some symptoms, and you are looking for answers. If this book has one message that I hope to convey to you, it's that no one should expect to heal significantly from a trauma condition involving several symptoms without appropriate therapy. That therapy should be directed at the root cause of the symptoms being experienced: the trauma energy that has been stored in the body. I know that "releasing trauma energy" sounds a bit like "hocus pocus" or something out of a science-fiction novel. (It did to me!) Nevertheless, after thirty years of witnessing trauma energy as it leaves a person's body (and feeling it leaving my own body), I'm convinced that it exists. I have no doubt that you probably will not be convinced until you feel trauma energy leaving your body. An important idea to understand is that if you have had traumatic experiences, there are some things that you can do to reduce some of the effects of the trauma energy currently stored in your body. Also, if you are a professional working with children or adults who have experienced traumatic events or a parent of a child who has experienced such events, you might find that you are experiencing what is known as "secondary trauma." This is a condition that is related to hearing details about traumatic events that others have experienced. It involves experiencing symptoms similar to the symptoms of trauma survivors, such as sleep issues, difficulty managing emotions, and increased levels of anxiety. The suggestions in this section might help with your secondary as well as primary trauma symptoms. I've tried most of the suggestions in this section myself, and the people participating in my project have reported back to me as they tried them. Certainly, the activities listed here are not guaranteed to help, but they might be somewhat helpful, at least in combination with therapy.

Remember that your body is working as it is designed to work

As explained earlier in this book (and other books in the reference section), our bodies are designed to help us deal with traumatic events. The first time we experience falling off a bike or a minor car accident, we might not feel any lasting repercussions at all. That is because the excess trauma energy is stored in our bodies in a way that has little effect on us. When trauma energy gets stored up, our nervous system's ability to store it can reach capacity, and symptoms can occur. These symptoms are the body's way of signaling to us that our nervous system has reached capacity. When I have explained this to people who have come to me for help, they have often said, "Does this mean that I'm not crazy?" When I say, "Yes, that's what it means," they respond that they are greatly relieved. In fact, after more explanation, some have left my office, saying that they are so relieved that they do not feel the need for additional therapy. Somehow, knowing that your body is working the way it should work versus feeling like it is permanently broken is a comforting thought. Indeed, your body might be giving you helpful signals that you can use to assist you in living a healthy life.

Truly take to heart the reservoir analogy

At the beginning of this book, I explained how the human body reacts to a series of traumatic events through an extended analogy and illustrations. (See Chapters 2 and 3 for the "reservoir analogy" and illustrations.) The reservoir analogy depicts how the human body serves as a reservoir of sorts that can store trauma energy that is left over after a traumatic event. After a series of traumatic events, this "reservoir" (or the body's capacity to store excess trauma energy) gets filled up, and "water" starts splashing over the dam. This "splashing water" represents the symptoms that our bodies start experiencing, which can serve as signals to us that our capacity to store trauma energy has been maxed out. If you keep this analogy in mind, you can adjust your circumstances and your reactions to events around you accordingly. Below is a continuum listing the "levels of caution" about which you should be alert and coordinated actions in which you might engage. You won't find this continuum anywhere but here; it isn't based on much more than my own experience as a human being who has experienced my own share of symptoms and on my experience as a trauma therapist who has worked with people for thirty years.

Attend to these levels of caution

Level #1

At Level #1, the body experiences some minor symptoms. For example, an eye might twitch a few times and then stop, the stomach might hurt for an hour or burp a few times, or a pain might shoot through the head a couple of times. A person might occasionally have trouble sleeping, like when facing a big speech or other important event. The person has no difficulty with exercising regularly and engages in social activities often and comfortably. The person can concentrate and learn with ease. The person works steadily and productively. The minor symptoms described above pass quickly, and there is no need to act on them or be concerned about them.

Level #2

At Level #2, the body experiences a few bothersome symptoms; that is, they are bothersome enough that the person seeks out some easily available remedy, such as an over-the-counter drug or a homeopathic remedy, or drinks alcohol sporadically. These remedies often work to relieve the symptoms being experienced. Examples of symptoms at this level include the following: the person takes twenty to thirty minutes to go to sleep; has heartburn or stomach acid when eating certain foods; skips breakfast or eats very little for breakfast; has occasional headaches; is sometimes irritable and grouchy; has minor aches and pains for no discernable reason; or feels anxious when late. The person may experience difficulty exercising on a regular daily schedule but does some exercise. The person continues to work and learn but less easily. Social activities continue but more sporadically. Sometimes the symptoms occurring at this level are considered to be permanent personality traits. Fortunately, they are actually symptoms that can be alleviated.

Level #3

At Level #3, the body is experiencing a number of serious symptoms that interrupt or hinder life in some way. For example, the person experiences sleep interruptions, sleeps for about five or six hours per night, is almost constantly in motion (leg jumping, cracking joints or knuckles), has chronic pain somewhere in the body, has migraines, feels tingles in the legs at night, eats minimally or sporadically (or overeats when stressed), skips periods, is fearful of others, feels anxious and depressed, has daily headaches, has frequent illnesses, and/or engages in self-harming behaviors (e.g., by cutting oneself). The person has some trouble concentrating and completing work or school tasks. Also, the person does not exercise much but may do so occasionally or only as required (as in gym class). At Level #3, people often seek the help of a professional such as a doctor with regard to obtaining a medication, like sleeping pills or medications for depression or anxiety. If they do not seek out this help, they may self-medicate with recreational drugs and/or alcohol.

Level #4

At Level #4, the body continues to experience serious symptoms as described above, but the person's behavior can no longer be ignored or excused by others or society. The person might not sleep more than three or four hours per night, eat only one meal a day, blackout when standing up, and not exercise at all. The person might avoid crowded environments, like crowded classrooms, stores, and community events. They might have panic attacks or become explosively angry when little things go wrong. They might be disciplined by school or work staff. They may not be able to concentrate at a level required by schoolwork and job tasks, and they are often unable to complete assignments. Children might get involved in fights and have few friends. Adults might get divorced or become involved in domestic violence and come to the attention of community authorities. They might seek out a new level or form of medication from a doctor or psychiatrist to add another prescription drug to other drugs being taken. The picture of water flowing over the dam in Figure 10 (Chapter 3) depicts people functioning at this level.

Level #5

At Level #5, symptoms have become so serious that the person is no longer able to function in the world in a normal way. The child may no longer be able to attend school, or, if allowed to stay in school, may be placed in a special class or special school for "behaviorally disturbed" children or students with learning disabilities. The adult may no longer be able to maintain a job for a variety of reasons, like lateness, noncompliance, and failure to complete work. The person might no longer drive a car or attend usual activities. Thereafter, the person might remain in the home, isolated from others, or depending on circumstances, might become homeless, placed in a residential facility, or be incarcerated. The picture of the dam showing water flooding the land below the dam in Figure 11 (Chapter 3) depicts people who are functioning at this level.

Summary

The five levels of caution related to a continuum of symptoms described above lists examples of symptoms that might occur at each level, but these examples are not set in stone for each level. As shown through the stories in this book, the people reported long lists of symptoms, and, although there were commonalities across the symptom lists, no list was like another one. The levels in this continuum are simply guides for you to use to judge the level of caution that you might apply to yourself as you consider your current state of health and the therapeutic services and activities in which you might engage. Of course, since this book shows the effectiveness of Somatic Experiencing, and since I can recommend it because of the experiences I've had, I will be recommending it here in relation to this continuum. Nevertheless, see books like Bessel Van der Kolk's *The Body Keeps the Score* and Appendix C in this book for references on therapies that might also be helpful.

As you might imagine, people who are functioning at Level #1 need not be concerned about seeking therapy for the minor symptoms being experienced. Importantly, if you are functioning at Level #1 and experience a traumatic event, be sure to attend to your symptoms after that event. If, for example, a single symptom becomes worrisome, like pain expressing itself daily in a part of the body and limiting activity, then medical attention is important to eliminate any serious injury (e.g., a broken bone) as a result of the traumatic event. Then therapy such as Somatic Experiencing may be accessed to alleviate any remaining symptoms.

On the other hand, if you are functioning at Level #2 and above, trauma therapy might immediately be needed. A person functioning at Level #2 might function at that level for years without serious repercussions. Nevertheless, if people functioning at Level #2 experience a traumatic event, they may be catapulted into Level #3 or #4 in terms of the seriousness of their symptoms. A good choice would be to participate in some trauma therapy at Level #2 to stave off serious repercussions at Levels #3 and #4 if a traumatic event comes along.

Engage in some potentially helpful activities

A number of activities might be helpful if your body is giving you signals that your "reservoir" (i.e., your capacity to deal with trauma energy) is approaching capacity or at capacity. These activities are not meant to be substitutes for trauma therapy. Some of them might be helpful on their own, in combination with each other, or in combination with therapy. As I said, I've engaged in most of them, as have the people who have worked with me, and, overall, they can be productive in giving you some symptom relief for short periods of time.

Please try to remember the general goals that you are trying to accomplish as you experiment with these activities. First, you won't want to add trauma energy to your reservoir. Thus, although accidents sometimes happen, do your best to avoid activities that might cause you harm. Second, one of your goals is to calm your sympathetic nervous system; this is the system that gears up so that you can fight or flee and that keeps you in a hyper-vigilant, hyper-alert, and hyper-active state. It is the system that got turned on during traumatic events and did not get turned off. Although therapy is the best way to turn off the sympathetic nervous system, anything else you can do to calm yourself and keep yourself calm will be helpful. For example, anything you can do to create a calm lifestyle is important. Figure 19 (p. 210) depicts what happens when your reservoir is constantly being filled by a rainstorm.

Figure 19: A filled reservoir, which has raindrops adding to its contents and causing splashing over the dam.

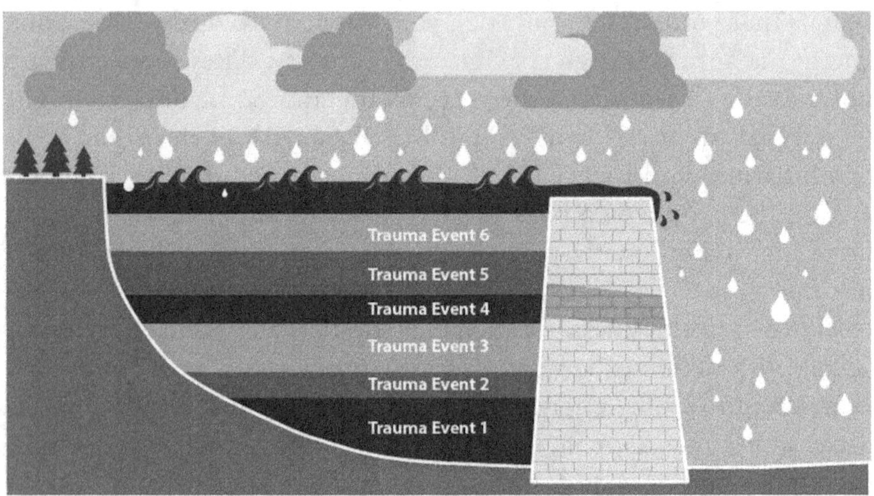

That rainstorm can be any kind of chaos that occurs in your environment. For example, your boss may engage in frequent yelling at employees. If no one knows when the boss will become angry, that uncertainty adds stress to the workplace. It adds "raindrops" to your reservoir. Likewise, fighting with your roommate or a business partner also can add "raindrops" to your reservoir. Although eliminating these types of stress from your life may be difficult, doing so is very important in terms of taking care of yourself.

Third, you will want to re-engage your parasympathetic nervous system; this is the system that shuts down many body functions during a traumatic event and puts a person into a "frozen" state. That may or may not have happened to you, but if you find yourself isolating from others, having a flat affect, daydreaming, not paying attention to activities around you, not able to "feel" anything, feeling numb in any body part, or not engaging in physical activities, then these symptoms may be a continuation of that frozen state. Again, therapy is the best way to bring you out of a frozen state. Nonetheless, some of the activities below might be helpful in re-engaging your parasympathetic nervous system; however, please don't expect the activities described below to take the place of therapy.

Protect yourself

Something you can do to calm your nervous system is to do all you can to protect yourself. To start, think about changes you might need to make in your environment to allow you a sense of safety. For example, you might need a security system and/or a new set of locks on your doors to help you feel more secure. You might feel safer if you have a dog or person who can accompany you on walks. You might feel safer if you have a mace or pepper-spray container in your pocket. Take time to think about your safety and what you can do to help create that sense of safety. Bottom line: Avoid risking your safety whenever possible.

Another way to protect yourself is to limit medical procedures that invade your body. Figure out the least invasive ways to get medical information for yourself. For example, choose to do a Cologuard test instead of a colonoscopy that involves general anesthesia. Any time you receive general anesthesia, the body senses that it is being poisoned and goes into fight or flight mode. For another example, if surgery is recommended for carpal tunnel syndrome, find and try other methods (e.g., physical therapy, rolfing, acupuncture) that can alleviate the pain and heal the problem. Every time a medical procedure is recommended for you, ask lots of questions and seek suggestions for alternatives to surgery and options for anesthesia. Unless your life and wellbeing are at stake, avoid elective procedures that invade your body.

Visit a "peaceful place"

Think of a peaceful place where you feel comfortable and safe. It can be real or imaginary. Examples of peaceful places chosen by people include their beds surrounded by pillows and stuffed animals, a place in nature such as a stream or a waterfall, a certain beach, a swing on the porch, a bathtub filled with warm water and suds, a hot spring in the mountains with a beautiful view, a tree climbed as a kid, a spot under a bush or porch for hiding, or a ski slope covered in six inches of powder. One teenager chose a painting in my home after saying he didn't feel safe anywhere. Once you've chosen that place, describe it to yourself in detail, including the color of the sky, the temperature, the season, and everything you can see in your mind's eye. Relax into the pleasant sensations that you have experienced or would experience in that place. Take time each day to visit that peaceful place in your mind. Allow your body to sink into the chair or mattress while visiting that peaceful place. Take pleasure in how your body feels.

Create order

Take a good look at your residence. The more orderly your residence is, the more likely you will feel peaceful and at rest. Starting small (e.g., with one cabinet), slowly go through each part of your home and eliminate or put away everything that is not needed, is cluttering up surfaces, or hasn't been used in a long time. File important papers in an organized way so that you can find them quickly and easily. Clean out cabinets and closets. Read a book or a blog on the internet about creating order in your environment, and follow the instructions, bit by bit.

Listen to and read peaceful information

Your auditory and visual channels are important influencers of your state of being. If the messages coming in through those channels are chaotic and scary, you are more likely to remain in a fearful state. For example, if you watch cable news off and on all day that focuses on disasters, wars, mass shootings, accidents, and other catastrophes, while playing the sounds of screams and chaos, you are more likely to be hyper-alert, hyper-fearful, and hyper-vigilant. Likewise, reading a newspaper every day that is filled with obituaries and reports of accidents and shootings is bound to set you "on edge." If you listen to peaceful, calming music and avoid those negative visual portrayals, you will be more likely to feel peaceful. Go to the internet, search for "relaxing music" or "calming music," and play it whenever possible. Search for programs on the radio and TV that teach you about something new instead of reporting traumatic events.

Provide excellent nutrition to your body

Engage a nutritionist to analyze the food that you are eating and the supplements that you are taking. Experiment with the suggestions that the nutritionist gives you. Certain foods might be better for your body type and blood type than others. (See Peter J. D'Adamo's book *Eat Right for your Type*. It's excellent and helped me eliminate pain in my body.) Also, drink the requisite six to eight glasses of water per day to keep your body hydrated. Additionally, you might do a complete workup of your body's medical composition to determine what supplements you need and what toxins to avoid. I recently found, for example, that I had mercury poisoning, microplastic poisoning, and excess iron in my body. I've since cut down on eating big fish, thrown out all my plastic containers, kitchen utensils, and cutting boards, and I'm taking a supplement that absorbs iron and carries it out of my body. All these kinds of measures are bound to help reduce stress on a person's body.

Engage in physical exercise

If possible, engage in some form of physical exercise. Try out different forms. For example, you might find that swimming or walking in a pool feels good, but running does not. Go slow. If you find that you can't do much exercise, just do what you can. For example, I started by walking half a block and then returning home. By gradually adding a block at a time and gradually increasing my speed, I found that I was able to do more than I originally expected. Over time, I was able to run a few miles. Alternatively, you can join a class, like a Zumba class or a dance class. You can go to a gym and use the weight machines, or you can lift small weights in your own home. Soon you can add some simple floor exercises. Some people find that participating in a yoga class a few times a week is very helpful in reducing symptoms. You may amaze yourself and feel better in the process. Choose an activity that fits with how you are feeling. If you don't want to be around other people, find something you can do on your own, like exercising while watching a recording of a yoga or exercise class at home. Be sure to consult your doctor about starting any new physical activity. Work with professionals who can ensure that you do not hurt yourself as you are beginning a new type of exercise.

Do the shower activity

If you are having difficulty feeling any part of your body, try this shower activity. Stand in the shower, with the water turned on at a comfortable temperature. Slowly put a different part of the body into the shower stream, and tell yourself what you are feeling. For example, say, "I feel the water on the back of my hands," or "I feel the water on the top of my head," or "I feel the water on my back." Gradually do that for every part of your body each day, taking plenty of time, and emphasizing parts of the body that are most numb to sensation. After doing this activity many times, you may start to feel sensations in different parts of your body. If you engage in appropriate therapy, you will likely regain sensations all over your body.

Minimize

If you find yourself running from one thing to another with barely enough time to catch your breath, being late, eating while working, multitasking, and making mistakes while doing so, slow down and take inventory. Make a list of your activities, and decide which ones are absolute priorities and which ones are not. Figure out what is important and why. Gradually move away from those activities that are taking up time and are not meaningful to you.

Take a sauna or mud bath

Saunas and mud baths are thought to reduce stress levels and promote relaxation. Other benefits that are often mentioned are improved immunity, improved circulation, and improved sleep. Infrared saunas, which heat the body from the inside out with dry heat and infrared light, have been shown in some research studies to reduce the level of cortisol in the body. Cortisol is one of the hormones that is triggered by traumatic events. Be sure to consult your doctor before you engage in any of these kinds of baths, and work with a reputable company.

Obtain body work

A variety of body work is available and can be helpful in reducing symptoms. It might not be appropriate for you, though, if you cannot tolerate someone touching your body. In such a case, obtain trauma therapy first, and work with your therapist in determining when you are ready to experiment with body work. Therapeutic massage, chiropractic adjustment, rolfing, physical therapy, craniosacral therapy, Reiki, acupressure, and acupuncture are among the many types of body work available today. You can do acupressure and some massage techniques yourself. Also, subtypes are available as well. For example, Swedish massage, hot stone massage, chair massage, and aromatherapy massage are among the many types of massages. Again, be sure to consult your doctor before you engage in particular types of body work to ensure that you are physically able to do so.

Meditate in some way

A wide variety of meditation methods are possible, including such practices as mindfulness meditation, transcendental meditation, spiritual meditation/prayer, mantra meditation, chanting, visualization meditation, grounding meditation, and movement meditation. Learn about these different methods, try some of them, and choose a method that fits your circumstances and personal style. Meditation is often paired with yoga and occurs at the end of yoga class. All of these methods require some investment of time and energy where you will focus quietly upon a particular subject, like an object, your breath, a visual image, or a mantra. Meditation can help you relax, keep your mood calm and steady, reduce stress and anxiety, and improve your ability to sleep. Be sure to seek out a guide who can help you learn to meditate if needed. Please understand that focusing on your breath or a part of your body can activate discomfort in your body. This is a signal that you will need to do some trauma therapy before you will be ready to meditate in this way. Work with your trauma therapist to determine when you are ready to meditate and what type of meditation you might try.

Engage in "forest bathing"

"Forest bathing" involves immersing oneself in nature and noticing all the beauty of nature. Research has shown that spending time in nature can reduce feelings of stress and improve health. When you visit natural surroundings, do so with the idea of being present and enjoying all the pleasant sensations around you. Listen for and look at the birds and other creatures; smell the vegetation and flowers; look at the details of everything, and feel the warmth of the sun on your skin. Combine "forest bathing" with a slow walk or at least ten minutes of meditation.

Identify and avoid "triggers"

When you experience a traumatic event, there are stimuli all around you that you may associate with that traumatic event. For example, when you have a car accident, it takes place at a certain place like an intersection and during a certain type of weather like a snowstorm, and it involves certain types of cars. The intersection, a snowstorm, and those types of cars are stimuli that might remind you of the accident. We call these stimuli "triggers" that might bring back the memory of the traumatic event and lead to discomfort in your body in some way. Sometimes, that discomfort can be debilitating, as during a panic attack or nausea and diarrhea. If you are experiencing debilitating discomfort of this type, you might take time to identify the triggers to which you are reacting. Once you know what the triggers are, you can choose to avoid them in the future. For example, you might avoid driving in a snowstorm or avoid a particular intersection. Of course, some stimuli might not be avoidable, at least not immediately. In such a case, seek out trauma therapy to deal with the particular traumatic event and to work with your therapist to find alternatives to experiencing those stimuli in the future.

Identify and avoid reenactment

Review your behavior patterns (and the patterns of people around you), and if you find that you are experiencing the same type of traumatic event over and over, work to change that pattern and, if needed, seek help with that pattern. For example, if you experienced abuse as a child and currently find that you are spending most of your time with abusive people, take time to evaluate that pattern. You may decide to start some new relationships and build those relationships in a way that accentuates the positive aspects of your life. You may decide to set your boundaries in new ways with regard to allowing others to act in abusive ways toward you. You may decide to gradually separate yourself from abusive people in your life. These remedies take time, so be patient with yourself. With time, you will find that you are experiencing fewer trauma symptoms in your life if you eliminate the reenactment of traumatic experiences.

Learn self-defense skills

Consider learning how to defend yourself physically by taking a series of self-defense lessons. If you know how to defend yourself, you will be more likely to feel safe. I took part in the program called Model Mugging and found it to be helpful. Other programs include karate, Jiu-Jitsu, Muay Thai, Krav Maga, and Taekwondo. A critical point to remember is that self-defense lessons may not be appropriate for people who have experienced a physical attack or rape. If you have experienced a physical attack or rape, consider engaging in self-defense lessons only after participating in Somatic Experiencing Therapy that fully addresses that traumatic attack and that results in a reduction of symptoms. Work with your therapist to determine the best time to begin self-defense lessons. If you engage in this activity without having adequate therapy, you are likely to experience extreme shaking, emotional upset, and an increase in symptoms.

Reengage with people

If you have experienced traumatic events, you are likely to have isolated yourself in some way after those events. You may be working at home and rarely interact with others face to face. You may have few friends. Your old friends might comment that you rarely interact with them. If this is the case, recognize that your isolation is a symptom and a result of your traumatic experiences. It's the result of your social faculties shutting down during the traumatic experiences as part of your parasympathetic nervous system's reaction to the trauma. (See information on biological connections in Appendix A.)

Once you have recognized that you are isolated, start working to remedy the situation. Little by little, start reaching out to other people. Call or send a text message to an old friend. Talk to the cashier at your grocery store, and learn the person's name. Greet that person by name and with a smile the next time you are in the store. Talk to someone at the gym, and learn that person's name, too. Each time you see that person at the gym, greet them and ask a question about their life. Briefly share something about your life. Gradually, gradually, one-by-one build a group of contacts in your everyday life. Having short interactions with these people will hopefully give you a sense that you are not alone. Gradually, gradually, you will be able to initiate activities with some of these contacts and enjoy engaging in them.

Build a community

Once you have made pleasant contact with a few acquaintances, you might be ready to join or build a community. This community can be relatively small, with just a few people who have a similar interest. Spend some time learning about interest groups or classes in your neighborhood or town. Talk to your contacts about what they do and the groups to which they belong. They might be in a book club, or they might play pickleball on certain days. They might volunteer for a charity or at a church or school. They might collect books for a sale at the library or for schools overseas. Ask if you can join, and attend the next event. Volunteer to help out during the activity, and provide help in any way that you can. Be generous in supplying your time, energy, and support, and you will find that you gradually will become a member of the group. Please understand that these things take time, and that you will be most successful if you have trauma therapy that enables you to engage your abilities to interact with others.

MAKE A PLAN

Now that you've read about the Levels of Caution (pp. 205-208), decide within which level you are (or someone close to you is) currently residing. Then list some of the recommended activities in which you would like to engage (or that you might suggest to someone close to you). (Please be realistic and choose wisely.)

LEVEL OF CAUTION

ACTIVITIES

CHAPTER 15
RECOMMENDATIONS FOR PARENTS

The stories in this book are about traumatic events that can easily happen to your child and the potential repercussions that can result. They include a wide variety of falls, accidents, injuries, attacks, and medical procedures. Most of them are common occurrences in our culture. Obviously, as a parent, you cannot protect your child from all possible traumatic events, and you probably do not want to be an overprotective parent. Many events happen randomly, and they cannot be avoided. Of course, now that you have read this book, you can keep the lessons learned about trauma in mind, and you can make decisions accordingly. Please know that the best way to protect your child from the effects of traumatic events is to prevent them from occurring.

Prevent childhood injuries

As your child explores the world, stay vigilant about dangers in the environment. Don't put your child in harm's way by not being attentive to these dangers. Below are examples of dangerous situations that have been reported to me and that resulted in stored trauma energy.

- Seating a child on a windowsill of an open window.
- Seating a child on the handlebars of a bike (or motorcycle).

- Seating a child in a seat on the back of a bike (or motorcycle).
- Not using a proper car seat or seat belt for your child.
- Putting a baby in a sink in a baby seat where the baby can reach the faucet handles and turn on the hot water.
- Allowing a child to jump off furniture near other furniture with sharp corners.
- Allowing a child to play on rusted, sharp, and/or old playground equipment.
- Allowing a child to run across a street or to be loose in a parking lot. (Never pit your child's body against the force of a 4,000 lb. vehicle or the asphalt!)
- Not insisting on standing well back from the street and having a hand on the child.
- Not closely supervising a younger child who is playing with an older child or a group of older children.
- Not supervising children around animals.
- Not remaining in the room when your child is being examined by medical personnel.
- Not securing potential weapons (e.g., knives and guns) and medications in locations that children cannot access.
- Allowing your child to sit on a couch with an older individual with a blanket over them.
- Allowing your child to participate in "slumber parties" with older individuals.
- Engaging in any type of physical abuse or restraint.
- Not choosing your "babysitter" extremely carefully.

Also, stay alert to the kinds of childhood accidents that are most likely to occur, and be extra vigilant in related situations. For example, childhood drowning is the most common cause of death between the ages of one to four years. For those children who survive a near drowning, the traumatic effects can be debilitating. Thus, be sure to obtain swimming lessons for your children. Insist that they wear life jackets in boats and near water. Stay close to them when they are in the water, even if the water is only a few inches deep. Never leave them unattended near water.

Biking and skateboarding are also frequent activities that result in childhood injuries. Make sure your children wear appropriate helmets and other equipment. Sign them up for a bike safety course. Teach them how to be safe and good citizens as they bike or skateboard on sidewalks and streets.

Dog bites are one of the most common childhood injuries seen in hospital emergency rooms. Thus, be especially vigilant when a dog is around your children. If you are walking on the sidewalk, stay well away from dogs in the area, pick up your child, or hold your child's hand. Teach your children how to approach a dog and its owner by asking if they may pet the dog and, after getting permission, holding out their hand to be sniffed by the dog. Teach them how to pet a dog gently. Warn them to never run after a dog, hit a dog, or tease a dog. Also teach them to recognize the warning signals that a dog does not want to be petted or approached (e.g., growling, bared teeth, hair standing on end). Any dogs, even your own dogs, will be especially protective of food they are eating. Teach your children never to approach a dog that is eating or that has a bone.

Fireworks can also be a danger to children. They can experience serious burns when they play with fireworks, and these burns are frequent statistics in hospital emergency rooms. Not only can burns be disfiguring, but they can also result in the storage of trauma energy. Thus, be especially vigilant, and provide close supervision in situations where children are having fun with fireworks or around a fire toasting marshmallows and hotdogs.

When your children get injured, give them your loving attention. Hold them and reassure them in a calm and loving voice that all will be well. Refrain from telling your child to stop crying. (Crying is a natural discharge of energy after an injury.) Despite your own upset, refrain from yelling at your child, regardless of what was done to cause the injury. If your child's body is shaking, reassure them that the shaking is a good sign of healing and that the body is doing what it is supposed to be doing to take care of the injury. Sit quietly with your child and allow the shaking to dissipate in its own time. Gently coach your child to breathe calmly and evenly. Of course, make sure your child receives appropriate medical attention as soon as possible.

Carefully monitor sports involvement

As seen in some of the stories in this book, participation in sports can result in injuries and stored trauma energy. The stored trauma energy from one major injury or a series of minor injuries can accumulate and eventually result in symptoms. As a parent, your job is to evaluate and choose the kinds of sports activities in which your children will participate. On the one hand, you will want to be protective so that future symptoms can be avoided. On the other hand, you will not want to be over-protective, especially if your child's friends are participating in a sport in which your child also wants to engage. Obviously, some sports are riskier than others, and some sports are more controlled than others, especially if referees are involved. Football and ice hockey are widely considered the most dangerous sports, but cheerleading and horseback riding are known to be even more dangerous. Take time to search the internet for information about the sports available to your children, training programs associated with those sports, the types of protective equipment available, and the types of injuries that can occur. Be particularly careful about choosing sports in which high rates of concussions occur because injuries to the brain are more likely to impair learning than a broken foot bone, for example. After your child has experienced a major sports injury or a series of injuries, be sure to seek professional help for the accumulation of trauma energy that will likely occur.

Carefully monitor technology use

More children are becoming anxious and depressed each year than in the past, and some of the blame is being aimed at their involvement with social media and computer games. A widely held notion is that the developers of these platforms and games have programmed them with the intent of addicting children to them. Additionally, social media platforms seem to be prime arenas for bullying. When children compare the number of friends they have to the number of friends other children have, compare their bodies to pictures they see on the internet, and compare photos of the fun other people are having to the amount of fun in their own lives, they start to feel left out and "less than." In addition to anxiety and depression, children are experiencing sleep problems, eating disorders, headaches, stomach aches, acid reflux, and other symptoms. At the extreme, they experience the symptoms of cutting themselves and attempting suicide.

Because children are so vulnerable in this regard, parents need to make several decisions *before** they allow their children to have cell phones. Here are some thoughts about decisions you can make that will help you protect your children.

- **Decide your purpose.** Consider the purpose of giving your children cell phones. Is your purpose to allow you to communicate with your children and vice versa, especially in emergencies? Is your purpose to allow them to communicate with close friends? If so, go into the venture with those purposes in mind.

- **Specify limits.** Consider limiting access to cell phones in a way that fits your purpose. For example, have your children

---

* Clearly, if your children have had phones for some time and have few limits, you will have to make adjustments to these suggestions and according to your children's behavior. If they are suffering from symptoms, seek help from a professional to make decisions and follow through on policies.

check their cell phones at the door as they enter your home and pick them up as they leave. That way, they won't be using them when they are eating dinner, playing with friends, interacting with you, completing homework, or supposed to be sleeping. Another limit might relate to how much time they can spend on their cell phones to communicate with friends each day after homework and chores are completed and where they are allowed to do that (e.g., in a central family area).

- **Make choices.** Set up privacy settings, go through them with your children, and explain the reasons you have chosen them. Consider what platforms your children can use. Stay alert to national news with regard to how different platforms are protecting or not protecting children and how they are affecting children. Allow your children to use certain platforms and not others, or simply don't allow them to use any social media. Closely monitor what they do in this regard.

- **Regularly review your children's use of devices.** Explain that while your child is growing and learning, you will share custody of the devices with them. Regularly go through the devices and talk about the interactions your children are having with others without judgment. Ask them how they like or dislike certain interactions. If they do not like certain ways that others are interacting, make a plan together on how to handle each situation, and follow through on the plan together. You may have to make a choice that your child does not like. For example, you may have to block a certain person's access to your children or your children's access to a certain site. If threats, bullying, or other abuse are occurring (either in person or online), contact school personnel and/or the bully's parents. If adults are interacting with your child, contact the police. Tell your children that you will have a "zero tolerance" policy for anyone who bullies or threatens them. Explain that your priority is their safety, and that setting boundaries about how they will allow themselves to be treated is important for their future health. Listen to your children's thoughts and feelings and allow them to feel heard and validated. Work with them to keep them safe. As they get older, have more experience, and show you that they are thinking about interactions in a positive way, allow them more space gradually over time with less frequent checks on their devices.

- **Teach them to be civil.** In addition to making these decisions and following through on them, teach your children how to interact with others on their phones and other devices. Explain that they need to be polite and nice to people when they interact with them on their phones. They should treat people as they want to be treated. Explain that if they treat others poorly, they may become the victims of bullying, pranks, and other types of abuse. Give them examples of words or phrases to say in certain situations, just like you would when they are interacting in person. Teach them to give compliments and be helpful to others.

- **Teach them the "What would Grandma say?" rule.** Ask your children to count to five before they post something and then ask themselves the question: "What would Grandma [or any other person that your child respects] say about what I have written?" If the answer is that Grandma would disapprove, they need to go back and redo the post. Teach them to be honest and truthful and never to post something that is not factual. Remind them that they should never forward something from another person or say something themselves that would be hurtful or that would harm others' reputations.

- **Teach them to protect themselves.** Explain that they should not interact with people whom they do not know. Teach them that anything they post will be there forever. There will be no way to remove any remark or photo or prevent anyone from showing it to others. In the case of email, texting, or social media, no one is to be trusted to keep anything private once it is posted. Anyone will be able to see it now and in the future, including future employers, teachers, potential dates, and people deciding to allow them into college or training programs. Teach your children never to risk their future reputations or success by posting something that others can access forever.

Protect your children from sexual trauma

On the surface, you might feel that this caution is not necessary. However, now that I have seen the incredible damage that occurs to children after experiencing sexual trauma and talked with the unsuspecting parents involved, I feel that you cannot take your mind off this issue, ever. The perpetrators of sexual trauma are everywhere. Older brothers and sisters, step-siblings, cousins, uncles and aunts, mothers, fathers, other relatives, mother's boyfriends, father's girlfriends, friends, caregivers, teachers, therapists, tutors, and babysitters are all possible perpetrators. Allowing a younger child to play with several older children without supervision is a recipe for disaster. The older children can gang up on the younger child and perpetrate physical and/or sexual abuse. Older siblings cannot be responsible for the safety of a younger sibling.

Preventing sexual trauma entails first educating children about their bodies and their boundaries. Explain that their bodies belong to them and that they can control who touches them. Teach them to watch for a sensation that indicates that they feel uncomfortable when some people touch them. Discuss appropriate and inappropriate touching and what they feel like. Teach your children about "consent" and what it means for people to ask for permission from each other and accept their answers. Explain that saying "No" or "Stop" when someone touches them without permission is okay. Likewise, it is equally important to respect someone who says "No." This is true in person, in texts, in posts, on the phone, on the internet, everywhere.

Have your children practice saying "No!" or "Don't touch me!" when someone is touching them in a way that is uncomfortable to them. Model how to pull away and run away from another person. Have them show you what they would say and how they would react if someone touched them inappropriately. All kinds of touching are suspect, including tickling, rough housing, wrestling, and cuddling. If your children tell you that they are uncomfortable about the way someone is touching them, listen carefully, believe your children, and restrict that person's access if necessary. Assure your children that you will listen to them, believe them, and address their concerns about uncomfortable touching. Also encourage the adults in your children's lives to ask for affection and to listen to the answer. Ask them yourself if they want to hug someone, and listen to their answer without shaming them, versus shaming them into hugging someone. For more information and games to play to prepare your children, see Levine and Kline's chapter (2007) on this topic in their book *Trauma through a Child's Eyes*.

Carefully evaluate all medical procedures

As also seen in the stories in this book, surgeries and other medical procedures can result in stored trauma energy and symptoms. Based on my experience, a series of surgeries can result in debilitating symptoms. Also, a surgery early in a child's life can cause the child to lose basic skills such as toilet training and language. It can harm the child's developmental progress. Although some surgeries are considered "business as usual" (e.g., tonsillectomies, circumcision), they can cause serious symptoms in a child or when the child becomes an adult. Always get a second opinion and read about the results of any surgeries that are recommended to you for your child. Explore all other avenues available to you (e.g., allergy testing and treatment, nutrient testing and treatment) before signing up for surgery. Any elective surgery warrants careful investigation and thought. Of course, emergency surgeries can certainly be lifesaving, and, because time is of the essence during an emergency, you may not have time to learn much about the surgery. Sometimes, you will have time to evaluate a serious elective surgery, such as an operation for an anterior cruciate ligament tear or an Achilles heel rupture.

For any surgery where you have time to evaluate, start by learning about the surgery. Go to the internet and/or the library to read about it. Become familiar with the terms associated with the particular body parts, so you can talk about them and understand what the doctor is saying to you. Be clear on whether there are surgical options among which you can choose. For example, some surgeons might choose to cut through the abdominal wall, and others might not for the particular surgery being considered. For another example, arthroscopic surgery (a minimally invasive procedure involving tiny incisions and the use of a tiny internal camera to aid the surgery) might be used by some surgeons, and not by others. You might want to find the option that is least invasive and involves the smallest incision(s). Less trauma will be associated with this option.

Once you understand your options and have selected the best option, look for a surgeon who is skilled in that option. Talk to your pediatrician, other health care providers, and friends. Be sure to ask them specifically about the surgeon's work with children and the outcomes of the surgeon's work with children. Interview different surgeons if more than one is available. Explain that you are interested in making sure the least amount of trauma will occur as a result of the surgery. Ask what procedures the surgeon is willing to use to reduce trauma. If the surgeon does not name any of the following procedures, state that you formally request them.

- A drape that will prevent your child from witnessing the surgery if the anesthesia wears off and the child awakens.

- A medication that will make your child drowsy before entering the operating room.

- A local anesthesia (in addition to any general anesthesia) that will deaden the sensation of being "cut" into. This can be a very localized shot, a shot in the main nerve in the area, or a shot in the spine (a spinal block).

- A general anesthesia that does not have side effects such as nightmares, hallucinations, memory issues, and other serious symptoms. Ask, for example, that Versed and ketamine not be used.
- A *slow* method of bringing your child back to consciousness versus a quick one.
- If they normally play music in the operating room, soft music playing in the operating room that your child knows and likes.

After talking with the surgeon and finding that the surgeon agrees to use these methods, make an appointment for your child to meet the surgeon for a few minutes. Also meet with the anesthesiologist who is assigned to the surgery. You might even start with the anesthesiologist before seeing the surgeon. Either way, be sure to see the anesthesiologist. Go through the same requests with that person.

I have found that some professionals are very agreeable with these requests. For example, the anesthesiologist who was present for my son's surgery said that he would make the same requests if he (or his child) were going through surgery. Medical research has shown for years that using these methods reduces pain, bleeding, complications, and time of recovery. I've been told that these methods are used in VA hospitals to reduce trauma in our veterans undergoing surgery. Some professionals might get defensive and refuse to use these methods or seem reluctant. They might state that giving a local anesthetic is time consuming and that they have a tight operating schedule. If they seem reluctant or refuse, you can decide to choose another surgeon.

Once you have found an agreeable surgeon (and associated anesthesiologist), prepare your child for the surgery. Explain what will happen and when in words your child will understand. Be honest. Answer any questions matter-of-factly. Don't make statements like, "It won't hurt," or "You'll be able to eat all the ice cream that you want!" These kinds of promises often do not come true, and then your child will lose trust in you. Make an appointment to tour the hospital and operating room with your child. Have the staff show your child the clothes and masks that will be worn during the surgery, and the transportation (e.g., gurneys, wagons) that will be used. Tour a hospital room like the one in which your child will stay. Meet and chat with the people who will be involved in the surgery and the aftercare. Specifically ask to meet the person who will be with your child in the recovery room so your child can recognize the person's face and voice. Practice having someone listen to your child's heart and looking into eyes and ears. In other words, give your child every opportunity to become familiar with the hospital setting, the people in it, and the basic equipment that will be used. This may reduce the amount of stress your child experiences on the day of the surgery and will hopefully reduce the amount of trauma energy that your child stores as a result of the surgery.

Before the day of the surgery, ask for permission to accompany your child from the hospital room to the operating room and to be in the recovery room when your child awakens. Also, before the day of the surgery, have your child choose a peaceful place, and practice visualizing that peaceful place with your child numerous times. Have your child describe that place and picture it mentally. On the day of the surgery, calmly accompany your child through all the pre-operation procedures. As the various procedures are occurring, prompt your child to visualize the peaceful place with you. This is important—if your child enters the anesthesia peacefully, she will be more likely to come out of it peacefully. As your child awakens from the anesthesia, speak softly and calmly. Explain that you are there to help in any way that you can. Refrain from giving any instructions or commands to your child. Just happily welcome your child back. If your child's body shakes, assure your child that shaking is okay. Explain that it's the body's way of healing.

If your child is spending the night in the hospital, bring familiar objects and decorations from home that your child likes. Arrange low lighting if possible. Make the necessary arrangements to spend the night in the hospital with your child. Ensure that pain medication is administered on time. Keep your child pain free as much as possible in the hospital and at home by following the pain prescription instructions in a timely way.

By all means, please understand that you can suffer from secondary trauma if your child or a loved one experiences a traumatic incident (especially one you witness) and suffers from trauma symptoms. Going into "fight or flight" is not uncommon if your child is in danger or experiences a traumatic event. Follow the suggestions in Chapter 14 about taking care of yourself whenever this happens.

If you are contemplating surgery for yourself, follow all the recommendations above. Make sure that you have an advocate accompany you to the hospital and remain present during the surgery, recovery, and hospital stay. Make sure your advocate knows details about your health, trauma history, and any allergies, and what requests you have made and why, since the advocate may be asked questions about you and may have to advocate for you. Ask your advocate to protect you from unwanted attention and needless interruptions so that you can spend your time healing.

Seek professional help for trauma symptoms

If your child experiences trauma symptoms (see Figure 12 in Chapter 3), be sure to determine whether they are related to a physical condition by checking with your medical doctor. If they are not, obtain trauma treatment for your child with a person who is experienced in working with children and certified as a trauma therapist. (See Appendix C for references for some potential therapies and links to therapist directories.) Also, books by Levine and Kline (2007, 2008) suggest simple activities you can do with your children to help them.

CHECKLIST FOR PARENTS

- ☐ The home is "child proofed."
- ☐ Dangerous corners and objects have been removed.
- ☐ Safety gear is available and rules are made.
- ☐ All weapons are locked up and not accessible.
- ☐ Windows and doors are locked
- ☐ Cell phone rules have been set.
- ☐ Cell phones are checked weekly.
- ☐ Medicines and hazardous materials are not accessible.
- ☐ Safety devices have been installed (on outlets and stairs).
- ☐ TV rules have been set.
- ☐ Video-gaming rules have been set.
- ☐ Slumber-party/overnight-stay rules have been set.
- ☐ Babysitter surveillance cameras are in place.

CHAPTER 16
RECOMMENDATIONS FOR TEACHERS

The people who told me the stories in this book are representative of some of the students in today's classrooms. They have encountered all kinds of abuse as witnesses and targets, and they have experienced a wide variety of falls, accidents, injuries, attacks, and medical procedures. They have lost loved ones. They are innocents. Based on the stories in this book, we know that they cannot concentrate and have difficulty learning. Their memory skills are lacking, and they cannot sustain reading for very long, even though they may know how to read. We also know that the personal space around their bodies in which they feel safe is an imaginary large circle with a radius of about eight feet. We know that they are extremely fearful, so they are likely to be very vigilant and reactive to any sign of danger, especially when they are in an environment with lots of people.

Additionally, we know that they cannot control their symptoms with their "thinking" brains. They cannot direct themselves to do assigned work in a way that works. We also know that people around them cannot control whether they do their work by telling them to do so. For example, despite being restricted in a room or a basement until they completed their work, children with whom I have worked could not and did not complete their work for days and even weeks. We now know that these individuals are highly intelligent because they earned advanced degrees once they received treatment for their traumatic experiences. In fact, in all the cases in this book where children were earning failing or barely passing grades, despite not receiving tutoring, special academic coaching, or being placed in special education programs, they became productive students after participating in Somatic Experiencing sessions.

The reason for this inability to voluntarily control symptoms is that the part of the brain that has been affected as a result of traumatic events is not the "thinking" brain. Instead, the "reptilian" brain has been affected; this is the part of the brain that is involved in responding to traumatic events. (For more detail on the biology behind this, read Appendix A in the current book or Besel Van der Kolk's excellent book *The Body Keeps the Score* [Van der Kolk, 2014].) This means that students cannot voluntarily control their symptoms. They are not able to suddenly concentrate or complete work because someone tells them to do so. No matter how hard someone might try to talk a student into controlling a symptom, no matter how loudly someone might shout at a student or how long someone might shame a student, that student cannot respond.

If you are someone who is charged with providing some sort of instruction for students like the ones described above (e.g., a teacher, occupational therapist, speech therapist, music therapist), then you are in a unique position to help them. Obviously, you may not have the time or needed training to provide trauma therapy to your students. Nevertheless, you can do quite a lot in terms of providing an environment that supports students with a history of traumatic experiences. Understandably, you will be busy as you do your work, and you may not have time to follow all the suggestions below, but anything you can do in terms of extending understanding toward them will help these children immeasurably.

Watch for signals that a student may have a traumatic history

Physical signals

Look at each student every day, perhaps by greeting them at the door to the classroom. Students who have a traumatic history may have glassy or fogged-out-looking eyes. They may be disheveled and ungroomed. They may have cuts and bruises or may have clothing covering every inch of their bodies, including their hands. All of their clothing might be black. Alternatively, they might have very little clothing on, even on the coldest days. They might have frequent injuries, like big bruises, sprained ankles, black eyes, or stubbed toes. When they sit at their desks, they don't sit up straight and may put their heads down and go to sleep. They might stare into space and not be alert when called upon.

Academic signals

When you look in your grade book, these students will not have handed in assignments. They might give you an excuse or say that they will hand in past-due work, but it will rarely appear. They might do well on tests while not completing assignments. They might have some skills (learned prior to their trauma history), but they have difficulty learning a new skill.

Behavioral signals

These students can present behaviors that occur on two sides of a continuum. On the one hand, they might be very quiet, fearful, compliant, isolated, and the target of bullies. They might cry and become emotional. They might be reactive to loud noises, voices, and anger. On the other hand, they might be noncompliant, defiant, and oppositional. They might be disruptive in class. They might throw tantrums or start yelling loudly when they do not get their way or when no one is understanding what they are trying to say. They might bully and attack others. Various parts of their bodies might be in perpetual motion. Because they are uncomfortable in a crowded space (your classroom), they may ask to go to the restroom often. You might find them doing school work while sitting on the bathroom floor. You might find them wandering the hallways or the outdoor areas. Punishing them by putting them at a desk in the hallway might have the opposite effect (it might function as a reward); they might feel more comfortable in the hallway away from other students.

Social signals

Regardless of the end of the continuum on which these students find themselves, they typically do not have friends. They have difficulty making and keeping friends; some of them may be constantly involved with interpersonal "drama." They may repeatedly be arguing with a variety of peers or making negative statements about peers. They may state that they are uncomfortable in cooperative-group activities. They might isolate themselves away from others such as during recess and other large-group activities. They might pull their chair away from the small group to which they've been assigned for a cooperative group activity and not participate in the group.

Summary

No matter what signals you witness, take care to watch for them over time and gather more information. Not every child who wears black or who gets bullied has a trauma history. Not every child who falls asleep at her desk has been abused; she might have an iron deficiency. An observed behavior might simply be a one-time occurrence, which has no relationship to anything that should concern you. Nevertheless, observing one or more signals repeatedly over time should be cause for concern. You may be the closest adult to these students' plight, and you have resources that you can use to help them. Children who have experienced a traumatic event or who are living in a traumatic environment are likely to be very fearful, hyper-vigilant, alert to danger, and very reactive. You might quietly ask to meet privately, explain calmly what you've observed, and then ask the student to share information about what is happening. Next, take your observations and the information the student has shared to the people in your building and district who have access to resources that can help. Feel certain in knowing that events in a child's life such as divorcing parents, domestic violence, family financial woes, serious parent illness, or a dying relative can be traumatizing and can exacerbate a situation in which a child has experienced a serious traumatic event personally in the past (e.g., a fall, injury, medical procedure, or inescapable attack).

Create a safe learning environment

An important step you can take in supporting children with a traumatic history as well as other children in your classroom is creating a safe learning environment. This means creating a classroom where everyone feels safe, valued, and protected. It means creating a place where you and the students work together to facilitate the learning of every student in the class and to ensure that students are encouraged to participate and perform at their best.

You can start by posting a large sign in your classroom that states, "SAFE CLASSROOM." On the first day of class, point to the sign and announce, "This is a safe classroom! This is a place where everyone feels safe." Ask the students to help you design a safe classroom by contributing their ideas about the characteristics of a safe classroom (e.g., "In a safe classroom... People listen. No one is shamed. People take turns. No one yells."). Make a list on the board of their contributions, and add your own contributions. Pledge to them that you will do everything you can to ensure they feel safe in your classroom. Ask them to pledge to make the classroom safe by signing a sheet listing the characteristics of the safe classroom that they designed. Post the signed list of characteristics in the classroom.

Hand in hand with this agreement to create and abide by the characteristics of a safe classroom must be an adherence to a zero-tolerance policy specifying that anyone who dishonors those characteristics will receive consequences for their actions. Work with the class to design consequences for breaking the "Safe Classroom Agreement." Your responsibility will be to specify that someone has broken the agreement and to administer the consequences. For example, if someone yells out instead of raising a hand to be recognized or laughs at someone's contribution, then take a moment to name the behavior (e.g., "Jamar, you just yelled out an answer instead of raising your hand;" or "Marta, you laughed at Peony's contribution. Remember that everyone's contribution has value."), and apply the consequence, which may be the loss of a point during the discussion. In contrast, students who adhere to the agreement should receive praise and attention for doing so. For example, they can receive points for their contributions. (See the *Talking Together Program* [Vernon, Deshler, and Schumaker, 2000] for a way to structure safe discussions.) Uniformly enforce the same rules and consequences for everyone.

Additionally, during the first few days of school, teach the students about the behaviors you expect in each class activity that will occur in your classroom. For example, separately teach them about a routine for each of the following activities: entering the classroom, leaving the classroom, passing out papers, collecting papers, working with a partner, working within a small group, and participating in a whole-class discussion. Give each routine a name (e.g., "Small-group work," "Paper passing," "Paper collecting," "Leaving class," "Transition between activities"). Make a list of the steps they are to follow in each routine, explain what they are to do for each step, have them practice the steps, and give them feedback. Post the steps on the board. If students understand what is expected in each activity, they will be able to predict what will happen next, and they will be more likely to feel safe and follow your instructions.

Another way to help students feel safe is to announce and post a standard schedule for activities in your classroom. Again, once students can predict what will happen next, they will experience less stress and anxiety, symptoms related to past traumatic events. When you know that you will be changing the schedule, give the students advance notice of the change. When new people will be visiting the classroom or when the students will be leaving the classroom for another place, prepare the students in advance for the visit. Explain what the students will be expected to do during the visit.

Create a learning community in your classroom

A learning community is a group of people who learn together. Each person's learning is just as important as another person's learning, and everyone contributes such that everyone can learn. To create a learning community, use available instructional programs* to teach social skills that students can use during class activities and elsewhere. For example, programs are available for teaching students to participate in whole-class discussions and to work with a partner to focus on schoolwork, follow instructions, organize materials, and take notes together. Programs are also available for teaching students to work cooperatively and productively in small groups to complete a project, to study for a test, to solve a problem, and to resolve an issue. Research has shown that as students learn social skills, they are more likely to have positive interactions and less likely to have negative interactions. As they treat each other with kindness, respect, and understanding, everyone feels included, and the well-being of everyone benefits. Additionally, research has shown that if students are taught to help each other and work together, they will better understand each other, like each other more, and learn more.

Focus on location and spacing

When you have identified a child who may be suffering symptoms related to traumatic events or living in a traumatic environment, focus on how you can help that student feel safe while present in your classroom. Remember that these students are very fearful and hyper-vigilant. That means that they need to be able to see what is

---

* For available programs that my colleagues and I have validated through research for building a learning community, see the website at www. edgeenterprisesinc.com, and click on the product menu for the *Community Building Series* and the *Cooperative Thinking Strategies*. For a list of references for those programs, please email jschumaker@ transcending-trauma.org.

happening around them in the classroom. Placing them in the front row makes their vigilance and fearfulness worse because they cannot see what is happening behind them. Clearly, if you have a class with twenty to thirty students, you won't have many options for safe places. One way to proceed is to quietly and privately chat with the student about choosing a location in the classroom that will alleviate some of the anxiety and fearfulness. The best location will probably be at the side of the class, toward the back of the class, with full view of the door to the classroom, and close to the door.

If you plan to use partner activities, choose a partner for the target student who is well-behaved and is likely to help the student. When you are going to assign a small-group activity, surround the student with safe students who are not likely to bully the student. Research has shown that bullying can easily occur in small-group activities, especially when students have not learned the social skills they should use in small groups. Also, place students around the target student who have high scores on the Hope Scale.* These students will be more likely to be supportive of other students.

Also, be aware of your personal behaviors when interacting with the identified student. When you approach the student, approach from the side or the front. Avoid approaching from behind or surprising the student. Be sure to stop at least three to four feet away. Crouch down or sit down in a seat near the child. Refrain from touching the child because the child may be hypersensitive to touching.

Attend to your expressions

Students may have experienced domestic violence complete with angry facial expressions, raised voices, yelling, and swearing. Thus, when you are interacting with students, use a friendly facial expression and gentle, smiling, kind eyes. Speak to them in a calm and quiet tone of voice. Use polite and respectful language. The muscles in

______

*　See the Hope Scale on p. 50 of Cathleen Beachboard's book *The School of Hope* (Beachboard, 2022).

your face and your voice tone give students clues about how much you are accepting of them. When they receive messages from you that they are safe with you, they will feel supported and nourished.

Engage in open and relaxed communication

Promote open communication, starting with the first moment of the first day that you meet students. After you present the "Safe Classroom" sign to them and explain what it means (see the section on "Creating a safe learning environment" above), tell them that you are interested in them, want to hear what their lives are like, and what they are thinking. Explain that you understand that everyone faces difficulties, and that you are willing to help them in any way that you can so that they have the best chance of learning in your classroom. Tell them that no topic is "off base," and you will listen to their concerns and issues. Give some examples of issues that might be bothering them or might interfere with their learning (e.g., "Not enough food," "Feeling unsafe," "Electricity cut off"), and ask them for other examples. Make a list on the board. Explain that you will listen to their concerns. If you cannot help them, you will find someone who can help them.

Certainly, active listening is a key element of open communication. When you ask students a question, give them plenty of time to answer. Hold back from answering for them or letting someone else answer for them. Give students space as you wait for an answer. Encourage an answer by nodding your head, smiling, and using soft and smiling eye contact.

If you see or learn that a student is upset (e.g., sad, crying, head on the desk), then ask the student to meet with you privately while the other students are working on an assignment. Encourage the student to tell you what is upsetting (e.g., "I see that you're upset. Are you willing to share with me what's upsetting you?"). Take time to gather information about the situation, including who is involved, what has happened, and the impact the situation is having on the student. Use short phrases or questions to encourage the student to tell you details about what has been happening (e.g., "Is that right?" "What happened next?" "What did you do?" "Please tell me more about that" "So how has this affected you?" "I'm so sorry you're going through this" "What can I do to help?" and "Is there someone you want me to contact?"). Try to determine whether a traumatic event has occurred, whether the student froze in the situation or was able to react, and what the outcome of the situation was. Explain what you can do and who you plan to contact to provide some help.

Also, try to figure out what the student's "triggers" are. These are stimuli that cause the student to be upset because they remind the student of a traumatic event or they activate the student's hyper-vigilance. For example, if a student has been beaten, that student might become upset when another student touches her, even gently. Alternatively, the student might state that not being able to see people behind her seat upsets her. For another example, if a student has immigrated from a war-torn nation and has experienced bombings, a loud noise may be a trigger for that student. This student will need special care on days when fire alarms or active shooter drills are planned.

As an alternative to oral exchanges, you can try exchanging some notes with students. A simple method can involve using 3" x 5" cards whereby you distribute a card to each student and ask them to write their names on the card and answer a question. The question can be as simple as, "How do you feel today?" Students can answer with a drawing of a smiley face or a frowning face, or they can write something. Cathleen Beachboard, in her book *The School of Hope* (Beachboard, 2022), suggests the use of a one-page Mental Health Check-in Form (p. 21 in her book) whereby students can report how they are doing. This can be followed up with a Daily Self-Care Plan (p. 24 in Beachboard's book) created by the student and teacher working together.

Additionally, you might engage in activities such as those suggested by Levine and Kline (2006, 2008) and Kline (2020). Regardless of what you choose to do in your classroom, be sure to communicate with other professionals in your school and district and work as a team with them to access resources and professionals who can provide services to the student and the student's family.

Use research-validated instructional procedures

When you are teaching a new skill or giving a new assignment, use instructional behaviors and programs* that have been shown through research to work, especially for students who have trouble learning. There's nothing more frustrating to students than not understanding what to do when an assignment has been made. The instructional behaviors that have been shown to work include the following.

Tell the students what to expect

Before beginning any instruction, explain what the instruction will be about. Explain what you will do and what they are expected to do. If they know what to expect, they will be less anxious and fearful.

Break the skill (or task) down into steps

Think about the skill you are teaching, and make a list of the steps you follow when you use the skill. Include thinking steps as well as overt physical steps.

Describe the steps

Tell the students explicitly about the steps to be used. Make a list for them to follow, and have them make a copy of the list to keep. Some students might need the list taped to the top of their desks.

---

* See example programs that have been validated through research as effective on the website at www.kucrl.ku.edu. Scroll down and click on the button "KUCRL Store."

Model the steps

Demonstrate all the steps for students. Be sure to include the thinking steps by stating your thinking aloud. Students need to hear how to think about a task as well as to see how to perform it.

Ensure students know the steps

Have students practice naming the steps until they can state all the steps. Create a variety of activities in which the students practice naming the steps, such as a team contest, paired-practice activities, or group-practice activities. Make lists of the steps available to them at their desks or posted in the classroom.

Have students practice the steps

At first, give the students easy practice activities until they can follow the steps without issue. Thereafter, gradually increase the difficulty of the practice activities until students can use the skill in a variety of ways. Give the students choices among practice activities as they practice new skills so that they can have a sense of agency in their lives. Always build on students' individual strengths and interests as they practice new skills whenever possible.

Provide feedback

As the students practice, be sure to give them frequent positive and corrective feedback. For targeted students, speak with them quietly and privately. Always tell them what they did correctly. Be generous with your praise. Also explain where they made errors and demonstrate how they are to perform in the future. Adjust what you expect in the future from a given student based on what you know about the student. In other words, you might differentiate how much work you expect, the quality of work you expect, and the amount of support you provide as a student is receiving treatment and dealing with symptoms. Then, as a student's concentration and performance improves, you will be able to adjust your expectations gradually.*

Promote hope in a variety of ways

Research has shown that high Hope Scores are correlated with lower anxiety in children. Thus, by promoting hope in your classroom, you may be helping students move forward with less fear. With less fear, they will be more likely to try new things and learn new skills. Cathleen Beachboard, in her book *The School of Hope* (Beachboard, 2022), suggests many ways to promote hope in a classroom. For one of her suggestions, she has designed a form called the "Children's Hope Scale" that students can fill out to indicate their level of hope (p. 50). Children who express high levels of hope tend to be more resilient to difficulties. They problem solve and continue to pursue their goals. Having all students in a class complete the Children's Hope Scale is an easy and quick way to find children who have high levels of hope and those who have low or no hope. Children with different levels of hope can be paired and can work helpfully together.

Deal with out-of-control students

One way to promote a safe classroom is to have a plan for and to deal respectfully with out-of-control students in ways that help everyone in the class. Students who are hyper-alert, hyper-vigilant, and hyper-fearful will only become more so if other students in the classroom are violent and out-of-control. You can prepare all students ahead of time for out-of-control situations by telling them about grounding techniques and having them practice using these techniques. (See Beachboard's table of grounding techniques on p. 32 [Beachboard, 2022].) You can guide a student through a grounding

---

* For a reference list for instructional programs that utilize the procedures described in this section, email jschumaker@transforming-trauma.org.

technique if the student has become upset. You can also teach the whole class a routine of how they are to react if you have to take someone out of the classroom when a student is upset. Specifically tell them what they are to work on and how they are to behave. Your first priority is to keep yourself and other students safe. To do so, follow your school's protocol for such incidents. Students who have been physically abused or who have witnessed violence can have a great deal of stored trauma energy that can take the form of rage when it is triggered. That rage is what you might see in your classroom in the form of shouting and throwing things.

Once you feel that you can keep everyone safe, ask to meet with the out-of-control student privately, such as in the hallway. Refrain from touching the student, and give the student plenty of space as you move toward the hallway. Refrain from escalating the situation in any way. Keep your voice quiet and calm, and refrain from reasoning, explaining, lecturing, and giving instructions. Keep in mind that the student is engaged in 'fight or flight' behaviors, in "survival mode," and cannot be expected to respond to reason. Your calming presence can be the solution to the crisis. Just ask the student to walk with you.

Once in the hallway, ask the student to take a few moments to become calm. Coach the student through one of the grounding techniques you've taught the class. When the student starts breathing normally, ask what happened to upset the student. Chat in a calm and normal voice tone. Seek to understand the situation, what happened to set off the out-of-control behavior, and learn how you can help. Use active listening to gather as much information as possible in the time you have available. Avoid arguing. Continue asking interested questions and show your concern. Once you understand the situation, provide the student with positive choices about what to do next. Help the student follow through on the choice made. Prompt or coach the student as needed. At a later time, teach the student privately how to handle a similar situation in the future.

Your goals

In summary, your goals related to students who have experienced traumatic events are many. Fortunately, these goals overlap with goals associated with teaching any student. First, creating a safe classroom is paramount. Students who feel safe are more likely to learn and be successful. Second, over time, creating a positive rapport with each student through open communication is important. You never know when a student will need your support. Third, gathering information about each student is helpful in order to be able to access resources that can help the student and in order to avoid triggers that can upset the student. Fourth, once you know that a student has experienced traumatic events, monitoring that student, especially during unstructured times, will become second nature. You will be able to prevent unfortunate situations among students and help the student avoid triggers. You will be able to facilitate the student's learning by providing instructional methods that will likely help the student. Finally, working with other professionals as a member of a team to help the student and the student's family will yield benefits for all involved. Know that you are the student's best hope because, chances are, you have gathered the most information about the student's situation and can use that information to get the best access to the right resources for that student.

As you work to help students, the following ideas will be helpful. First, try not to make assumptions about students. Take time to gather information instead. Just because a student is the target of bullying does not mean that that student has been abused. It is only one sign that abuse *might* have occurred, and that sign requires future exploration. Also always try to act as if a student has no conscious control over a symptom. Telling a student to stop touching other students will not enable the student to control that behavior. In other words, know that you cannot "fix" a student who has experienced traumatic situations. The student will need professional help, which you can assist the student in obtaining. Finally, know that each student who is having trouble concentrating and focusing on schoolwork can become a better learner if given that professional help. Indeed, the stories in this book have shown that students who seem to have trouble learning can become very productive learners once they receive SE Therapy related to their traumatic experiences.

CHECKLIST FOR TEACHERS

- ☐ Create a safe learning environment.
- ☐ Create a learning community.
- ☐ Create positive rapport with each student.
- ☐ Promote open communication.
- ☐ Gather information about each student.
- ☐ Focus on location and spacing.
- ☐ Attend to your expressions.
- ☐ Use research-validated instructional procedures.
- ☐ Promote hope.
- ☐ Prepare students to react calmly for any difficult or unexpected situation.

CHAPTER 17

RECOMMENDATIONS FOR OUR SOCIETY

The lessons presented here have been drawn from my personal experience, which I admit may be somewhat limited. All the stories in this book are also limited to the treatment of childhood trauma; however, all the adults whose stories are in this book had also experienced traumatic events during their adulthoods. The stories do not cover such traumatic events as war, generational trauma, historical trauma, cultural trauma, social injustice, and other types of traumatic events that are typically experienced by adults and families. Nevertheless, if the lessons that I have learned hold true, our society would do well to consider some adjustments in our thinking and policies. Below are some adaptations that might be helpful.

Discard the stigma of "mental illness"

If the symptoms that are associated with the condition typically called "mental illness" are caused by a biological phenomenon that our bodies are naturally programmed to perform as a way of protecting us, then we need a new term for this condition. Certainly, it is not an "illness" since all of us have the mechanism biologically programmed into our bodies. Also, since trauma energy is stored throughout our bodies, we can no longer call the condition a "mental" condition. Clearly, some symptoms are directly associated with the brain, like concentration and memory problems, but others involve other parts of the body like stomach ailments. Additionally, we can no longer cast aspersions on individuals exhibiting the condition. If ALL our bodies are programmed to work this way, such programming is a human condition that we all share, like the beating of our hearts or the inhaling of our lungs. Singling out individuals as "mentally ill" no longer makes sense. Each individual is simply experiencing more or fewer symptoms than other individuals.

Reconsider the practice of pairing labels or diagnoses with one symptom

As we have seen in the stories in this book, people not only experience more than one symptom simultaneously, but they can experience large numbers of symptoms, even as children. Therefore, tying a label or a diagnosis to one symptom does not make sense. Not surprisingly, because of the many symptoms reported by the people highlighted in this book, they have received several different diagnoses from various health-care professionals. Children who are having difficulty learning are said to be suffering from learning disabilities, attention deficit hyperactivity disorder (ADHD), oppositional defiant disorder, conduct disorder, and behavioral disorders. Many of these children also experience anxiety and mood fluctuations. Interestingly, about two-thirds of children diagnosed with learning disabilities are boys. Additionally, almost four times as many boys as girls are diagnosed with ADHD. Whether these differences are related to traumatic events in early childhood (e.g., circumcision, rougher play, more injuries) or genetic gender differences is unknown. Perhaps genetic differences related to resilience (e.g., a person's capacity to store trauma energy) also play a role, but there is currently no way to measure such resilience. Clearly, a new way of characterizing or describing individuals with symptoms needs to be developed.

Reconsider the practice of pairing medication with one symptom

Many of the people highlighted in this book and who received a diagnosis paired with one symptom were prescribed medication for that symptom. For example, they were given an anti-depressant for depression or an anti-anxiety medication for anxiety. When the medication did not work, they went back to the same professional who prescribed a second medication to take along with the first one. Sometimes, they stopped taking the medication because they did not like the way they felt while taking it. Often, they went to another professional who prescribed a different medication. After trying a series of medications or a group of medications (one for anxiety, one for depression, one for acid reflux, and one for sleeplessness), many reported to me that they stopped taking any medication at all. This is not surprising because most of the people with whom I have worked were experiencing a whole constellation of symptoms. It is also not surprising to meet individuals who have been taking as many as seventeen medications at once. Thus, our culture needs a new way of working with medications and linking them with individuals experiencing a constellation of symptoms.

Reconsider the way children who have difficulty learning are diagnosed and labelled

As shown in some of the stories in this book, children who have experienced traumatic events had difficulty learning. This difficulty remained with them for years until they received Somatic Experiencing Therapy. Only then were they able to learn again and improve in their academic activities. They were able to concentrate, complete tasks, and remember information to such an extent that they were able to earn degrees and perform complicated professional work. In other words, their difficulties with academics were not permanent. None of them required special tutoring or education. They simply engaged in educational pursuits in which they were already enrolled with their peers. As a professional who spent my whole career in the field of special education, I was amazed by this!

Recently, I've begun to understand that most of the people with whom I have worked had a chance to learn many of the basic skills of reading, math, and writing before they experienced traumatic situations. Therefore, once they participated in therapy, they were able to use those skills. Children who experience serious traumatic events at an early age (e.g., first and second grade) are a different case though. These children may not learn the basic skills (e.g., phonics and addition and then the skills that follow). Once they engage in therapy in later years, they do not have access to the most basic of skills to help them even though they can concentrate. Thus, as a society, we need to be very careful about identifying traumatized children at an early age and providing the therapy they need so that they can learn the basic skills and function effectively when schooling becomes difficult.

Engage in surgery as a last resort

Certainly, surgery can be a life saver and a life extender. Our surgeons are miracle workers in so many ways, and our culture seems properly focused on their many accomplishments. Obviously, surgery is a critical part of our lives. As a culture, though, we have not learned to respect the after-effects of surgery. About sixty percent of newborn boys are circumcised in the first few days of their lives. This is an elective procedure, based primarily on times when showers and baths were not readily available. Parents can choose to avoid this option for their sons.

In fact, eighty percent of *all* surgeries are elective surgeries. Since surgeries are likely to result in stored trauma energy, people need to be aware of what they are risking in terms of symptoms after the surgery. When they are told about the potential side effects and consequences of the surgery, they need to be told about potential symptoms that might occur as a result of the anesthesia and the surgery itself. Their doctors need to assess the level of symptoms patients are experiencing before surgery and the likelihood that they might become dysfunctional after the surgery. Potential surgery patients need to have wide-open eyes about these risks before they go into surgery. They need to refrain from getting caught up in the latest surgical "fad" like joint-replacement surgeries and body improvement surgeries. They need to learn what the recovery from a particular surgery entails. They need to hear stories and read about examples of people who have had the surgery and how these individuals have engaged in trauma therapy after surgery to alleviate their symptoms. Trauma therapy needs to be made available for surgical patients as a part of their insurance coverage for the surgery. People trained in trauma therapy need to be part of hospital staffs and need to provide treatment to post-operative patients as part of the whole sequence of activities related to each type of surgery.

Combine local anesthesia with general anesthesia as a matter of course

In cases where the body is being invaded in any way, the body will begin responding as if it is facing serious danger. For example, an incision can be sensed by the body as a potential mortal wound. Thus, local anesthesia should be used to reduce the body's ability to sense the invasion. General anesthesia does not mask the body's ability to sense the invasion. Additionally, the use of local anesthesia has been shown through medical research to reduce bleeding, reduce complications, reduce recovery time, and reduce pain after surgery. Its use is a win-win all around. Unfortunately, because local anesthesia takes a few minutes to administer and take effect, it is not used routinely. It often must be requested. Our society would do well to make its use a standard practice.

Develop more safety measures

Our society, in many respects, focuses on the development of safety measures. We have developed seat belts, car seats, and cars that stop automatically. Clearly, these safety measures save a lot of lives; nevertheless, we need to continue work in this area. For example, although we have air bags that inflate during a car accident, they explode with such force that they cause injuries such as deep bruises and cuts. They also release a gas that burns people's eyes. These events result in stored trauma energy that has to be discharged, in addition to the trauma energy related to the car accident. In another area, although progress has been made in creating football helmets that are more protective, and rules of the game prohibit targeting another player's head, football players are still suffering debilitating concussions. After several concussions, they can suffer from chronic traumatic encephalopathy (CTE) and behavioral changes. From my experience, concussions are among the more difficult traumatic events to treat. As a society, we need to continue to work on developments that will reduce the chances of injuries, trauma symptoms, and future debilitation. Policies and rules need to be changed in addition to developing better technology and equipment.

Create and implement a new service-delivery model

In our current service-delivery model, individuals experience a symptom (e.g., trouble going to sleep) and typically go to the pharmacy to purchase over-the-counter drugs matched to their symptom. When they have several symptoms, they purchase more drugs or sometimes start self-medicating with alcohol or recreational drugs. When a symptom worsens (e.g., sleeping only a few hours), they go to a medical doctor who prescribes a more powerful drug matched to their symptom. When the drug does not work or when other symptoms accumulate and interfere with the person's life, the medical doctor refers the person to a psychiatrist who, in turn, prescribes an even more powerful drug or group of drugs. Therapy may or may not be recommended in addition to the medication. When one medication does not work, another is prescribed to strengthen the first medication. When one medication causes complications or new symptoms, another medication is prescribed to deal with those additional symptoms.

This service-delivery model seems to be set up to exacerbate the phenomenon related to the accumulation of trauma energy. Instead of people getting appropriate trauma therapy when they first experience a symptom, treatment is delayed until trauma energy has accumulated to the point that they become dysfunctional or close to dysfunctional. In other words, the current service-delivery model needs to be turned upside down so that people can be treated for a trauma symptom when it first occurs or even *before* it occurs. For example, if children who have experienced a broken bone or a dog bite were to receive trauma therapy soon after the incident, the trauma energy that has been stored could be discharged, and the child could avoid future symptoms related to that incident. Trauma energy would not accumulate, and the child would not become dysfunctional at some unspecified and unexpected time.

This new service-delivery model would necessitate trauma therapists to be integrated within and throughout the health-care system so that they could immediately serve people after traumatic events. For example, they would need to be on hospital staffs and be assigned to help people directly after surgeries and after accidents. They would need to be integrated within primary-care doctors' offices and urgent care offices so that they can be assigned to individuals who need trauma therapy after traumatic events like falls, injuries, attacks, and other medical procedures. Our culture should value this treatment such that it would be covered by insurance since it would serve to prevent future problems for individuals.

Stop "letting off" people who abuse, molest, or rape others

Throughout the stories in this book, we have seen how children's lives are severely affected when they are physically attacked, molested, and raped. They simply cannot function as learners, which is their main occupation as children. They are singled out as behaviorally unacceptable, are attacked by others, and are sometimes hospitalized.

They cannot focus or concentrate, have poor memories, and cannot complete tasks. Sometimes, they cannot speak. If they are abused at an early age, they cannot learn the most basic of skills (e.g., adding, subtracting, phonics, handwriting, writing sentences), so that when these skills are needed in secondary grades to learn more difficult skills (e.g., algebra, writing paragraphs and themes, reading for comprehension), they cannot meet those demands. Children who have been abused in these ways have numerous symptoms that often result in academic failure and dysfunctional lives.

Nevertheless, our society continues to sentence their perpetrators to "probation." Prosecutors make the mistake of charging these perpetrators with low-level crimes, such that when they plea bargain the charges down, the only sentence can be probation. These predators are not punished in a way that is equivalent to their crimes, which involves destroying another person's ability to learn and live a productive life. Meanwhile, other would-be predators are not deterred from committing the same crime. The reasoning seems to be that because the victim is a child, the crime should be a low-level crime. That's not the case, when the crime is potentially destroying a person's life forever. Our culture needs to severely punish perpetrators at a level commensurate with the damage that they are inflicting on others. Only until this happens will perpetrators stop engaging in abusive behavior. Additionally, they need to have court-ordered treatment that helps them understand and deal with their own traumatic histories. Sometimes, a whole family might need court-ordered treatment depending on the extent of involvement of other family members in the abuse and the concealment of the abuse. Finding that a grandmother, mother, and daughter have all been victims of childhood sexual abuse is not uncommon, and all of the victims are likely to need some help and support, along with other family members, if, for example, a father is sent away to prison and the parents are eventually divorced. In such a case, all the children in the family are likely to suffer from the grief they feel related to their father's loss and the divorce.

Stop marginalizing traumatized segments of the population

Our society has isolated whole segments of the population who are stigmatized and marginalized because of the traumatic events they have experienced. Examples are children in foster care, children in need of care, children who have been adjudicated in the juvenile justice system because of incest and rape or criminal behavior, battered women, homeless people, recreational drug users and addicts, immigrants, military veterans, and victims of mass shootings. We need to understand, as a culture, that at the root of these people's issues are the trauma symptoms that they are experiencing, and we need to ensure they get proper treatment to alleviate those symptoms. Indeed, these people might be considered the most traumatized people in our culture. We need to create policies and programs that address their symptoms and help them get on their feet so that they might be productive citizens within our culture.

Fund and conduct future research related to trauma

As I explained in the Preface, this book is a compilation of stories through which I have observed some patterns that have come together into a coherent explanation of how traumatic events affect our lives. Although my findings as described in this book can be characterized as "case-study research," this research is not meant to be hard-core research. It is limited to my experiences and the experiences that people have described to me. It is also limited to my skills as a therapist, and I specifically chose to use only one type of therapy (Somatic Experiencing). Additionally, it is limited to the types of people who were willing to work with me and share their stories with the public because they wanted to help others. It does not include people who are suffering from domestic trauma, combat trauma, intergenerational trauma, and cultural trauma.

In contrast, rigorous research requires experimental and control groups that are randomly selected while controlling as many external factors as possible. Unfortunately, the factors associated with trauma and traumatic events are very complicated and difficult to control. Finding a group of people who have experienced one type of traumatic event to the exclusion of other traumatic events or one symptom to the exclusion of others is difficult if not impossible. Throughout the stories in this book, we've seen that people experience many traumatic events and many symptoms. Finding even two people who match up with regard to traumatic events and symptoms is nearly impossible.

Nevertheless, as a society, we need to further investigate these phenomena. We need to develop ways of measuring symptoms and improvements. We need to try out a new model of service-delivery and determine whether it prevents future symptoms and dysfunctionality. We need to compare the results of different types of trauma therapy to determine which ones work best, most efficiently, and in what combinations. Surely, some combinations of therapies might work more efficiently than others. We need to find the best ways to discharge trauma energy quickly. We need to develop the best ways to train people to provide the therapy. We also need to determine whether people can learn to discharge trauma energy adequately on their own over the long term once they have emptied their reservoirs and are not experiencing symptoms. This will require longitudinal studies that follow individuals across years and future encounters with traumatic events. Such studies will also allow data gathering with regard to reenactment of past traumatic events and factors that can control reenactment.

Provide education about trauma that permeates our culture

As we learn more about our bodies as a society, the phenomena associated with traumatic events, and the best ways to provide trauma therapy to people, we will need to communicate these findings in ways that will help people take part in keeping their bodies safe and functional. The information should be as integral a part of our society as knowledge about seat belts and car seats. Children will need to learn about these phenomena in their health classes in school, and parents will need to learn about them in parenting classes. People will need to understand how to avoid the accumulation of trauma energy, the best ways of treating symptoms, and the ways to access such treatment. They need to learn how to best reduce the frequency of stress and traumatic events in their environment so that their symptoms are not triggered and do not become overwhelming. In essence, they need to learn how to live lives that promote good health and a minimum of symptoms.

Summary

In conclusion, as a society we have a great deal of work to do to rectify the current situation related to our common understandings about trauma and the effects of traumatic events on people's lives. We need to reduce the frequency of traumatic events. We need to stop labeling and marginalizing people who have experienced traumatic events. We need to develop a new treatment model that permeates our health system and truly helps people heal from the consequences of traumatic events. We need to do more research on the best combinations of therapy and educate the public about them.

All in all, I sincerely hope that you have found some hope as you have read the stories and as you digested the themes that were woven throughout those stories. I also hope that, if you (or your loved ones) are suffering from symptoms that are interfering in your life, you will seek out therapy that will give you some relief. If you are interested in obtaining Somatic Experiencing Therapy, look online for the list of therapists in your area, and choose a therapist who is a certified Somatic Experiencing Practitioner (i.e., look for the letters "SEP" after the person's name). If you are a professional working directly with individuals who have experienced one or more traumatic events, and you wish to be trained as an SEP, go to Somatic Experiencing International (https://traumahealing.org), and look for information on the training program. My sincere wish is that your life has benefited from learning a new way of looking at and understanding trauma, and I hope you will engage in making the needed changes in your corner of the world.

ACTION PLAN

Now that you understand trauma and have thought about the recommendations for our society related to trauma, please use this page to brainstorm any actions you can take to make a difference. Perhaps you have ideas on how you can promote trauma-informed care in your profession or community. What can you do?

ACTION IDEAS

APPENDIX A
BIOLOGICAL CONNECTIONS

This section is for readers who want to understand a bit more about the biology related to the symptoms that result from traumatic events. The information in this section is not meant to cover every aspect of the biological story associated with trauma; instead, it covers just the highlights. Many, many of the details have been omitted. It portrays the major differences between what happens in our bodies during typical daily events versus traumatic events in a very simplified way. (For more information, see van der Kolk, 2014.)

The Voluntary Pathway

To begin the story, a good jumping-off place relates to what happens in your body in a typical life experience. Figure 20 (p. 264) shows what happens in your body when you decide to do something voluntarily. For example, you wake up in the morning and look out your window. The part of your brain that gathers information from your eyes, ears, and skin, the **Thalamus (1),** takes in that information and combines it. You can see that it is a beautiful day with a blue sky and wispy clouds, and you can hear the birds singing. Your window thermometer states seventy-two degrees Fahrenheit. This information is quickly passed to your **Hippocampus (2),** the part of your brain that evaluates how this information relates to your previous experiences.

Figure 20: The Voluntary Pathway

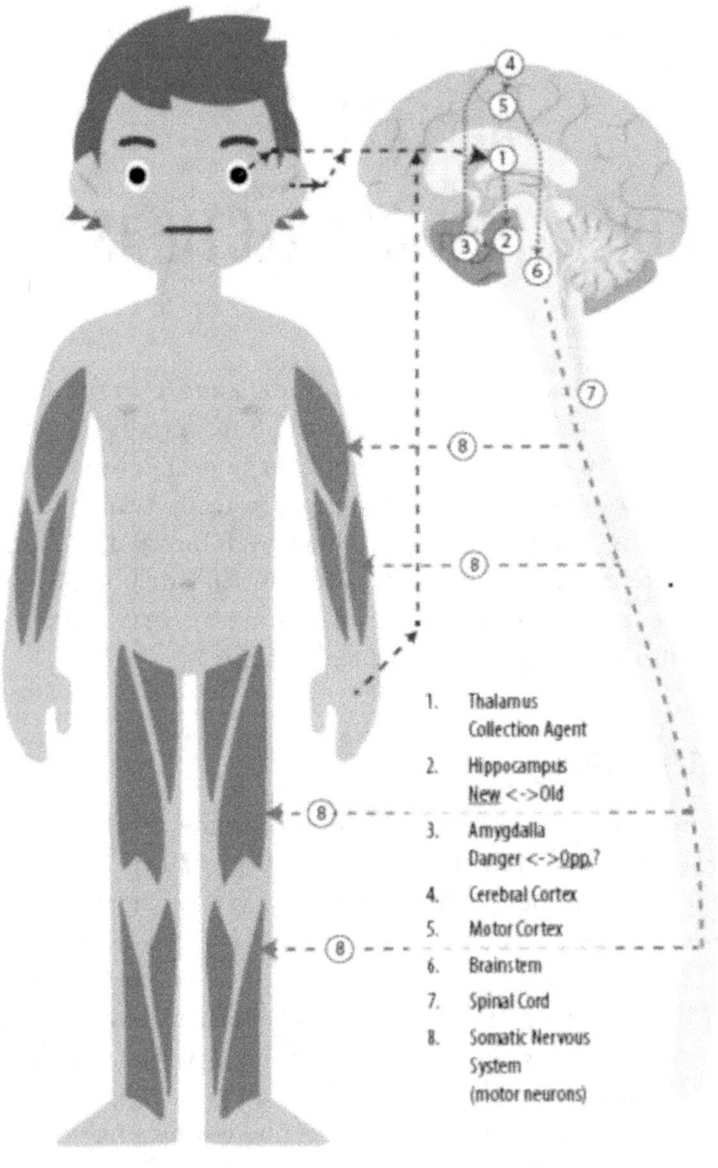

In other words, the hippocampus determines how the current weather compares to previous weather you've experienced. Has this type of weather proved to be perfect for taking a run? If it passes this test (e.g., this weather has proved perfect for a run in the past), then the information quickly passes to the **Amygdala (3),** another part of the brain, which determines whether this situation constitutes a danger or an opportunity. Since the good weather seems like an opportunity, the information is quickly sent to the **Cerebral Cortex (4)** of your brain, which begins to plan what you will wear when running, where you will run, and when you will run. You might also announce that you're going running and invite someone to go with you.

Next, the **Motor Cortex (5)** of your brain begins to carry out your plan. It sends messages through the nerves in the **Brainstem (6)** and the **Spinal Cord (7)** to the **Somatic Nervous System (8).** This system consists of motor neurons that activate your muscles voluntarily. As a result, you can get dressed, walk outside, and begin running.

This sequence from the thalamus through to the somatic nervous system can be considered the **Voluntary Pathway** through key parts of your nervous system. It is under your control through the use of several parts of your brain, including the cerebral cortex, motor cortex, the brainstem, the spinal cord, and the somatic nervous system. Figure 20 is a very simplified illustration of how your body typically works under voluntary control. Of course, as you begin to run, various parts of your body will begin to respond to the requirements of running. For example, your heart will beat faster, your lungs will breathe deeper, and some adrenaline will provide additional power to your body. When you stop running, your body will naturally return to a resting state.

The Involuntary Pathway

An entirely different neural pathway, which we will call the **Involuntary Pathway,** is used during a traumatic incident. It is portrayed in Figure 21 (p. 266).

Figure 21: The Involuntary Pathway

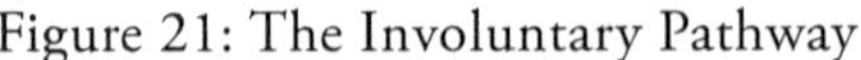

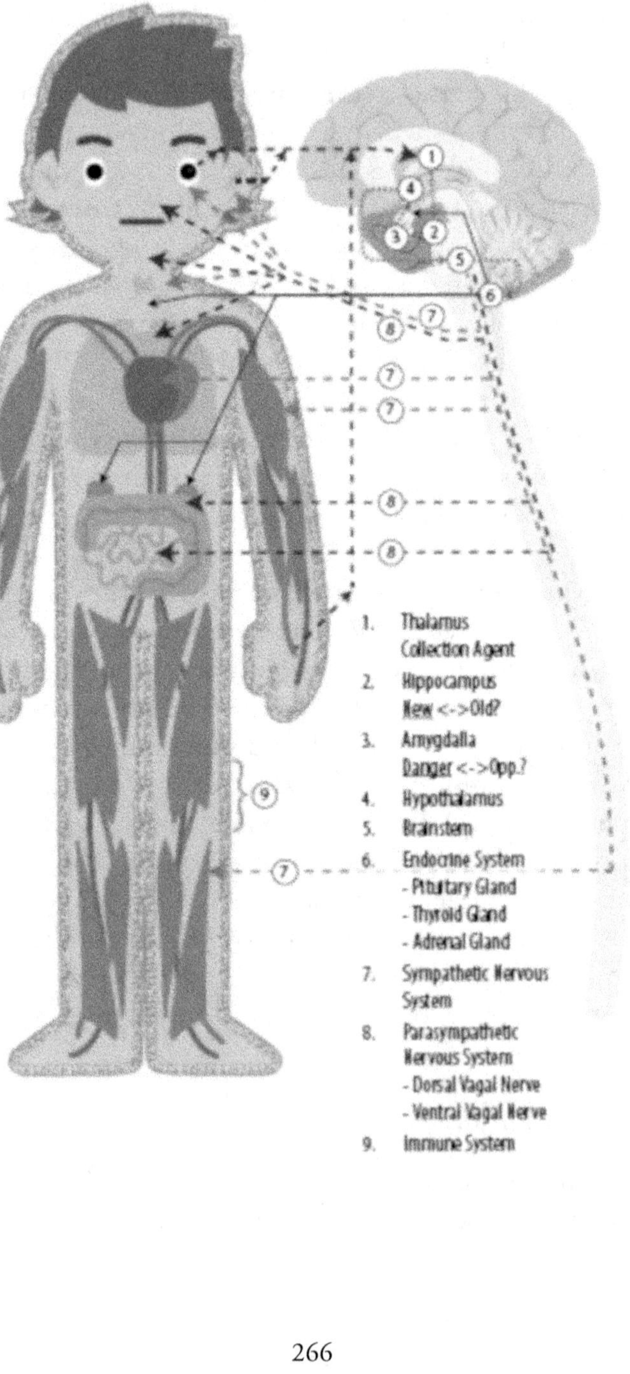

Similar to the Voluntary Pathway, the eyes, ears, and skin gather information, and the thalamus acts to combine that information in a meaningful way. For example, if you see a car coming through an intersection toward your car that is going through the same intersection, the thalamus gathers information about such factors as the speed of the other car, the direction of the car, the color of the traffic light, and the attention of the driver of the other car. This information is immediately shared with the **Hippocampus (2),** which compares this situation to previously encountered situations like it. Are the speed and direction of the car appropriate to this particular intersection? Are they appropriate to the color of the traffic light? Is the driver talking on a cell phone? After this comparison is made, the information is sent to the **Amygdala (3),** which determines whether the situation is dangerous or an opportunity. This sequence of messages and determinations happens instantaneously.

If danger is detected by the amygdala, an immediate message is sent to the **Hypothalamus (4).** This part of the brain sits on top of the **Brainstem (5)** and works with it to help your body respond to a potentially traumatic event in a way that promotes your survival. The brainstem controls the body's involuntary functions. These are the jobs within the body that do not require you to think about them. Your body just does them. For example, you do not have to think about making your heart beat or about making your lungs take in air. Likewise, a healthy person does not have to think about waking up, sleeping, breathing, circulating blood, and ovulating. These functions just happen. Moreover, many of these involuntary functions happen according to a certain schedule. For example, if all is well, healthy people's hearts beat about sixty to eighty beats per minute, they get hungry and eat about three times per day, and they sleep about seven to eight hours per night. Women's menstrual cycles are about thirty days long.

The job of the **Hypothalamus (4)** and the **Brainstem (5),** then, is to work together to ensure that you have the best chance of surviving a traumatic event by *increasing* those involuntary functions of the body that promote fighting and fleeing AND by *decreasing* those functions that take so much energy that they will interfere with fighting and fleeing. For example, they ensure that enough blood is pumped into the muscles of the arms and legs that these limbs can perform well in a fight or in a full-out sprint. For another example, they ensure that extra energy is available to these limbs by shutting down the gastrointestinal system, which requires a lot of energy to digest food.

In order to get this survival process started, the hypothalamus starts a chain reaction within the **Endocrine System (6),** a group of glands that release hormones into the blood that target certain organs in the body and activate those organs to perform in certain ways. As a first step, the hypothalamus produces corticotropin-releasing hormone (CRH), which stimulates the pituitary gland to produce adrenocorticotropic hormone. This hormone in turn stimulates the adrenal glands to produce adrenaline and cortisol. Adrenaline is needed by the muscles to perform well. Cortisol helps the body process the sugars, proteins, and fats needed when fighting or fleeing. It also enables a person to gather enough rage to fight. Additionally, cortisol reduces inflammation, which might appear when the body is wounded during a fight. The hypothalamus also produces thyrotropin-releasing hormone, which stimulates the pituitary gland to produce thyroid-stimulating hormone, which in turn activates the thyroid gland to produce thyroxine. Thyroxine is used by the body to increase the metabolic rate or the amount of oxygen used by the body. In other words, the hypothalamus sets in motion a number of chemical events within your body to make it stronger, more efficient, and more able to heal. Once these events are set in motion, they keep performing their responsibilities.

Meanwhile, at the same time, the hypothalamus and the brainstem engage the **Autonomic Nervous System** in sending messages to parts of the body to perform in certain ways. The autonomic nervous system, which regulates all involuntary functions in the body, has two parts: the **Sympathetic Nervous System (7)** and the **Parasympathetic Nervous System (8).** The sympathetic nervous system (SNS) serves to speed up all systems in the body so that they can participate in fighting or fleeing. The hypothalamus and brainstem send messages through the spinal cord and the sympathetic nerves to open your pupils wider so you can see better, turn your head in the direction of the danger, increase your heart rate, widen your bronchial passages, activate sweating to cool your skin, raise your blood pressure, and get your muscles ready to punch or run. To return to our example, all of these changes take place within a few seconds of you sensing that you might be in a car accident. Thus, you may grip the steering wheel more tightly and swerve the car to avoid a collision.

In contrast, if the collision takes place before you can react or if it takes place and you cannot get out of the car because you are seat-belted in or trapped by the air bag, the hypothalamus and brainstem activate the **Parasympathetic Nervous System (8) (PNS).** This system regulates your body when you cannot fight or flee. Under normal conditions, it helps the body rest, digest, urinate, and reproduce. During and after a traumatic event in which you cannot use the energy that has been accumulated to be able to fight or flee, the parasympathetic nervous system freezes your body. It has two branches. The dorsal vagal branch extends to the head and chest area and regulates the larynx, esophagus, tongue, face, heart, and lungs. Because of its activity, you might find that you cannot speak or scream during a traumatic event because your larynx is "frozen." It also controls your facial muscles, which may become less expressive. Because of the dorsal vagal branch's involvement in the freeze process, a person's social interactivity may also become frozen during the person's post-trauma life. The ventral vagal branch extends to the stomach and intestines. Because of its activity, your stomach and intestines stop working, or you might suddenly have diarrhea. The parasympathetic nervous system also triggers the release of acetylcholine throughout your body, which slows your breathing, relaxes your muscles, and calms you down. It also triggers your **Immune System (9)** to fight off any pathogens and other invaders, in the case of being wounded. Unfortunately, your immune system, once triggered like this, can overreact and continue producing extra numbers of cells to fight off invaders, even when invaders are not present. Once this happens, the body can be diagnosed with an autoimmune disease where the body starts attacking itself.

Comparing the Voluntary and Involuntary Pathways

Thus, there are two major pathways through the nervous system: the **Voluntary Pathway** and the **Involuntary Pathway.** The Voluntary Pathway is the pathway that our bodies use on a minute-to-minute basis to move about the world, interact with others, and live our lives. It is responsible for conscious, voluntary control of muscle movements. We walk, sit, feed ourselves, run, drive a car, go to the gym and lift weights, and hit a punching bag. In contrast, the Involuntary Pathway is the pathway that is triggered when an occasional traumatic event occurs. It enables us to survive the event by fighting, fleeing, or freezing.

Comparing the pathways leads to several important ideas related to trauma. First, the Voluntary Pathway involves the use of the executive cortex, known as the rational brain; the Involuntary Pathway does not. In fact, during traumatic events, the executive cortex often shuts down, and decision-making abilities go offline. Survivors of traumatic events often report that they could not think or speak during traumatic incidents. In other words, in most instances, the executive cortex is not involved in a meaningful way in triggering anything that happens in the body during a traumatic event. The hypothalamus and brainstem are primarily involved in sending messages and directing changes in the parts of the body involved in helping the body survive.

Another important idea that a comparison between the two pathways reveals is that the Involuntary Pathway specifically targets organs and structures that are aligned with symptoms that trauma survivors experience; the Voluntary Pathway does not. That is, the Involuntary Pathway involves control of all the organs and body parts involved in involuntary functions like sleeping, breathing, heart beats, and digestion. Survivors of trauma often report symptoms related to these body parts and functions. They have trouble sleeping and experience other sleep disturbances; they have numerous stomach and digestion problems; they feel pressure on their chests; and they report heart arrythmia. Sometimes, they have panic attacks where their hearts beat very fast, and they can't catch their breath. Since the Involuntary Pathway results in trauma symptoms and others related to continuing hormone release and autoimmune functions, it stands to reason that it needs to be involved in treatments aimed at helping trauma survivors.

The comparison of the two pathways reveals the folly of calling the symptoms reported by trauma survivors "mental illness." Indeed, the whole body is involved in the phenomena that occur during a traumatic incident. "Mental" typically refers to the rational brain, the brain structures involved in executive processing and decision making. Nevertheless, we've seen that the cerebral cortex is often offline during traumatic incidents and not involved in the Involuntary Pathway. Thus, "talk" therapy and other therapies targeting the rational brain can be missing the correct target. Parts of the Involuntary Pathway need to be targeted instead. The brainstem, the key structure operating the Involuntary Pathway and involuntary functions, is not involved in language or reason in any way.* Likewise, simply instructing trauma survivors to "shape up" or stop acting in certain ways does not work because the functions are not under their rational control. Their rational brains cannot turn off the processes started by the hypothalamus and brainstem. Also, an important point is the idea that although people in certain cultures might view some traumatic situations as more or less serious than others, the body decides. In other words, the amount of trauma energy stored is based on the person's biology and heredity, and the effects of that trauma energy depend a lot on the person's capacity to store trauma energy.

A further comparison of the Voluntary Pathway with the Involuntary Pathway reveals that the two pathways use different parts of the nervous system. The Voluntary Pathway utilizes the somatic nervous system.

---

* This statement is not meant to disrespect or disparage "talk therapy" in any way. Indeed, "talk therapy" can be helpful in a variety of ways.

This nervous system is involved in actions that a person *chooses* to undertake. It is not involved in involuntary fight or flight activities during traumatic situations. Thus, engaging the somatic nervous system by choosing to hit a punching bag or run five miles does not produce the results of trauma therapy. Although daily exercise is helpful for anyone with regard to general health and may relieve some of the jitteriness that trauma survivors feel, it does not necessarily resolve trauma symptoms through the discharge of trauma energy.

On the other hand, the Involuntary Pathway utilizes the autonomic nervous system, which has two components: the sympathetic nervous system and the parasympathetic nervous system. The sympathetic nervous system engages the body in fight or flight activities. The parasympathetic nervous system triggers shut down or freeze. These activities are directly related to the symptoms people experience. Thus, engaging the sympathetic and parasympathetic nervous systems in treatment can be productive in reducing trauma symptoms.

Summary

To summarize, choosing a trauma therapy that is directed at the parts of the body and nervous system that are involved in the Involuntary Pathway during traumatic incidents is important. In other words, the therapy needs to result in the discharge of the energy that is stored in the body to be ready to fight or flee or is built up in the body before the body freezes. (See Chapters 2 and 3 for the reservoir analogy.) A few therapies that involve the discharge of energy and fulfill this requirement are available. One of them, Somatic Experiencing Therapy, is covered in this book. (See Chapter 4 for a brief description.) Other therapies are also available (see Appendix C for some references and Van der Kolk [2014] for descriptions).

APPENDIX B
LESSONS LEARNED SUMMARY

Traumatic Events

Traumatic events come in lots of shapes and sizes.

A whole continuum of events can result in stored trauma energy from a simple cut to a catastrophic accident or attack. Trauma is not limited to combat and rape events.

Common events can result in stored trauma energy.

Sports injuries and medical procedures like elective surgeries can result in stored trauma energy. Any other event where the individual could not act in order to survive or help an endangered loved one can result in stored trauma energy.

Symptoms

The number of symptoms that people can experience has no end.

People can experience dozens of symptoms related to stored trauma energy, many of which are considered to be common occurrences in our society, like headaches and sleep disturbances.

Stored trauma energy has no expiration date.

An individual who has experienced a traumatic event as a toddler can still be experiencing symptoms related to that event as a senior citizen.

Trauma has no prejudice.

Trauma does not discriminate. People who experience trauma symptoms represent all walks of life, at all ages, and all groups.

Symptoms are not permanent.

People who have experienced serious symptoms for years can heal and be free of those symptoms after participating in Somatic Experiencing Therapy. They can learn, work, interact socially, and lead productive lives.

Trauma symptoms cannot be cognitively controlled.

Individuals who are experiencing a symptom cannot will themselves to stop experiencing that symptom. That is, they cannot tell themselves to stop being anxious or depressed. They cannot tell themselves to stop having panic attacks.

Individuals have their unique trauma-symptom profiles.

People are unique in the way that they experience trauma symptoms. Thus, their symptom profiles are unique. Although some symptoms might overlap between two people, other symptoms will not.

Trauma symptoms can be mitigated at any age.

Because anyone at any age can be relieved of symptoms after participating in SE Therapy sessions, people can be encouraged to participate in therapy well into their senior years.

Symptoms can return after additional traumatic situations.

Even though people become symptom free while participating in therapy, they can experience another traumatic event. When this happens, they can start experiencing symptoms again, typically some of the same symptoms as reported originally, but usually fewer symptoms. Healing can occur again and again.

Stored trauma energy can exceed people's capacity for storage, and they can become dysfunctional.

Individuals' symptoms can build up in seriousness such that they no longer are able to go to school, work, shopping, or social events. They can no longer lead productive and enjoyable lives.

Energy Discharge

Energy discharge occurs in distinct body parts that have been injured.

When someone has broken a leg bone, energy discharge during an SE session may occur in that leg close to the break. When someone has had surgery in the throat, energy discharge occurs in the back of the mouth and neck. These are examples of the location of energy discharge that can occur anywhere in the body.

Energy discharge in particular body parts slows down across SE sessions and stops.

When energy discharge occurs in a body part, it can be strong at first. For example, the person might experience pain in the first session in a given part, tingling in the next session, and slight itching in following sessions. Finally, there is no discharge from that part.

Energy discharge occurs in certain patterns across people.

People who experience similar types of traumatic events also experience similar patterns of energy discharge in SE sessions. For example, individuals who have experienced surgery are likely to run during sessions. Individuals who have experienced a car accident are likely to engage in arching their backs.

Involuntary Functions

Involuntary functions can be disrupted after traumatic events.

Such involuntary functions as eating and sleeping can be disrupted as a result of the storage of trauma energy. Symptoms related to these functions can vary widely.

Involuntary functions can be restored through Somatic Experiencing Therapy.

People who had no appetite become hungry and start eating. People who could sleep only a few hours each night sleep more and more hours. Women with no periods start having periods.

Physical Coordination

Physical coordination can be disrupted after traumatic events.

People who experience traumatic events typically do not engage in physical activities. They report that they do not feel comfortable engaging in those activities.

Physical coordination can be restored through Somatic Experiencing Therapy.

People who participate in Somatic Experiencing Therapy often start participating in physical activities. They report that they feel coordinated and energetic.

Cognitive Functions

Cognitive functions can be disrupted after traumatic events.

Memory, concentration, and motivation to learn can be affected after traumatic events. As a result, people may not be able to complete academic or work tasks.

Cognitive functions can be restored through Somatic Experiencing Therapy.

Individuals who were failing in school and have participated in SE Therapy have become successful learners and completed degrees. People who were not able to work have found jobs and become successful employees.

Social Engagement

Social engagement can be disrupted after traumatic events.

Individuals who have experienced traumatic events can isolate themselves from the rest of the world. They avoid crowded places like classrooms and stores and tend not to interact with others.

Social engagement can be reinstated through Somatic Experiencing Therapy.

People who participate in SE Therapy begin to participate in social events. They go to lunch or the movies with friends, join clubs, sign up for yoga classes, and volunteer for charity events.

Physical Health

Physical health can be negatively affected after traumatic events.

Individuals who have experienced traumatic events are more likely than others to get colds and infections. They seem to be "always sick." They have asthma, fibromyalgia, high blood pressure, and other ailments.

Physical health can improve after Somatic Experiencing Therapy.

People who participate in SE Therapy become healthier over time. Eventually, they attend school and work without interruption. Chronic health conditions fade away, and in some cases, medications are no longer needed.

"Mental Illness" Symptoms

Symptoms associated with the term "mental illness" can appear after traumatic events.

Such symptoms as depression, anxiety, panic attacks, and intrusive thoughts are commonly reported by people who have experienced traumatic events.

Symptoms associated with the term "mental illness" can disappear after Somatic Experiencing Therapy.

Individuals who participate in SE Therapy report that they no longer experience depression, anxiety, panic attacks, and invasive thoughts.

Three Caveats

Caveat #1: The storage and discharge of Trauma Energy is a dynamic phenomenon.

Although SE Therapy might serve to eliminate trauma symptoms, some of the same symptoms can reoccur as a result of future traumatic experiences. They can also be eliminated again as a result of therapy.

Caveat #2: : The body's reactivity to traumatic events appears to decrease over time, with fewer symptoms arising over years.

Fewer and fewer symptoms will appear over additional traumatic events if SE Therapy is used to eliminate initial symptoms. Some symptoms may not reappear.

Caveat #3: People can reenact previous traumatic events.

People who have experienced a certain type of traumatic event might repeatedly experience that same type of event.

APPENDIX C
REFERENCES

REFERENCES FOR THE TEXT

American Psychiatric Association. (2022). *Diagnostic and statistical manual of mental disorders (5th edition, text rev.)*. APA.

Beachboard, C. (2022). *The school of hope: The journey from trauma and anxiety to achievement, happiness, and resilience*. Thousand Oaks, CA: Corwin Press.

D'Adamo, P. J. (1996). *Eat right for your type: The individualized solution to staying healthy, living longer, & achieving your ideal weight*. New York: C.P. Putnam's Sons.

Kline, M. (2020). *Brain-changing strategies to trauma-proof our schools: A heart-centered movement for wiring well-being*. Berkeley, CA: North Atlantic Books.

Lenz, B. K. (2003). *Learning expressways*. Lawrence, KS: Edge Enterprises, Inc.

Levine, P. (1994). *Beginning training module for Somatic Experiencing Practitioners*. Circle Broomfield, CO: Somatic Experiencing International.

Levine, P. (1996). *Advanced training module of Somatic Experiencing Practitioners*. Circle Broomfield, CO: Somatic Experiencing International.

Levine, P., & Kline, M. (2007, 2019). *Trauma through a child's eyes: Awakening the ordinary miracle of healing-Infancy through adolescence.* Berkeley, CA: North Atlantic Books.

Levine, P. A., & Kline, M. (2008). *Trauma proofing your kids: A parents' guide for instilling confidence, joy and resilience.* Berkeley, CA: North Atlantic Books.

Van der Kolk, B. (2014). *The body keeps the score: Brain, mind, and body in the healing of trauma.* New York: Penguin Books.

Vernon, D. S., Deshler, D. D., & Schumaker, J. B. (2000). *Talking together.* Lawrence, KS: Edge Enterprises, Inc.

REFERENCES ON TRAUMA AND TRAUMA THERAPY

General References

Heller, D. P. (2019). *The power of attachment: How to create deep and lasting intimate relationships.* Boulder, CO: Sounds True.

Heller, D. P., & Heller, L. S. (2001). *Crash course: A self-healing guide to auto accident trauma & recovery.* Berkeley, CA: North Atlantic Books.

Heller, L., & LaPierre, A. (2012). *Healing developmental trauma: How early trauma affects self-regulation, self-image, and the capacity for relationship.* Berkeley, CA: North Atlantic Books.

Kline, M. (2020). *Brain-changing strategies to trauma-proof our schools: A heart-centered movement for wiring well-being.* Berkeley, CA: North Atlantic Books.

Massachusetts Advocates for Children. (2005). *Helping traumatized children learn: A report and policy agenda.* www.massadvocates.org

Sanders, M. R., & Thompson, G. R. (2022). *Polyvagal theory and the developing child: Systems of care for strengthening kids, families, and communities.* New York: W. W. Norton & Co.

Walker, P. (2014). *Complex PTSD: From thriving to striving, a guide and map for recovering from childhood trauma.* Lafayette, CA: Azure Coyote Books.

Van der Kolk, B. (2014). *The body keeps the score: Brain, mind, and body in the healing of trauma.* Westminster, London: Penguin Books.

References on Somatic Experiencing (SE)*

Levine, P. A. (2003). *Sexual healing: Transforming the sacred wound (Audio CD).* Boulder, CO: Sounds True.

Levine, P. A. (2005). *Healing trauma: A pioneering program for restoring the wisdom of your body.* Boulder, CO: Sounds True.

Levine, P. A. (2010). *In an unspoken voice: How the body releases trauma and restores goodness.* Berkeley, CA: North Atlantic Books.

Levine, P. A. (2015). *Trauma and memory: Brain and body in search for the living past.* Berkeley, CA: North Atlantic Books.

Levine, P. A. (2024). *An autobiography of trauma: A healing journey.* New York: Simon & Schuster.

Levine, P. A., & Frederick, A. (1997). *Waking the tiger: Healing trauma.* Berkeley, CA: North Atlantic Books.

Levine, P. A., & Kline, M. (2007, 2019). *Trauma through a child's eyes: Awakening the ordinary miracle of healing.* Berkeley, CA: North Atlantic Books.

Levine, P. A., & Kline, M. (2008). *Trauma proofing your kids: A parents' guide for instilling confidence, joy and resilience.* Berkeley, CA: North Atlantic Books.

Levine, P. A., & Phillips, M. (2012). *Freedom from pain: Discover your body's power to overcome physical pain.* Boulder, CO: Sounds True.

---

* For more on Somatic Experiencing, go to Somatic Experiencing International at <traumahealing.org>. To contact a Somatic Experiencing Practitioner (SEP) in your area, go to <directory.traumahealing.org> or look for "SEP" in the credentials of therapists in your area.

References on the Emotional Freedom Technique (EFT/Tapping)*

Cason, T. (2023). *All things EFT Tapping manual.* Little Sage Enterprises, LLC.

Craig, G. (2010). *The EFT manual.* Wake Forest, NC: Bane Publishing.

Ortner, N. (2014). *The tapping solution: A revolutionary system for stress-free living.* Carlsbad, CA: Hay House, Inc.

Ortner, N. (2015). *The tapping solution to pain relief.* Carlsbad, CA: Hay House, Inc.

References on Eye Movement Desensitization and Reprocessing (EMDR)**

Knipe, J. (2019). *EMDR toolbox: Theory and treatment of complex PTSD and dissociation.* New York: Springer Publishing Co.

Luber, M. (2019). *EMDR therapy: Scripted protocols and summary sheets.* New York: Springer Publishing Co.

Shapiro, F. (2017). *Eye movement desensitization and reprocessing (EMDR) Therapy: Basic principles, protocols, and procedures.* Switzerland: Springer International Publishing.

Shapiro, F. & Forrest, M. S. (2016). *EMDR: The breakthrough therapy for overcoming anxiety, stress, and trauma.* Seattle, WA: Thrift Books.

---

* To find an EFT practitioner, go to: <eftinternational.org>, and click on the link for "Find an EFT Practitioner or mentor." To learn more about EFT, go to the EFT website at <www.the tappingsolution.com/blog>

** To find an EMDR therapist, go to: https://www.emdria.org/find-an-emdr-therapist.

ACKNOWLEDGMENTS

I am indebted to Dr. Peter Levine for his mentorship, instruction, and therapy. From the moment I read an initial draft of his book that would become *Waking the Tiger* (1997), I was hooked! (I owe many thanks to Elaine Brewer for loaning me a draft of that book, which changed my life!) Also, I would like to thank Dr. Diane Heller, who was Peter's assistant during the five years that I participated in initial training workshops to become a Somatic Experiencing Practitioner and in many other training workshops thereafter when I became *their* assistant. Their understanding of trauma, their writings, and their exquisite and intuitive skills at implementing Somatic Experiencing (SE) formed the foundation for my research endeavors related to this book. Thanks to the two of them and my fellow trainees—who were also my therapists as we practiced doing SE work on each other—I was able to discharge stored trauma energy that was negatively affecting my life, and I am happily enjoying a calm and healthy life. I can't thank them all enough for the gift of my life!

I would also like to thank everyone who has supported and encouraged me through the creation of this book. First and foremost are the people whose stories are contained herein. Without hesitation, in our initial encounter, they all said that if I were giving them an opportunity to help others suffering from symptoms like their own symptoms, they would do it. When I was able to track most of them, in some cases twenty-some years after our last encounter, they agreed to help me, read what I had written about them, made corrections, and shared their current lives with me. I was so happy to communicate with them again and very gratified to hear about their lives. They have been so generous to share the stories of their lives with me (and with you!).

Significant others have also helped me in a variety of ways. Belinda Schuman, my dear friend for forty-some years, continues to make my work look beautiful and professional. Gary Bricker, my personal editor, has been an invaluable supporter of my life and my work. Dr. Don Deshler, my professional partner, has encouraged my pursuit of this project for years. Along with the readers/reviewers of this book, including Janice Bragg, Michel Loomis, Susan Schott, Paula Martin, Molly Glauner, Stephen Hazel, Rosemary Tralli, Kristin Vernon, Ty Tigner, and Naomi Tigner, they have read and provided edits for this book and discussed with me many of the issues that this book addresses. I have been grateful for their ideas and concerns. Their loving contributions to my work and my life have meant the world to me.

THE AUTHOR

Jean Bragg Schumaker, Ph.D., S.E.P., has been guiding Somatic Experiencing sessions for more than thirty years. In her day job, she is the President of Edge Enterprises, Inc. a research and publishing company devoted to developing and distributing instructional programs for students who have difficulty learning. She is a Professor Emeritus at the University of Kansas where she earned her doctorate in developmental and child psychology in 1975 and worked for fifty years. She has extensive research experience in the area of teaching struggling learners. She has developed and validated fifteen programs for teaching complex learning strategies that students can use to complete tasks at the secondary and post-secondary levels of education. She has developed and validated more than ten Content Enhancement Routines for subject-area teachers. She has written and published more than 100 research articles and many books as well as paper-based and digital instructional programs. She was the Principal Investigator on grants funded for more than $80 million.

Dr. Schumaker received the Division for Learning Disabilities, Council of Exceptional Children (CEC) Award for Outstanding Contributions to the Field of Learning Disabilities in 1996 and the same organization's Jeannette Fleishner Award for her research accomplishments in 2006. She received the Distinguished Achievement Award from her alma mater, Lawrence University, in 2004. She has served on the Professional Advisory Board for the Learning Disabilities Association of America, and she is a past President of the Division for Learning Disabilities (DLD), the largest division of the CEC. She received the Samuel A. Kirk Award for Outstanding

Publication from DLD in 2010 and in 2021 and the Don Deshler Leadership Award from the Instructional Coaching Group in 2014. She was named to the list of the World's Best Research Scientists by *Research.com* starting in 2023 and the list of Top Scholars by *Scholars GPS* starting in 2024.